GenTech

Advance Praise for
GenTech and Dr. Rick Chromey

"In *GenTech: An American Story of Technology, Change and Who We Really Are*, Rick Chromey does far more than remap generational categories bequeathed to us by conventional theorists. He gives us a new way to think about generational identity as a whole, demonstrating the shaping influence of technology on age-related cohorts. He rightly argues that generational identity and personality are guided as much by the technologies we use as by key historical events. The book is poignantly insightful and richly illustrative...a must-read for those who wish to deepen their understanding of our time and place in history."

—**Dr. Charles J. Conniry**, Jr., Vice President
of Academic Affairs, Western Seminary

"The generational labels provided in many books and articles have always confused me. Rick Chromey's more dynamic view of generations makes much more sense to me and better explains who I am, how I see the world, how I communicate, and, more significantly, how all of us relate to others from different technological generations. *GenTech* is especially valuable for leaders of churches, groups, ministries, and businesses."

—**Michael C. Mack**, Author, *Christian Standard* editor,
and founder of SmallGroupLeadership.com.

"Whether you're a technology nerd or wizard, this intriguing book will help you connect the digital dots. You'll see how technology is profoundly shaping our culture—and you, like it or not. Plus you'll discover how technology affects each generation differently, for better or worse."

— **Thom Schultz**, Founder and president, Group Publishing,
Author, *Why Nobody Wants to Go to Church Anymore*
and Filmmaker, *When God Left the Building*

GenTech

An American Story of Technology,
Change and Who We *Really* Are
(1900-present)

Dr. Rick Chromey

NEW YORK

LONDON • NASHVILLE • MELBOURNE • VANCOUVER

GenTech
An American Story of Technology, Change and Who We *Really* Are (1900-present)

Published in New York, New York, by Morgan James Publishing. Morgan James is a trademark of Morgan James, LLC. www.MorganJamesPublishing.com

Scriptures taken from the Holy Bible, New International Version®, NIV®. Copyright © 1973, 1978, 1984, 2011 by Biblica, Inc.™ Used by permission of Zondervan. All rights reserved worldwide. www.zondervan.com The "NIV" and "New International Version" are trademarks registered in the United States Patent and Trademark Office by Biblica, Inc.™

ISBN 978-1-64279-671-1 paperback
ISBN 978-1-64279-672-8 eBook
Library of Congress Control Number: 2019907495

Cover Design by:
Christopher Kirk
GFSstudio.com

Morgan James is a proud partner of Habitat for Humanity Peninsula and Greater Williamsburg. Partners in building since 2006.

Get involved today! Visit
www.MorganJamesBuilds.com

Dedicated to my grandchildren, the future generation:
Logan, Dallas, Aliyah, Scottlyn, Lucy, Caroline

Table of Contents

Foreword

"God's truth endures from generation to generation"
Psalm 100:5

The "Seventh Generation Rule" is a philosophy of life that factors the impact of every decision and deed as far as seven generations into the future.

"Seven Generations" is a principle most often associated with the Iroquois Nation, who first codified the concept in its constitution as a confederacy. But the philosophy of integrating future generations into one's deliberations, and to seeing oneself as the benefactor of previous generations' labors, is common to many indigenous tribes and cultures, not just in the U.S. but around the world.

In this work, Rick Chromey not only encourages us to ponder the "truth that endures from generation to generation," but ultimately explores a digital generation ("GenTech") which, for the first time in history, routinely exists side-by-side five other generations, soon to expand to six and even seven. For the first time in history we are living simultaneously with what our ancestors could only conceive of sequentially from a three generation, Abraham-Isaac-Jacob biblical perspective—the kind Marilynne Robinson explored in such riveting fashion in her Pulitzer Prize winning novel *Gilead* (2004), or that Nature Valley portrayed in its commercial called "Rediscover Nature."

The Nature Valley energy snack company talked to three generations and asked them one simple question: What did you like to do for fun as a kid? The oldest generation gave answers like gardening and fishing. The middle generation gave answers like playing hide and seek and building forts and tree houses with neighborhood kids. The youngest generation gave answers that talked about video games, watching YouTube, and texting on cell phones. One young girl even said she would "die" without her tablet.

I call the "GenTech" digital generations (also known as Gen Z and Gen Alpha in some circles), the 22nd century generations (22C). From an actuarial standpoint they are likely to live well into the 22nd century. Think what it was like to have no memory of life before books. These generations will have no memory of life before the Internet. They are the first generations of a New Era—not an era of change, but a change of era. What makes this book so valuable is Chromey's probing analysis of the role of technology (increasingly the GRAIN technology of Genetic engineering, Robotics, Artificial Intelligence, Infotech, and Nanotechnology) in the shaping of generations, and his masterful guidance on how to bring fresh understanding and bold undertakings to these change-of-era 22C generations.

"Every generation loses the messiah it has failed to deserve."
–Key plank in the Hasidic theory of the Tzaddik Ha-Dor

If history is any guide, the insights of one generation cannot be passed on to the next; they can only be explored and earned by each generation. Each generation discovers for itself and thinks it's the one who first invented it. Besides technology, what has shaped all generations, and ties all the generations together, are Story Dynasties. Five bodies of lore have galvanized us and gathered us together: *Star Wars* (11 films), *Harry Potter* (7 story arcs), *Games of Thrones* (8 seasons, 71 episodes), *Lord of the Rings* (6 books), *Marvel Universe* (22 story arcs).

Dr. Rick Chromey is someone who brailles the culture for new trends and movements with savvy and skill. He has now written a book that is a story of America and her generations—a narrative for the emerging 22C generations.

It's a story of change and challenge, if only we will listen, and apply the Seventh Generation Rule.

—**Dr. Leonard Sweet**, theologian, semiotician,
church historian, pastor and author

Introduction

What in the World Happened?

All things are wearisome, more than one can say.
The eye never has enough of seeing, nor the ear its fill of hearing.
What has been will be again, what has been done
will be done again; there is nothing new under the sun.
Is there anything of which one can say, "Look! This is something new"?
It was here already, long ago; it was here before our time.
Ecclesiastes 1:8-10

Midnight. December 31, 1999.

It was the dawn of a new century and another millennium.

This wasn't your typical New Year's Eve. Some believed the age of Aquarius was at hand. Some believed Jesus could return. Some thought technological hell would explode due to a mysterious Y2K bug.

December 31, 1999 was different. And everyone *felt* it.

My family ushered in the new millennium with a peaceful evening at home. We played board games, ate junk food, and watched *Dick Clark's Rockin' New Year's Eve*. We popped the cork on some sparkling cider, enjoyed a DVD movie on a big, boxy beast of a television and waited for the ball to drop. We used our landline phone to communicate new year's greetings to kinfolk far away (our family cell phone was reserved for calls when a regular phone wasn't available). I emailed a few friends via our Juno email account.

In 1999, the Internet was still young. There was no social media. No Facebook. No Twitter. No YouTube. No Instagram, Pinterest, or Snapchat. No podcasts, video chats, streaming services, robo calls or "apps." Most people used the web for information—not interaction. Chat rooms and message boards were popular, but blogs had yet to catch on. Google was somewhat unknown. Altavista and "Ask Jeeves" were preferred search engines. Amazon was making noise though. In 1999, Jeff Bezos was named *Time Magazine's* "Man of the Year." The new millennium would make him rich beyond imagination.

Meanwhile, Steve Jobs was busy resurrecting his computer company, trying desperately to get the masses to bite into the Apple. Yes, they had the iMac, but only hard-core Apple aficionados bought the machine. Most personal computers were pre-loaded with Microsoft Windows operating systems. People used Word, Excel, and PowerPoint. In the mid '90s, Apple Inc. was on life support. Steve Jobs had the company thinking "different" by 1999 and two years later they'd launch a revolutionary new music player named the iPod. In 1999, the first portable MP3 players appeared…but they weren't good—or pretty.

New Year's Eve 1999 was predicted to be an IT department's worst nightmare.

Most computers that controlled the infrastructure in America—particularly power grids—operated with internal clocks that couldn't compute 01/01/00. Technology experts and IT personnel worked feverishly to figure out a fix. Fear was widespread that the "Y2K Bug" would freeze networks, crash hard drives, and short-circuit servers that coordinated communications, banking, electricity, and other utilities.

Apocalyptic scenarios abounded.

Maybe Prince was right.

In 1982, the pop-funk star had hinted at a global Armageddon in his song titled "1999." The best we could do on such a perilous eve, Prince intoned, was to "party." For many people around the planet, his purple majesty seemed insightfully correct.

Two thousand, zero, zero…oops, *out of time.*

But we weren't out of time. Not by a long shot. It's been almost a quarter of a century since that millennium night and—*surprise, surprise*—we've survived. The world didn't end. Our computers didn't crash. Prince and those doomsday preachers were wrong. The Y2K bug was hype. With exception to a few isolated incidents, life continued as usual. We all woke up on New Year's Day 2000 to a parade and football. Nothing had changed.

Except that everything *would*. And soon. The first twenty years of the new millennium would transform the world.

Think about the technological change we've experienced since the calendar turned to January 1, 2000. From social media to GPS to smart phones to 3-D printing to cloud-based tech to self-driving cars, our world has experienced more change in the first twenty years of the millennium than in the previous 500 years *combined*.

And if that thought causes some pause, trust me, the next fifty years will produce revolutionary changes we cannot even yet imagine. Far bigger change is on the way.

I hope you're buckled in for this flight.

C-C-C-C-C-CHANGES

I was born May 29, 1963 in central Montana.

I grew up in a radically different "technological" world. My lower middle-class family watched three stations on a black and white television with rabbit ears—and two channels were "snowy." Between midnight and 6 a.m., television programming was a color test page. We started and ended every broadcast day with the national anthem. I still remember when we had cable television installed. We then enjoyed twelve crystal clear channels. Our new television had remote control. That was a nice innovation. For most of my childhood, I was the remote control. "Go change the channel," my dad would bark, and I did. *Click. Click. Click.*

Telephones were connected to a wall. I phoned family and friends with just a four or five number dial. In the rural regions of my central Montana world, there were "party lines." Essentially, several homes were hooked to the *same* phone line. It meant if rancher John was on the phone with his city brother Jerry that farmer Judy three doors down (and several miles away) could listen in on the conversation, waiting her turn for the line. Telephones had rotary (*click, click, click*) dials and bell rings. If you missed a call, you missed a call. Only rich people had answering machines, and I wasn't rich until 1983. Shoot, for most of my childhood, I was also the answering machine. "Get the phone, Rick!" my mom would yell. And I did. *Hello? This is the Chromeys.* That's another thing. We always announced our names at hello. It was proper phone etiquette. I still do it to this day.

On my tenth birthday, my parents gave me my first vinyl record. It was The Osmond's *Crazy Horses* album and I wore out the grooves. We had a huge console stereo in the living room. My dad was into old country (Patsy Cline, Hank Williams, Johnny Cash) and my mom favored rock (Elvis, Beatles, Stones). I had a portable record player in my bedroom with a tin can speaker, cardboard back, and plastic tone arm. When the needle dropped on that vinyl, I was transported to faraway places. My dad was a trucker. One day he came home with a large case of 8-track cassettes. He liked to listen to his favorite artists as he trucked down the road. Just imagine: your music of choice…on the go…in the car…*what a concept.*

Looking back, I was born at just the right time to experience the greatest technological shift in the history of mankind.

I watched a black and white world of newspapers and television morph into countless technicolor technologies. In junior high school, I took my first computer class and we didn't even have a computer in the classroom. In high school, I learned to type, a skill that remains handy. In 1986, to survive grad school, I bought my first computer (a double 5.25" floppy disk, no hard drive desktop). In 1988, I paid over a grand for a VHS camcorder. I filmed my kids' childhoods and still have boxes of home movies in the garage. If you're over forty-five, I bet you do too.

I've seen it all. The rise (and fall) of cassettes, VHS, CDs, and DVDs. The launch of MTV, CNN, ESPN, and entire channels devoted to shopping, home repair, and weather. The advent of GPS, MP3, JPEG, email, cyber-shopping, texting, tweeting, Google, and Facebook.

Today, I type on a laptop computer superior in muscle, battery life, speed, and memory than all my previous laptops *combined.* My FitBit watch is more powerful than the computers that put man on the moon in 1969. My satellite television delivers hundreds of channels, music, and movies (and is only hampered by real snow). I can read articles, listen to music, find an address, research a restaurant, video chat, and watch a baseball game *on my phone*. I save everything to something called "the cloud." I can get a degree, buy a home, attend church, plan a vacation, watch a movie, and order my groceries...*online*. My car is smart. My home is smart. I have smart speakers, smart phones, and smart kids.

And yet, I still have a DVD player with a blinking light (nothing a little black electrical tape can't fix).

Do I even dare to peek into our technological future?

On the horizon are robots, holograms, smart clothes, and self-driving cars. Our children's children will face new bio-ethical questions as they print 3-D organs and limbs to replace what's been damaged or diseased. We'll live in a world of screens that appear (and disappear) at will. Computers will be quicker than the brains that program them.

Yes, the world is changing...*fast*.

And every generation will experience those changes differently.

It's why we need to re-think, even reimagine, how we perceive and define generations today.

The Future is Rooted to the Past

It's not the first time the world has changed.

World history is filled with interesting patterns. One pattern is how massive cultural shifts happen roughly every 500 years. Several years ago, I formulated a concept called Cultural Language Theory. I theorized that technology—particularly certain "mega-tech" technologies—has the power to change cultural languages. These cultural languages are what societies use to guide learning, commerce, entertainment, and communication. Consequently, they influence all cultural institutions from the home to the church, from politics to business. When a cultural language changes, a whole new world emerges.

It's why we need people to read the cultural tea leaves. It's critical to understand the world and hold conversations about where we need to go. We need to make sense of what's happening.

In the science of geology, it's stated *the key to the past is the present*. Essentially, we understand what happened in former ages by studying what we see in the rocks today. We interpret the past through the sediment in which the fossil was found. Similarly, in cultural explorations, we rely upon a parallel concept: *the key to the future is the past.* You might say a good futurist is a great historian. He or she can look into the past, detect the patterns of history, and make a prediction that's fairly reliable.

Weather forecasters do it every day.

Every weather forecast is rooted to patterns of the past. The ability to accurately predict the weather only happens because someone has learned meteorological science, reviewed the weather records, recognized particular jet stream patterns, and identified that if A happens then B is likely to follow (especially if there's a pattern that whenever A occurs then B nearly always happens too). Satellite and Doppler radar technology have improved the potential for correct assumptions and astute projections.

But you don't need a meteorological degree to interpret seasonal weather changes.

For example, we know winter is approaching because we see the leaves turn colors and drop to the ground. When fall happens, we know (based upon past experience) that colder temperatures and snow will eventually come. A futurist simply reads the cultural leaves and then, like good weather forecasters, proposes educated predictions based upon what has happened in the past and present. Futurists study history, specifically obsolescence, to project what might happen in the years ahead.

Let me give one example of something we enjoy today—a piece of technology— that will likely be a dinosaur tomorrow. I know it will be hard to hear this prophecy because it's a true page turner.

I'm talking about the book as a printed publication.

Despite the proliferation of printed books today, including the one with paper pages you might be turning, there is growing concern about the future of printed materials. After all, the phone book is already a dead medium. Just like the scroll—a primary way of communicating for centuries—grew obsolete in the wake of Gutenberg technology, the printed book is potentially seeing its sunset as a new digital age emerges.

Still not convinced? Let's consider two print technologies that have seen better days.

Can You Picture That?

The photograph was the undisputed king of the modern paper culture, emerging as a bona fide cultural phenomenon in the mid 1800s. The photograph changed our world. It allowed us to see things as they truly are (not as an artist wanted us to see). For example, the Civil War was horrifically documented through the lens of the camera. Photographs played a major role in what we know about that war. Abraham Lincoln was the first U.S. president to be photographed. Cameras documented the opening of the West: from the gold rushes to the Oregon trail to the Indian Wars.

In the late 1800s, Eastman Kodak emerged as the camera (and film) to buy.

For over a century, Kodak was the first and last word in print photography. We bought Kodak cameras, Kodak film, and Kodak photo paper. We developed our photographs through Kodak technology, materials, and solutions. Anybody remember waiting several *days* to see how a roll of photos developed?

Kodak also led the cutting edge of a new medium: digital photography.

In 1990, Kodak developed the first Photo CD system and a year later released the first professional digital camera (with a $13,000 price tag!). In 1994, Kodak sold the first memory card (1 MB) and two years later was the first company to use an internal storage drive.[1] But for all its contributions to this new emerging technological world, Kodak preferred the sanctuary of its past and wanted the photograph to stay *on paper*. This explains why Kodak's most notable contribution was photographic film long after film began its death march. Even though Kodak recognized digital was the wave of the future, they held tightly to the old technology that made them "Kodak." And why not? For decades, the majority of cameras used Kodak film to capture special moments, historical events, and timeless beauty.

We called them "Kodak" moments.

Yes, Kodak initially led the pack in digital photography but, for whatever reason, resisted a complete transition to this new world. Other competitors like Canon, Olympus, and Nikon edged out Kodak by the late 1990s. Consequently, Kodak grew increasingly out of touch. It lost cultural traction and eventually filed for bankruptcy.[2] In 2012, Kodak ceased film sales and development. The age of developing every photograph (on paper) had ended. Digital photography was now the predominant media. Oh sure, there remains a space for those who still need a paper version of their photo but it's a niche market. With the rise of Facebook, Snapchat, and Instagram, the digital photo had better appeal. We used to print every photo we snapped. Now we just print very special ones.

Camera film is dead technology.

Copy That Story

Similarly, newspapers have come on hard times in recent years. For most of the twentieth century, newspapers were the go-to media for news, commentary, weather, sports, obituaries, and classifieds. But, by the year 2000, the Internet had changed how we interacted with current events. Websites could publish and push news as it happened while newspapers had natural delays in printing and delivery. This was never more evident than on September 11, 2001. As live television, for the first time, carried the unfolding story of a terror attack upon New York City and Washington, the Millennial and Gen X generations were furiously clicking the computer mouse, scrolling for news and information. By the time the newspapers printed headline stories about 9-11 and dropped them on America's doorsteps, it was *old* news.

The world had changed. Newspapers were no longer relevant.

As social media—particularly Facebook, YouTube, and Twitter—emerged, news and commentary were further reduced to 140-character word bites and four-minute video clips. Micro media changed how we consumed current events. Even televised news—both mainstream and cable—found viewership in decline. Younger generations gravitated toward Internet news sites like the *Huffington Post*, *Breitbart*, *The Daily Beast*, and *Drudge*. Facebook singlehandedly became the new commentary for current events. With social media, every person could be a broadcaster, videographer, commentator, and storyteller. And it doesn't take long for fake news to brew with a cocktail of contributors producing varying views, perceptions, and ideas.

Social media spelled doom for newspapers. Newsprint suddenly became useful for little more than lining bird cages, starting fires, and packing boxes.

Consequently, between 2008 and 2010, more than 166 newspapers stopped their presses. Since then, dozens of major newspapers—including the *Rocky*

Mountain News and *Tucson Citizen*—ceased publication.[3] Dozens more reduced their staff to skeletal crews to stave off closure. Some newspapers, like *The Detroit News*, now only deliver to homes a few times a week.[4] Every major newspaper has lost print readers.[5]

The advent of social media, apps, and smartphones instantaneously broadcasted news, often raw and unedited, for human consumption and interpretation. News is continuously feeding our feeds.

Many predict the newspaper will be a dinosaur in a decade. Most people under forty don't read them. It's the same with magazines. I recently converted thousands of air miles into subscriptions to various periodicals, from *People* to *The New Yorker*. Every week, I received a half dozen magazines. I perused the covers and table of contents...and laid them aside. In a week or two I tossed them...mostly *unread*. It's old news. If I'm curious about something, I google it. If I'm interested in certain topics, my Facebook feed brings them to me.

It's why some predict the *printed* book will be history by 2050.

After all, printed books take up space and weight. They literally have a shelf life in a web culture. In contrast, digital books occupy little cyber real estate and entire libraries can be contained on a flash drive, tablet, or smart phone. As younger generations grow up, naturally wired to read and interact with digital materials, the printed book will seem antiquated, heavy, and irrelevant. It won't fit the future lifestyle and living quarters of tomorrow's world citizen.

The irony is that the printed book was once the T. rex of the modern culture. It was at the top of the media food chain. When other media faltered, failed, or faded, the book hung in there. But today, the digital book is also flourishing. In fact, more and more digital books are published every day. The proverbial writing is on the wall. Digitization is changing everything.

But it's not just the book.

Other media is growing obsolete and extinct, like the "silver" disc (CD and DVD). Streaming media continues to grow as the primary choice of younger generations. Consequently, the physical disk is losing steam. Pawn shops specialize in flipping stuff and they won't buy a CD collection anymore. Like vinyl records in the 1990s, local thrift shops are now well-stocked with CDs that people can't sell in their yard sales or on Craig's List.

Obsolete or Soon-To-Be Obsolete Technology (Since 1970)

Adding Machines

Cassette/CD Players (Walkman, Discman)

Calculators

GPS Navigation Systems (stand alone models)

Pagers and Beepers

Typewriters

Altavista Search Engine

Compact Discs

Compact Cassette

Instant Cameras (Polaroid)

Personal Digital Assistants (PDAs, Blackberries)

Videocassettes

Analog Radio Transmission

Computer Mouse

Dot Matrix Printers

LaserDisc

Phone Books

Video Game Disc Systems (Atari 2600, Nintendo)

Answering Machines

Desktop Computer

Fax Machines

Mimeograph

Portable Dictation Devices

8-Track Cassettes

DVDs and Portable DVD Players

Filmstrip

MiniDiscs and MiniDisc Players

Portable Gaming Devices (Gameboy, Gamegear)

Betamax

Dial-Up Modems

Film Cameras, Film and Film Developing

MP3 Players (including the iPod)

Public Pay Phones

Cathode Ray Tube Televisions

Digital Audi Tapes (DAT)

Floppy Disks (8", 5.25", 3.5")

NTSC Television Broadcasting

Rotary Dial Telephones and Landlines

Car Phones

Digital Versatile Disc (DVD) and HD DVD

Folding Maps

Overhead Projectors

Slides and Slide Projectors

You can also soon say goodbye to satellite and cable television. Streaming options and YouTube are the preferred way to watch television for the under-thirty crowd. If you're investing in DirecTV, Dish Network, BlueRay, and RedBox... consider yourself warned.

But this isn't the first time the world has changed...and it won't be the last. If that's an unsettling idea, I get it. The technology that influences our lives, particularly in youth and young adulthood, will mark us for life. In fact, technology has significantly tattooed every American generation since 1900. We are generations of technology.

Transportation and telephone. Motion pictures. Radio. Television. Space. Video games. Personal computers. Cellphones. Internet. Robotics.

We are Americans and this is *our* technology.

It's become our unique, collective story.

A story that needs to be told.

And that's why I wrote this book.

Chapter One

Generations

"Technology shows up and changes the culture. The culture then enables new industries and movements, which further change the culture. And then technology shows up and puts an end to the system we were all used to."
—Seth Godin

Generations come and generations go.

It's been that way since the beginning of time. It's the "story" in hi*story*. Every generation contributes a phrase or paragraph, a comment or chapter to the greater digest of mankind. In the larger book of recorded history, the lines can eventually blur, fade, and disappear. Unless highlighted by the conscientious, a generation can easily be forgotten once the reader turns pages into the future.

And yet, without the contribution of each generation, just like a single sentence in a book, the overall work can suffer. That doesn't mean every generation should be treated the same. Some generations live in the shadows of greater ones. Others are marked by negative circumstances, horrific struggles, and misplaced values.

Still others prove idealistic, positive, and influential. Every generation has its own psyche and personality.

It's what flavors and colors history. The stories within the story create the chronicles of a generation, a people, and mankind.

It wasn't until the last half of the twentieth century that sociologists seriously charted, studied, and considered generations. At best, certain distinctive birth cohorts were labeled in the literature of their day. For example, the term "Gen X" was employed by Douglas Coupland in his 1991 fiction novel titled *Gen X: Tales for an Accelerated Culture*. Prior to 1991, this cohort of babies were known as "baby busters."[6] In the same year as Coupland's novel, William Strauss and Neil Howe penned *Generations: The History of America's Future, 1584–2069*, a landmark book that launched a national conversation about who we really are. In this epic historical and sociological tome, the authors reimagined generations into cycles with four "turnings" inside each cycle. Not only did Strauss and Howe create fresh boundary lines and labels for various generations, but they also saw patterns and repetitions. Strauss and Howe inspired the tag of "Millennial" for the generational cohort being born at the time their book was published (supplanting the generic "Generation Y" label).[7]

"As is the generation of leaves, so too of man
At one time the wind shakes the leaves to the ground
but then the flourishing woods
Gives birth, and the season of spring comes into existence,
so it is with the generations of men,
which alternately come forth and pass away."
Homer, *The Illiad, sixth book*

While there is academic criticism regarding Strauss and Howe's socio-historical views, particularly in how certain generations are framed and labeled, there has also been general acceptance of their theoretical ideas.[8]

Talkin' 'Bout My Generation

What exactly constitutes a "generation?" How is a generational cohort defined? How long is a generation? What is its sociological nature? These are critical questions that form the foundation for any conversation about "generations."

According to social scientists, developmental psychologists and cultural historians, a new generation is born approximately every twenty years. Since the majority of babies are born during our "young adult" years (ages twenty-forty)—a span of two decades—it's fair to conclude a different generation emerges approximately every twenty years.[9] This seems sensible at face value, but it's also problematic. After all, every year a new cohort of people turn twenty. Essentially, that could mean every year a new generation is being born.

It's why we need additional markers—historical and societal—to demarcate a generation. Human development only gives the *length* of a generation (approximately twenty years), but it cannot provide an accurate "start" and "finish" to a generational frame.

"A generation is composed of people whose common location in history lends them a collective persona. The span of one generation is roughly the length of a phase of life. Generations come in four archetypes, always in the same order, whose phase-of-life positions comprise a constellation."
William Strauss and **Neil Howe**

Historically, the best frames are created by circumstance. A generation is a group of people who experienced a similar life path; that is, they endured the same events over time.

One of the earliest numerical references to a generation is in the Old Testament: '*The Lord is slow to anger, abounding in love and forgiving sin and rebellion. Yet he does not leave the guilty unpunished; he punishes the children for the sin of the* **parents to the third and fourth generation**' (Numbers 14:18). This framework will eventually prove true for the ancient, disobedient Israelites, who wandered in the desert and were prohibited entrance into their "promised land" for four decades or two generations of twenty years (Numbers 32:13). In other biblical texts, a twenty-year-old is considered an adult and subject to "adult" roles and responsibilities, from military service (Numbers 1:20) to taxation (Exodus 38:25–27). Consequently, at least from a biblical view, there is merit to a generation lasting two decades.

In addition, every generation also possesses a collective personality that drives cultural attitudes and behaviors. This persona is influenced via the social, political, spiritual, and historical contexts in which a cohort of people journey. Consequently, every generation inherits a unique cultural clock and cloak that they wear their entire life. A Baby Boomer raised in a post-World War II landscape differs from a Millennial raised during the War on Terror. There might be similar stressors and even occasional common themes (fear of nuclear war) but, in general, no one would see these two generations as being similar.

This is where technology offers some help. Baby boomers experienced a radio and primitive television world in their youth and these technologies shaded their generational psyche all their lives. Boomers tend to see things more "black and white" and idealistic. They marched for peace and "flower power" in the 1960s, promoted women's rights and sexual revolution in the 1970s, and became soccer moms and "conscientious" politicians in the 1980s and 1990s. In contrast, Millennials grew up in a web and digital culture with email, texting, downloads, and uploads. In adolescence and young adulthood, Millennials were the first adopters of social media. The world for them is more multi-dimensional, multi-cultural, and multi-visual. Consequently, Millennials view life with more "color" (diversity, harmony, and tolerance).

It's the technology of a generation that influences its personality.

Furthermore, every generation is framed by certain major socio-historical events that mark their inner psyche. These events guide each generation with a collective historical consciousness. Using Strauss and Howe's generational frames, in part, it's easy to witness the impact and influence of these cultural events[10]:

- G.I. Generation (1901–1924): *World War I, Great Depression, Pearl Harbor, World War II*
- Silent Generation (1925–1942): *Great Depression, Pearl Harbor, World War II, and Korea*

- Boomer Generation (1943–1960): *Sputnik, Eisenhower, JFK, Vietnam, man on the moon, Watergate*
- Gen X (1961–1981): *Man on the moon, Watergate, Iran hostages, Reagan, Challenger, Desert Storm*
- Millennials (1982–1999): *Desert Storm, OJ, Columbine, Clinton, 9/11/01, Katrina, War on Terror, Great Recession*
- iTech (2000–present): *Great Recession, War on Terror, Parkland school shooting*

In fact, what we *can't* historically remember might be as important as what we do. Every generation is tattooed by a certain "mega" event that the next generation *cannot* recall, and it's precisely because we can't remember it that we differ from the previous generations.

Every Boomer, for example, can recount where they were on November 22, 1963. John F. Kennedy's assassination galvanized an emerging generation of young Americans. On the other hand, Gen X was too young to remember Kennedy. It's why the classic Boomer birth frame (1946–1964) fails. The post-WWII baby boom actually began in 1943 (not 1946) when soldiers initially returned home from European battlefields[11] Furthermore, the post-war "baby boom" culturally ended in 1960 with the introduction of oral contraception[12] Strauss and Howe rightly reset the "Boomer" birth years to 1943–1960 for this reason. Gen X (or the "Baby Busters" for their lower generational birth rate) is more appropriately framed between 1961–1981.

"There is a mysterious cycle in human events. To some generations much is given. Of other generations much is expected. This generation has a rendezvous with destiny."
Franklin D. Roosevelt

Most of us begin to retain memory of cultural events between the ages of five and seven[13] Consequently, it's very difficult for anyone to truly recall the Kennedy assassination if they were born *after* 1958! What we remember most from our preschool years are "passed on" memories from significant adults through stories and photographs. I'm a classic case of this misidentification. I was born May 29, 1963. I was six months old when President Kennedy was assassinated. I don't remember anything about that tragic day. And yet, I've been tagged a "baby boomer" (1946–1964) all my life. It's not true. My generational psyche was formed by other events, most notably man walking on the moon in 1969 (the first significant news story I recall). From this perspective, every generation has an experience they *can't* remember, and this event is so big in the American cultural fabric that it powerfully shapes the emerging generation:

- G.I. Generation (1901–1924) cannot recall: *Great San Francisco Earthquake (1906)*
- Silent Generation (1925–1942) cannot recall: *Stock Market Crash (1929)*
- Boomer Generation (1943–1960) cannot recall: *Hiroshima/Nagasaki atom bomb (1945)*
- Gen X (1961–1981) cannot recall: *Assassination of John F. Kennedy (1963)*
- Millennials (1982–1998) cannot recall: *Challenger explosion (1986)*
- iTech (1999–present) cannot recall: *Terror attacks on New York and Washington (2001)*

In this book, I'll argue for a technological framework to understand American generations. Nevertheless, we cannot underestimate the power of historical events. There are just certain occurrences that change us and how we look at our world.[14]

Another interesting twist on generational cohorts are the identifiable phases or "waves." Every generation has a clear "early" and "late" phase (of about ten years). It's why an early member of a particular generation might seem different than later members. Strauss and Howe noted these "waves" in their description of the G.I. Generation (b. 1901–1923).[15] The Boom generation clearly has a two-phase personality: Elvis boomers (b. 1943–1952) and Beatle boomers (b. 1953–1960). Similarly, Gen X has two distinct phases: Pong and Pacman Xers (b. 1961–1971) and Mario Brothers Xers (b. 1972–1981). The Millennials are often (and lazily) reduced to a "Y" and "Z" but in reality, these are just early and late phases of the same generation. Early "Y" Millennials are Bush/Clinton Millennials (1982–1991) while later "Z" members are Clinton/Bush

Millennials (1992–1999). Even the iTechs reveal two phases: Cell phone iTechs (b. 2000–2009) and Smartphone iTechs (b. 2011–present).

The Generations

Currently, there are six living generations in America today. The oldest is the "G.I. Generation" (born 1901–1923), but this "greatest generation" is dying off fast. The youngest G.I.s are in their upper '90s in 2020. The newest American generation is the iTechs (born since 2000). In 2017, this generation graduated its first high school class.

Before I give a brief overview of these living American generations, it's necessary to address the cyclical nature of generations. This was the novel thesis proposed by Strauss and Howe. They argued that just like a calendar year contains four seasons, there is a four-part cycle to the generations:[16]

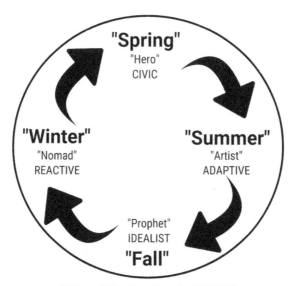

Neil Howe and William Strauss "Generations" Cycle (1991)

These generations repeat approximately every eighty years (creating a four-part cycle). A major, prolonged crisis that completely rearranges the American cultural landscape is the spark for a new cycle. It's not hard to see these "crises" in our history, each one starting with a significant tragic event that has repercussions for years:

- 2001–2016: September 11, 2001 Terrorist attacks, War on Terror, and Great Recession
- 1929–1945: Black Friday, Great Depression, Pearl Harbor, World War II
- 1860–1865: Election of Abraham Lincoln, secession of southern states, Civil War
- 1773–1783: Boston Tea Party, Lexington/Concord, Revolutionary War

According to Strauss and Howe's generational cycle theory, we are currently on the back end of what they label "The Millennial Cycle." This post-WWII cycle began with the *Idealist* Boom generation (1943–1960), followed by the *Reactive* Gen X generation (1961–1981), *Civic* Millennial generation (1982–2004), and the *Adaptive* Homeland generation (born since 2005).[17] It's interesting to note that the next great American generation is about to be born and, if it follows the pattern, will be "idealistic" like the Boomers.

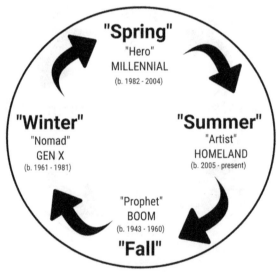

Neil Howe and William Strauss Millennial Cycle (1943-present)

In this work, I offer this frame for generations as way of introduction. However, my working thesis will rattle this prevalent idea and propose generations that are less fixed and more fluid, less sequential and more interactive, less tattooed by cultural events and more guided by technology that informs their unique generational identity and personality. Strauss and Howe speak to technological change and influence in their generational explanations but tend to focus more on historical events as markers that make a generation what it is. And while I agree that events do influence a generation, I would argue the *awareness* of these events would not be possible without technology. The news of the Civil War was helped significantly by telegraph. Pearl Harbor would've been far less momentous without radio, film, and photography to capture it. September 11 was horrific, but without the Internet and cable news, a much different matter.

Here is a brief overview of each living generation born since 1900.

G.I. Generation (b. 1901–1924)
Front "coming of age" event: World War I
Back "coming of age" event: World War II
Strauss and Howe Archetype: Hero

The G.I. Generation was the sons and daughters of the Lost Generation of the late 1800s. From birth, they were protected, honored, and serviced. They were the first American generation to drink pasteurized milk and receive vaccinations. They were the first Boy and Girl Scouts. Tom Brokaw later dubbed this cohort of Americans as the "greatest generation."[18] Strauss and Howe suggested the acronym "G.I." meant they were "government issued" or "general issued" in nature. Consequently, it's helpful to view them as more than just a "war time" cohort, but also grooved by their cultural elders to value citizenship, appreciate homogeneity, and accept general principles of duty, respect, and hard work.

The G.I. generation was raised in a new world of technology: telephones, radio, automobiles, and planes. After they fought in two world wars (collectively saving the world from fascism and tyranny) and survived the Great Depression, they came home to build suburbs, dams, interstates, McDonalds, and Disneyland. As a generation, they have produced great leaders, including a three-decade string of U.S. Presidents from John F. Kennedy to H.W. Bush. This is the generation of John Wayne, Billy Graham, Bob Hope, and Jimmy Stewart. In fact, no other movie personifies the G.I. Generation more than the 1946 Christmas classic *It's A Wonderful Life*. In elderhood, the G.I. generation retired early (many to sunbelt states like Florida or Arizona), devoted their spare time to travel, and enjoyed "senior citizen" discounts, pensions, and government perks like Social Security and Medicaid. The G.I. Generation created the "silver" (over fifty-five) American cultural dream to save early, retire right, and live long.

For the G.I. Generation, life threw some early curve balls, but they finished well.

Silent Generation (b. 1925–1942)

Front "coming of age" event: Atomic Bomb
Back "coming of age" event: Yuri Gagarin space flight
Strauss and Howe Archetype: Artist

The Silent Generation has purportedly been a quiet generation. Unlike their G.I. elders who fought in two world wars, the Silents earned their military stripes in Korea (a.k.a. The Forgotten War, 1950–1953). Korea wasn't even tagged a war originally but a "police action." Korean War veterans were the last to receive a monument in Washington, D.C. (1995). By comparison to other American generations, it's also a small cohort number—due to the economic hardship and insecurity of the Great Depression, when most of the Silents were born.

The Silent Generation—a term coined by a 1951 *Time* magazine article on American youth—is the only American generation to not produce a U.S. president, although it generated its fair share of hopefuls from Michael Dukakis to John McCain. It did produce a few U.S. Vice Presidents, including Walter Mondale, Dick Cheney, and Joe Biden, and some notable first ladies like Barbara Bush, Rosalyn Carter, and Jacqueline Kennedy.[19]

Some have argued the "silent" term refers to this generation's "focus on careers over activism" and that may be true. This was the generation that produced the popular business book *How To Succeed In Business Without Really Trying* (1952) and "pop" business leaders like Zig Ziglar, Jim Rohn, and Wayne Dyer. The Silent Generation came of age in a post-World War II America and were "rebels without a cause." As young adults, they enjoyed peace time and the long prosperous shadow created by their G.I. elders. In fact, many opted for silence during the McCarthy era.

The Silent also experienced its fair share of tragedy, losing its most influential voices far too early and many in the prime of their life, including Martin Luther

King, Jr, Malcolm X, Robert Kennedy, Marilyn Monroe, James Dean, Buddy Holly, Elvis Presley, Marvin Gaye, Jimi Hendrix, and John Lennon.

Boom Generation (b. 1943–1960)

Front "coming of age" event: John F. Kennedy assassination
Back "coming or age" event: John Lennon assassination
Strauss and Howe Archetype: Prophet

No generation has been more celebrated, labeled, and discussed than the "Boom" Generation birthed in a post-World War II America. They were originally known as "Spock Babies" due to elders who raised them by the parenting wisdom of pediatrician Benjamin Spock and his bestselling book *Baby and Child Care* (1946). However, the "boomers" were also festooned with other nicknames: flower children, Woodstock Gen, Me Gen, yuppies, soccer moms, and, most recently, silver surfers. As a cohort, they have always been about movements, whether it was anti-war, civil rights, "Jesus," feminism, LGTBQ rights, or abortion. Consequently, they were dubbed draft dodgers, peaceniks, Black Panthers, hippies, and Jesus freaks, to name a few additional monikers.

The Boomers grew up in a cultural Disneyland where fathers knew best and "liked Ike." They dined upon a new music known as rock 'n roll (Elvis, Beatles, Dylan) and worshipped sports heroes like Jackie Robinson, Willie Mays, Joe DiMaggio, and Mickey Mantle. When the Russians beat America to space in 1957 (Sputnik), a cold war fear, anti-Communism spirit brewed that forced Boomer kids to "duck and cover" under school desks and in backyard bomb shelters.

Not surprisingly, Boomers have used their "flower power" to change America. They've been successful, whether in public morality (civil, gay, women rights), faith/religion (new age and megachurch movements) or technology (television, microwaves, video cassette recorders, computers). What the Boomers never saw coming was the Great Recession. Just as they retired (or intended to retire), the mid-00s economy tanked, home prices crashed, and layoffs gutted the American work force. Many Boomers couldn't afford to retire and so they continued to work (forcing Gen Xers in their wake to stall or lose their own careers).

Now in their "silver surfer" years, these boomer seniors continue to rewrite social norms. Seventy is the new sixty. Sixty is the new fifty. And Disneyland dreams still happen for those who wish upon a star.

Gen X (b. 1961–1981)

Front "coming of age" event: Iran Hostage Crisis
Back "coming of age" event: Clinton Impeachment
Strauss and Howe Archetype: Nomad

If there's anything revealing for how a generation is described and characterized, it's the label of Generation X. Sandwiched between the beautiful and blessed boomers and the precocious and innocuous Millennials, Gen X is clearly the "Jan Brady" of America generations. They're stuck in the middle on a horse with no name. "X" marks the spot. "X" means crossed off. "X" is for the illiterate and illegitimate. And Gen X is all those things.

Gen X is the title of a Douglas Coupland novel that found traction with a cohort once called "baby busters."[20] In reality, there was a "bust" and a birthing well for Gen X, first due to the introduction of the Pill (1960) and later the legalization of abortion (1973). Consequently, Gen X youth were unwanted before birth and often ignored, abandoned, forgotten, and demonized after birth. Gen X was aborted, daycared, and latchkeyed. They were the first generation to experience the widespread divorce of their parents, cohabitation, a drug culture, and an AIDS epidemic.

In the media, Gen X was portrayed as blank, dumb, or slackers.[21] They were a *Nation at Risk*—the title of an educational analysis by the Reagan administration (1983).[22] In the movies, Gen Xers were goonies, bad news bears, nerds, breakfast club delinquents, children of the damned, and exorcist kids. Consequently, Gen X grew up with a cultural chip on their shoulder. They were as happy as underachiever Bart Simpson to flip the bird to their parents, teachers, preachers, and other authorities who never gave them a break. Xers introduced two new forms of edgy American music to the world: rap and grunge. They also led the Silicon Valley dotcom boom, extreme sport, emerging church, and #MeToo movements.

As a generation who experienced first Richard Nixon's lies and then Bill Clinton's perjury, it's no wonder Gen X opted to drain the swamp and elect a nonpolitical outsider like Donald Trump for president.[23] His crass, narcissistic, and punishing presidential manners are quintessential Gen X. After all, similar to the trajectory and explosion of Challenger (1986), Gen X equally views itself on a collective catastrophic trip to implosion. The Great Recession and housing crisis of 2007–2009 were just the start. That's when many older Gen X men lost their middle management jobs and never recovered (most downsized, accepted lower pay, worked part-time, or became entrepreneurs). Gen Xers doubt they'll enjoy a retirement like their parents and grandparents. Their savings are already slim, thanks to the Recession, inflation, and covering high college tuition for their Millennial kids.

But Gen X will figure out a way to survive. They always have and always will.

Millennials (b. 1982–1999)

Front "coming of age" event: Columbine School Shooting
Back "coming of age" event: Parkland School Shooting
Strauss and Howe Archetype: Hero

In the early 1980s, a "baby on board" generation was born, mostly to late Boomers and young Gen Xers. For the next two decades, these "millennial" babies—a term widely attributed to William Strauss and Neil Howe in their watershed work *Generations*—refocused America on youth and family.

The Millennials proved a "www" generation: *wanted, watched, and worthy.* Maternity wards and mini-vans were full. Babies R Us stores launched. Babies were everywhere, even in the movies (*Three Men and a Baby, Baby Boom,* and *Look Who's Talking*). Millennials were also protected (by parent and politician): baby monitors, bike helmets, car seats, air bags, kid-proof medicine caps, Amber alerts, and school metal detectors. It takes a village was the word, and helicopter parenting proved the trend. The Millennials were also culturally blessed. They were awarded participation trophies and "student of the month" honors, sent on mission trips, given Hollywood leads, scored Top 40 hits, and secured book deals.

The Millennials were the early adopters of emerging technology. They are a cell phone generation that grew up on the tech ABCs: jpeg, pdf, mpeg, mp3, mp4, gps, url, org, com, usb, mov, edu, dvd, cd, and cd-rom. Millennials are the first digital generation and the first to dive into social media. In fact, it was a few Millennials named Kevin Systrom (1983), Mark Zuckerberg (1984), Bobby Murphy (1988), and Evan Spiegel (1990) who launched Instagram, Facebook, and Snapchat, respectfully.

The Millennial generation hasn't been without trouble, however. They were also the first to experience mass school shootings by peers (Columbine), the terrorist attacks on American soil (September 11, 2001), and the Great Recession (2007–2009). Millennials have always been tolerant, relaxed, experiential, and sensitive. In the wake of the 2016 elections, the term "snowflake" was attached to some Millennials, a derisive label to suggest they were an entitled generation that was fragile, over-sensitive, and easily offended, in need of coddling, safe places, easy workloads, and needless praise.

In reality, the Millennials are proving highly resilient to cultural change, open to fresh ideas and emerging technology. In Strauss and Howe's theoretical frame, the Millennials are a "hero" generation like their great grandfathers and great grandmothers. Time will tell whether history and historians will look back on the Millennials like Tom Brokaw did with the G.I. Generation and bless them as yet another "great" American generation.

The iTech Generation (b. 2000–present)

Front "coming of age" event: 2020 Presidential Election
Back "coming of age" event: Yet to be Determined
Strauss and Howe Archetype: Artist

The iTech Generation has had its own share of labels, most of which have not stuck. Strauss and Howe call them the post-9-11 "Homeland Generation." Psychologist Jean Twenge refers to them as "iGen."[24] Others tag them as Gen Z, Gen Wii, Plurals, Digital Natives, or NetGen.[25] Several years ago, as I watched this generation emerge and studied their cultural frame, I noted how Apple "i" technology guided their historical context:

- 1998: iMac
- 1999: iBook (laptop)
- 2001: iPod, iTunes
- 2007: iPhone
- 2010: iPad
- 2015: iWatch

Each of these "i" technologies significantly moved the world forward into a digital, downloadable, touchscreen, social media world. The iPod killed the compact disc. The iPhone introduced the smartphone experience. The iPad changed how we read, consumed entertainment, played games, and worked. The iWatch brought time back to our wrists (among other things).

The iTech generation was raised in a swipe and pinch, screen and cloud world. They've known nothing but social media (Facebook, Twitter, YouTube) and cloud-based programming (Netflix, Hulu, Pandora, Amazon Prime, Sling). Everything happens for them on screens…and these touch screens are interactive. This highly personal—trending narcissistic—technological culture creates the "i" in iTech. Deep down, this emerging generation is self-designed, self-empowered, and self-centered. They personalize everything to create a unique, individualistic social mark. Their number of followers determines self-worth. Some iTechers have millions of hits on their YouTube videos, as well as millions of followers on Twitter, Facebook, and Instagram. In fact, some of the most "famous" iTechs—not to mention wealthy—are social media moguls. Teenagers like Mr. Monkey and Skylander Girl (YouTube), Kristina Pimenova (Instagram), and Shae Bennett (vlogger).

The iTechs have no recollection of the terrorist attacks on September 11, 2001—but that doesn't mean they haven't known terror. In fact, their generation has experienced even more troubles than their Millennial, Gen X, and Boomer elders. These children and teens have lived through the Great Recession (2007–2009), Islamic extremist bombings, school shootings, and terrible catastrophes and human crises. And they've done so with more awareness of these perils due to 24/7 news cycles, social media, memes, blogs, and podcasts. They've always had a phone in their pocket. They've had drone parents hovering overhead. Sociologist Neil

Howe comments, "Carefully raised by hands-on Gen-X parents, who don't dare let their own kids take the same risks they themselves took, Homelanders literally spend more time "at home" (with their multiple digital platforms) than any earlier child generation in history."[26]

In 2018, the first iTech class graduated high school and trotted off to college, even though online learning is a common educational strategy. The iTech Generation, as the first purely cyber generation, will no doubt reimagine how we work, worship, learn, interact, and amuse ourselves.

Generations come and go. But they always leave a mark.

Certainly, cultural events and historical happenings can tattoo a generational psyche, but the rise of the post-modern generations (Gen X, Millennials, and iTechs) suggests that technology plays a critical role in how we demarcate and label a generation. In fact, as we survey the technological landscape since 1900, it's clear that emerging technologies carved the path and framed the cohorts we call "generations." We are uniquely shaped by innovations that influenced us during our "coming of age" years (ages ten to twenty-five). It's the technological interactions in our adolescence and college years that guide our generational frames more than anything.

We are generations of technology.

We are GenTech.

Chapter Two

Waves

"Think of a tree. Does it go through a straight linear growth process?
Well, yes—it grows from one year to the next, straight ahead through time.
But no—because that time is a cyclical experience of seasons:
Winter, summer latency, activity.

For animals and humans, it's sleep, waking, work, rest, morning, night.
Life is a loopy linear cycle: progress, set-back, breakthrough, slowdown,
Growth, pruning, same thing, cyclically but different too, year after year."
Leonard Sweet

It's a wet and loopy world. We live in a culture of curves, ripples, rings, and waves. We used to live in a world that was more squared. It was a world of boxes featuring cultural corners that directed us, societal frames that defined us, and collective labels that limited us. For hundreds of years, the technology we used constricted our universe into identifiable truths. Photographs revealed the *real* story. Video captured life *as it was happening*. Newspapers and television reported *known* facts. It was a world that was predictable, secure, and reasonable.

17

In a word, modernity was about *control*.

This confident (some might argue arrogant) modern worldview spawned dozens of deterministic ideas, including Darwinian evolution, behavioral psychology and theological atheism. It's no wonder nineteenth-century philosopher Friedrich Nietzsche's famously quipped that "God is dead."[27] After all, if man can put God in a box (philosophically and theologically), it's not all that difficult to suffocate Him altogether.

But we don't live in that world anymore. In a post-modern cyber culture, the boxes are gone. The world is fast, flat, fluid…and spiritual.

———————

"Maybe the most certain of all philosophical problems is the problem of the present time, of what we are, in this very moment."
Michel Foucault

———————

We now live in a multiverse where technology frees every person to produce, write, create, film, barter, comment, and sell. Photographs can be doctored. Video can be manipulated. Fake news is what the "other guy" reports, the one with whom you disagree. In a world where we surf the web and create our own waves, there is no predictability and no security. Nothing has to make sense.

In a word, we happily live and thrive inside *chaos*.

It's this wet, chaotic, digital, and cyber world that forces us to think differently about who we are, where we came from, and where we're going. What used to be definable is now blurred. What used to be reasonable is now nonsense. What used to be predictable is now spontaneous and uncontrollable.

———————

"Here at home, we're in a world of right angles and human construct, so whether it's cement or plastic or steel, everything is at an angle. But nature is chaos theory in full play. So having that uniqueness of what nature is gives me a sense of rejuvenation and scale."
Conrad Anker

———————

The World Wide Web is our best example. At its root, it's simply one computer linking to another computer, hyperlinks connecting to other hyperlinks, wireless activity buzzing through invisible, interactive wires. It seems so ordered, defined, and connected. And yet, as we step back and move further away from these zillions of microscopic connections, we see beautiful waves of chaotic human interaction. These breakers reveal patterns filled with curvatures, concaves, and conversions. Like ocean waves striking the shores of humanity, the World Wide Web is best observed through the human sands that it sifts and shifts. The shoreline is constantly changing, moving with the tides, washing in and washing away. Similarly, the World Wide Web features countless websites that operate like mythic sandcastles. The water lapping against these cyber fortresses creates small changes but it's the occasional rogue wave that washes them away in an instant. Any cyber permanence is subject to the surf of time, culture, and popularity. Anybody remember Friendster? Or Ask Jeeves? Or Pets.com? Or Altavista?

This is why I've come to view generations of man differently. Rather than linear, I see loopy. Rather than fixed, I see fluid. I see generations that experience life more like tidal waves than tidy boxes.

"During the 1960s…a general intellectual mood of change and the dissolution of old paradigms was joined by spectacular political upheaval and struggle throughout the world, along with the emergence of new forms of thought, culture, technology and life, which would produce the matrix for the postmodern turn."
Steven Best and **Douglas Kellner**

Approximately every twenty years a new generation rises, but that's the only defining mark we enjoy. Generations can be short or long, idealistic or realistic, positive or negative, large or small. Like breakers in the surf, every generation rises in youth, swells in young adulthood, breaks into a roaring crash in middle adulthood, and gently washes the shores of time in elderhood.

Breaking Out of the Box

Generational theory has long been guided by a linear, fixed approach. For decades, sociologists and historians have put generations inside boxes and brackets, with clever labels and defining monikers. This labeling worked because a post-Enlightenment culture was building the boxes. Let's create a box that identifies a Boomer, a Gen Xer, or a Millennial. These frames worked because we *willed* them to work. We found security inside our boxes and some sanctuary within our generational tags.

They also made *sense* to us.

Control, expedience, and logic ruled the modern world.

Until the late twentieth century, there was no rhyme or reason for how generations rolled through time. To be honest, few people deeply considered how generations interacted with each other. One generation followed another generation, that followed another generation, that followed yet another generation. If there was any rhyme, it was a linear perspective. Generations were laid down like inches on a ruler.

It wasn't until William Strauss and Neil Howe proposed a cyclical view to generations that we began to see our world in a different light. In their writings, they charted these cycles as far back in Anglo-American history as "The Arthurian Generation" (AD 1433–1460):[28]

Like a tree's rings, this outline gives a helpful overview of American history. But Strauss and Howe primarily focused on cultural and historical events to define various generations. I'd like to propose a fresh perspective and a new template piloted by *technological* change. My general thesis is that technology shapes the personality of a generation far more than random events and cultural micro-changes. Technology is what creates our cultural awareness. It could be argued that the "printing press" generations were more "aware" because of Gutenberg's invention. The historical events that shaped them were exposed and explained *through* print technology. The same could be said for radio generations or television generations or web generations. The automobile and airplane allowed people to travel great distances, to personally experience what they once only heard through story or read in print.

AMERICAN GENERATION ARCHETYPES

HERO	ARTIST	PROPHET	NOMAD
ARTHURIAN (AD 1433-1460	HUMANIST (AD 1460-1482)	REFORMATION (AD 1483-1511)	REPRISAL (AD 1512-1540)
ELIZABETHAN (AD 1541-1565)	PARLIAMENTARY (AD 1566-1587)	PURITAN (AD 1588-1617)	CAVALIER (AD 1618-1647)
GLORIOUS (AD 1648-1673)	ENLIGHTENMENT (AD 1674-1700)	AWAKENING (AD 1701-1723)	LIBERTY (AD 1724-1741)
REPUBLICAN (AD 1742-1766)	COMPROMISE (AD 1767-1791)	TRANSCENDENTAL (AD 1792-1821)	GILDED (AD 1822-1842)
---	PROGRESSIVE (AD 1843-1859)	MISSIONARY (AD 1860-1882)	LOST (AD 1883-1900)
G.I. (AD 1901-1924)	SILENT (AD 1925-1942)	BOOM (AD 1943-1960)	GENERATION X (AD 1961-1981)
MILLENNIAL (AD 1982-2004)	HOMELANDERS (AD 2005-present)		

Notes:

1. The significant human loss in the Civil War completely decimated an American generation and removed a "hero" spoke in the generation constellation.
2. Strauss and Howe dates for Millennials (1982–2004) and Homelanders (2005–present) are unique.
3. Most sociologists and generational historians end the Millennial Generation birth by the year 2000.

The Baby Boom generation cut their teeth on primitive television, but it was Gen X that was truly raised on television. Television (color, cable, video games, and VCRs) significantly influenced the Gen X personality, far more than any cultural or historical event after 1961. In fact, without television, these events—from man walking on the moon and Watergate to the Challenger explosion and the fall of the Berlin Wall—would've been less significant and influential. Television tattooed these events upon Gen X's psyche. Similarly, the Millennial generation suckled on a computer and cyber culture. They embraced new "windows" that offered a digital and electronic view, whether it was a computer or the Internet or a cell phone.

Technology matters to every generation. It's how we communicate, play, learn, and lead.

I don't oppose previous frames for generations. They are helpful to our conversations. However, I no longer believe they provide the best understanding for who we are and the stories we tell our children.

Stories that often flow through the technology our generation embraced in youth.

Coming of Age

Every generation "comes of age." That is, we journey through a season of maturation into adulthood. We "come of age" when we are self-sufficient and responsible for our actions, choices, and ideas.

"Coming of age" also happens when a person is officially recognized as an "adult" within his or her community. Unfortunately, there is no strong agreement for *when* that blessing happens, as every cultural context is different. Nevertheless, there are several markers that determine when a person "comes of age."

We come of age when we are physically and cognitively mature. Biologically, that age could be as young as eleven or twelve, at least for females (who can then reproduce).[29] From a cognitive perspective, the ability to think abstractly and critically doesn't emerge until the preteen years (ages ten to fourteen). Cognitive theorist Jean Piaget argued that abstract reasoning skills (formal operations) blossomed between ages eleven and sixteen.[30] Some developmental psychologists believe abstract reasoning can occur even earlier.

We come of age when we are recognized as "of age" to embrace personal faith. In some strains of evangelical Christianity, that can be as young as five years of age, but, in general, it's between ten and fifteen. In Catholicism, a child as tender as seven may receive first communion.[31] In Jewish culture, a child's bar or bat mitzvah at age thirteen makes the mark.[32] In the Bahai faith, a child becomes "spiritually mature" at fifteen. The Amish practice "adult baptism" only for candidates older than sixteen.[33] In Buddhism, it's age twenty when boys go through a Shinbyu ritual.[34]

We come of age when we experience a defining societal rite. Some see the "sweet sixteen" birthday as that marker. Others say it's when we can legally drive, drink, or vote. Still others argue it's when we assume adult roles and responsibilities (e.g., military service, leaving home for college, living alone, working full-time, getting married, home ownership). If that's the case, some children will never "come of age," while others will do so fairly young. In certain cultures, it's not unusual to see preteen children working and producing an income for their families. Consequently, any specific "coming of age" determination is limiting and contextualized. A child might be considered an adult in one culture and not in another.

I would propose there's less a specific "time" or event when we mature into adulthood and more a season in our life when we *grow* into adulthood. As I survey the developmental, cultural, religious, and social markers for "coming of age," it seems that most humans experience "maturity" sometime between the ages of ten and twenty-five. This is our "season" for "coming of age." Every developmental marker from rites of passage to puberty fit within this frame.

It's also a fifteen-year span of time when we uniquely interact with the technology of our historical time period. For children and adolescents in the 1930s it was radio. For kids in the 1950s it was television. For young people in the 1990s it was personal computers. Today, most American children receive their first smartphone around ten years of age.[35] I've long theorized the music we enjoyed between the ages of ten and twenty-five becomes the "soundtrack" for our entire life. It's our "comfort music" and what "takes us back" to our past. It's where we go when we need to relax, reminisce and relive.

That is why ages ten to twenty-five is an interesting period in lifespan development. It's a frame of time when we change how we look (biological growth), interact (social growth), think (cognitive growth), and believe (spiritual growth). These fifteen years of maturation could be the most important years of our life.

What does this have to do with generational theory? Actually...*everything*.

It's the technology that we experience during this fifteen-year "coming of age" window that carves our true generational identity. This technology, interacting with historical events, is what flavors a generation. Generationally, we aren't boxes at all. We are more like surfers who catch a great wave and leaves behind a story. The waves are particular emerging technologies that influenced us between ages ten and twenty-five.

Consequently, we aren't so much "baby boomers" (named after a birth demographic) as we are a "vinyl" or "television" generation (technologies that found cultural traction between 1940 and 1970). We aren't so much ambiguous Gen Xers as we are a "space" and "gamer" generation (due to 1960s and 1970s technologies like satellites and space rockets, video games, and remote controls). We aren't so much "Millennials" because of the year 2000 as much as we are a "personal computer" and "net" generation (due to the emergence of PCs, the Internet, and web-connected devices).

Technology is what truly shapes a generation.

Windows to the World

Every generation has its mood.

Mostly because every generation is born into a different historical context. At the root, there are only two primary dispositions: optimistic or pessimistic. It's interesting that when we study the moods of those born between 1900–1920—commonly dubbed "The Greatest Generation"—we witness a rather rosy temperament. It's this "can-do" view that launched airplanes and rockets, invented vaccines and television, liberated Europe, and dammed the Colorado river. However, the Depression generation (1920–1940) possessed a more somber sentiment. This generation faced Prohibition, economic hardship, the bombing of Pearl Harbor, and World War II.

Strauss and Howe would identify the two optimistic generations as "hero" and "prophet" and the two pessimistic generations as "artist" and "nomad."

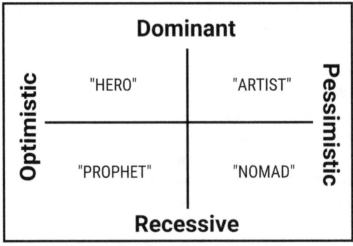

Neil Howe and William Strauss: Four Generation Archetypes (1991)

Furthermore, every generation operates either as dominant or recessive in its interactions with other generations. Neil Howe and William Strauss used this generational gene to construct their four-part generational constellation.[36] A dominant persuasion is more proactive and idealistic, while a recessive persuasion is more reactive and pragmatic. This explains the vast difference between the G.I. (b. 1901–1924) and Boom (b. 1943–1960) generations. Both the G.I. and Boom generations were *optimistic* in their moods but differed in how they interacted with other generations. The G.I. was proactive and rooted to cultural ethics of faith, family, hard work, and grit. The Boom children were reactive and idealistic. They wanted to change the world through "flower power" and mantras like "turn on, tune in, and drop out." Boomers optimistically *reacted* to the institutions that the G.I. generation had *proactively* built and venerated: societal, political, educational, and religious. This reactive nature guided the Boomers their entire life. It's what seeded every Boom-driven movement from anti-war to gay rights to the evangelical megachurch.

It also explains the original "generation gap" between Boom kids and their G.I. parents.

Both the Boom and G.I. generations were optimistic in nature, but again were different in orientation. This explains why the Boom generation was politically and socially dominated by their elders until the 1990s when the G.I.s either retired or died. It also helps us understand why Boomers are equally at odds with younger "dominant" Millennials (who are cut from the same generational genetic as the G.I.s). This is particularly evident in our national politics. The rise of new Millennial lawmakers on Capitol Hill like Alexandria Ocasio-Cortez (D-NY) and Ilhan Omar (D-MN) have irritated elder lawmakers on both sides of the aisle. However, Millennials are just getting started politically. They will make legislative noise, as Ocasio-Cortez has proven with her "Green New Deal."[37] The first Millennial to run for president in 2020 was Pete Buttigieg (born in 1982). But this generational and political dominance isn't confined to Capitol Hill. Millennials can be found in school boards, city councils and statehouses, too.

When you blend these generational characteristics, four distinct styles emerge:

- DOMINANT/OPTIMISTIC: a proactive and idealistic generation *(John Wayne)*
- DOMINANT/PESSIMISTIC: a proactive and realistic generation *(John McCain)*
- RECESSIVE/OPTIMISTIC: a reactive and idealistic generation *(John Lennon)*
- RECESSIVE/PESSIMISTIC: a reactive and realistic generation *(Johnny Depp)*

Dominant

Optimistic

Pessimistic

"HERO"

G.I. Generation (b. 1901 - 1923)
Millennial (b. 1982 - 2004)

John Wayne

"ARTIST"

Silent Generation (b. 1924 0 1942)
Homeland (b. since 2005)

John McCain

Boom (b. 1943 - 1960)

John Lennon

Gen X (b. 1961 - 1981)

Johnny Depp

"PROPHET"

"NOMAD"

Recessive

These four generational personalities also follow a particular order in U.S. history: dominant/optimist, dominant/pessimist, recessive/optimist, and recessive/pessimist. Consequently, as already noted, a pattern or cycle emerges that repeats over and over again.

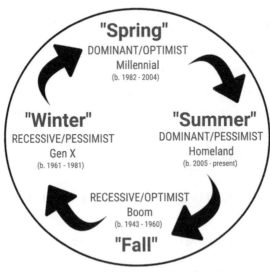

Generations: Dominant-Recessive and Optimist-Pessimist

Strauss and Howe noted how these four archetype personalities produce different "callings.":[38]

- DOMINANT/OPTIMISTIC: preachers, writers, radicals, publishers, and teachers.
- DOMINANT/PESSIMISTIC: statesmen, scientists, economists, diplomats
- RECESSIVE/OPTIMISTIC: artists, lawyers, therapists, legislators, statisticians
- RECESSIVE/PESSIMISTIC: entrepreneurs, generals, salesmen, industrialists

Every generation has its own unique style…and, as we will soon discover, their own technology that drives this personality.

That's *My* Tech!

Think about the technology that influenced you most between the ages of ten and twenty-five. How did it change you? What unique impact did it have upon wider culture?

Is any of this technology now obsolete?

Think about all the technology that now is dispatched to the garbage dumps of history. Stuff like rotary phones, 8-track tapes, transistor radios, black and white television, and Polaroid cameras. If you're under twenty-five, you probably marvel that people once walked to a wall to answer a phone (with no idea who was calling). Or that we manipulated something called rabbit ears to remove the snow from one of only three stations available to view. Or that we had to wait days to see what developed on a roll of film. Or that we had to "dial up" our Internet.

It's these engagements or stories with technology that make us who we are. It describes our generational contexts.

Of course, some retroactive tech has its niche popularity. Vinyl records are currently fashionable among affluent Millennials. Recently, I met a young man who professed his undying affection for vinyl records. He enjoyed the experience of dropping a needle, the sound of "rice krispies" (snaps, crackles, and pops) and turning the record over to side B. I found his technological enthusiasm for vinyl intriguing and ironic. Even though I grew up playing vinyl records and still own a large record collection, I prefer clean, digital recordings. Listening to a digital recording is far superior to the pops, skips, and clicks. It's better than needles that get stuck in a groove to repeat, to repeat, to repeat (ruining a good song). As a technology, vinyl is hardly final. It's easily scratched and scuffed. Records melt in heat and snap in cold. You also can't take records anywhere. Vinyl is too big to take jogging, go to the beach, play in the car, or enjoy at work. Vinyl is a limiting type of technology.

Nevertheless, vinyl was significant to a controlling modern culture. It came in square packaging, stored best in crates, and was played inside a box (record player). To change songs or switch sides, the listener had to place the needle or turn over the record. You had to go to a specific place at a particular time to hear the record play. Vinyl thrived in a box culture.

But in a fast and fluid world, vinyl is too constrictive. We want our music to go *everywhere*. We want a personalized soundtrack for our daily tasks. Digital music allows us to listen to music 24/7/365. We can listen underwater, on a plane, at the supermarket, while we learn, ride a bike, fall asleep, and wake up. In a digital economy, music is our life.

This is why certain technologies have a way of framing our entire existence. As a fifty-something, I'm still drawn to record bins at thrift stores just to sift through the well-worn vinyl of Barbra Streisand, Herp Alpert and the Tijuana Brass, the Osmonds, and Rod Stewart. I still have boxes of audio and video cassettes in the garage. I still own a VCR. The irony is that I can't remember the last time I played a record or videocassette.

The reason is pretty simple. It doesn't fit my world *anymore*.

And yet, these technologies grooved my "coming of age" between 1973 and 1988. The video cassette recorder, record player, and boom box (with radio and cassette) ruled my adolescence and young adult years. I didn't buy my first computer until 1987, my first compact disc until 1990, or my first DVD until 2000. I didn't have an email address prior to 1996. I didn't even buy my first smartphone until 2013. I use these technologies, but my story is rooted in older technology.

I still get excited when I see Pong or Pacman video games. I enjoy the sound of scrolling across a radio dial to tune in a station. I love *Brady Bunch* and *M*A*S*H* marathons. I like to dial a number on a rotary phone. And, yes, I still think a vinyl record is *fun* to play. I can hear that needle drop just thinking about it.

Our "coming of age" technology is like comfort food. It makes us feel *good*.

Think Different

So, it's time to reconsider the way we frame generations.

What if we viewed generations with more blends, curves, and fluidity? What if the influence of technology defined a generation more than some random event? If so, someone born with access to computers (like young boomers Bill Gates or Steve Jobs) might have more in common with the generation that first used these technologies (Gen X). What defines Bill Gates or Steve Jobs as "boomers" is currently rooted to their birth dates in history and their cultural memories. But, in reality, these two 1955 "boomers" were born into a "television" and "space" culture. They came of age between 1965 and 1980. Is it any wonder that both men pioneered personal computing in the 1970s (with devices that looked like television sets)? Is it any wonder that both men led personal computing into the Internet age (which relies upon satellite technology)? Gates and Jobs aren't just "boomers." They rode the surf of two great technological eras: television and space.

Consequently, I propose generations aren't constrained as much to birth dates but rather technological experiences between the ages of ten and twenty-five. The one thing all generations experience *together* is technological *change*. We just experience different technology in different times. My great grandfather learning to drive a Model T is no different than my adventures in learning to compute or my son figuring out his Fitbit. New technology creates confusion, disturbance, and even opposition. Not everybody found the horseless carriage a good thing. Radio and television were both met with opposition. Every generation experiences emerging technology in a way later generations will not.

Furthermore, if there's fluidity, then there's also tipping points. If you pour too much water into a glass that's leaning, it will eventually tip and spill the water. Our culture naturally leans into the future.

Not all technology tips us.

But the ones that do change our future.

Chapter Three

Tipping Points

"There is a simple way to package information that,
under the right circumstances, can make it irresistible.
All you have to do is find it."
Malcolm Gladwell

In 1979, this device was heralded as the next "must-have" technology. Television commercials proclaimed its value.[39] Tech experts extolled its superior performance. The market seemed ready to move. But this new "must-have" technology never found widespread popular appeal. Perhaps because it was slightly more expensive. Maybe because it targeted more niche markets. Possibly because its competitor flooded the market better.

Whatever the reason, Betamax lost the technology war to VHS cassette tapes and recorders. Today, it's another forgotten brand and obsolete technology. It simply never found its cultural "tipping point." It wasn't "sticky" enough as a product. The kicker? The "max" in Betamax stood for "greatness" (something it never quite achieved).[40]

I traveled to the African continent for the first time in the summer of 2013.

My training team worked in a small, rural village on the eastern slopes of Mount Kilimanjaro near Moshi, Tanzania. The conditions were primitive for our presentations. We used no PowerPoint or projection technology. We didn't incorporate Western learning strategies into our presentations. Our audiences were rural Tanzanians, many of whom walked miles each day simply to participate in our workshops.

Our team leader warned us about using too much technology around the Africans. Our job was to help them become better teachers and leaders without introducing resources—particularly "high-tech" ones—that were unavailable or too expensive. So here I was packing a smartphone, high-def video camera, MacBook Pro laptop, and iPad. I was used to presenting with video and presentation technology. But during that trip we used paper on an easel to communicate our points. I kept my personal tech hidden from my Tanzanian friends. My use was strictly limited to the privacy of my room.

I quickly discovered the lone technology these African leaders and teachers possessed were old-style flip phones. These devices were only for phone conversations. Despite the fact that two-thirds of all Africans don't have proper drainage or piped water, and half still travel on unpaved roads, nine in ten Africans owned a cell phone and service.[41] These rural Tanzanians were no different. They were all packing flip phones.

I traveled back to Tanzania in 2014 and there was little change, except this time I saw the Masai (Africa's version of the Amish) using phones as they walked their herds alongside the highway. Two years later, I traveled to South Africa and Uganda and witnessed for the first time a few smartphones and occasional texting.

And then I visited the Ivory Coast of West Africa in September 2018.

It was a true technological sea change. Every African had a smartphone. In fact, I don't remember seeing a single flip phone during my stay in Abidjan, Cote d'Ivoire. The conference where I spoke featured seventeen different African nations, including Cameroon, Nigeria, Togo, Ghana, and Sierra Leone. *Everyone* had smartphones, and they used them for multiple purposes, from filming the event to surfing the net to texting and connecting on WhatsApp. Their favorite activity was "snapping" (or what Americans know as the "selfie"). And they were pretty good at it. All our presentations used projected PowerPoint technology. These West Africans were conditioned to visual communication.

I learned the emergence of the smartphone was recent in West Africa, less than a few years. But it had a significant "tipping point" influence. The smartphone revolutionized how these Africans lived, learned, worked, and communicated. They went from a contextualized conversation technology to an immersive technology that connected them to different worlds far from their African homes.

The smartphone's adoption and assimilation into African culture, at least the West African culture that I observed in 2018, has been swift and powerful. It's also not without consequence. Because of limited transportation, most Africans walk, and now they're walking with their eyes glued to their smartphones (sound familiar?). It's the African version of texting while driving (except they're walking!). I witnessed a few close calls in my travels around Abidjan, including one overly-engaged smartphone user who nearly met his Maker. Many Africans, especially older generations, are growing concerned about how technology has impacted young African brains.

It's all about "tipping points," and every technology that survives and changes a culture has a "tipping point." Some techs (like the smartphone) find it. And some (like Betamax) do not.

Tipping points are those moments when a technology is used by the majority of individuals within a culture. A machine might be invented in a particular year, but that doesn't mean it has popular appeal or widespread use. The printing press, for example, took over a hundred years to find cultural traction.

"The tipping point is that magic moment when an idea, trend, or social behavior crosses a threshold, tips, and spreads like wildfire."
Malcolm Gladwell

Another recent example is the commercial airplane. The airplane was an early twentieth-century invention but had little commercial use for decades. It was primarily used in war, agriculture, and sightseeing. Commercial flight was very expensive for most of the twentieth century, reserved for the rich and famous. Consequently, the commercial airplane's tipping point happened in the 1970s when deregulation, lower flight prices, plane capacity, and routes permitted more people to fly the friendly skies. The tipping point for flight travel was decades in the making.

Television was introduced to the American buyer in 1949 but did not enjoy a cultural tipping point until the early 1960s. That's when the true power of television was unleashed. From 1963–1964, a trifecta of significant "televised" events occurred that reimagined America: Martin Luther King's "I Have A Dream" speech (August 28, 1963)[42], John F. Kennedy's assassination (November 22, 1963)[43], and the arrival of the Beatles in America (February 9, 1964).[44] From those days forward, television was our window to the world.

Oral contraception was introduced to the American public in 1960. However, it took five years before a generation of women favored it as "the" form of birth control. The impact was swift and identifiable, as live birth rates fell for the first time below the 20 percent watermark. They never rose above it again.[45]

Tipping points are different. Some happen quick while others rise after decades of usage. Some tipping points never happen at all. Maybe we should call those that never happen "Betamax Moments."

Time Keeps Tech-ing Away

The world has changed dramatically in a century.

We've moved from the Model T to the Prius, from radio to YouTube, from black and white pictures to high-definition, 3-D, computer-generated images. It's unbelievable how much technological change there's been in our world.

Between 1800 and 1900 several significant technologies emerged that set the stage for modern innovation, including: the telegraph (1816), photograph (1826), railroad (1831), repeating handgun (1836), telephone (1876), electric light bulb (1879), automobile (1885), and motion picture (1892). The discovery of electricity fueled many technological improvements, especially those connected to communications. All these technological advances rearranged and pushed civilized cultures into the Industrial and Information ages. The scope of this work will intentionally concentrate on technologies that have appeared (or experienced "tipping points") since 1900 and how they uniquely shaped American generational personalities.

Here is a selected list of technologies, advancements, and discoveries (scientific, medical, cultural) that have arrived since 1900, all of which improved and influenced society. I have listed them alphabetically, rather than by date of invention or cultural tipping point:

3D Printing
16mm film
Adhesives/Tape
Adobe PDF
Aerosol sprays
American-made cars
Airbags
Air conditioning
Airplanes/Helicopters/Jets
Aluminum Foil
Answering Machines
Artificial heart
Artificial Intelligence (AI)
Atomic Bomb
Atomic Power
Bakelite (plastics)
Ballistic missiles
Barcodes
Birth control/oral contraception
Blender
Bulletproof vests
Cable/satellite television
Cassette
Calculator
Camcorder
Cell Phone/Smart Phone
Chain Saw
Cloning
Cochlear Implants
Color motion picture
Compact Disc (CD/CD-R)

Computer (desktop/laptop)
Computer (supercomputer/quantum)
Credit cards
Dams (Hoover, Grand Coulee)
Digital camera   Snowmobiles
Digital readers/books (Kindle)
Digital watches (iWatch, FitBit)
DNA/molecular biology
Doppler radar
Digital Versatile Disc (DVD/DVD-R/
    Blu-Ray)
Digital Video Recording (DVR)
Electric blanket
Electronic commerce (eBay, Amazon)
Electronic mail   Television (Black/
    White, Color, Hi-Def, 3D)
Electronic learning (online education)
Electronic payments (ApplePay)
Electronic photographs (JPEG)s
Electronic video (MP4, MOV, AVI)
Ethernet
Farm tractor
Flash Freezing (frozen foods)
Floppy Disk
Fluorescent Lamps
Freon (refrigeration)
Freeze-Dried Food
Global Positioning Systems (GPS)
Google
Home refrigeration
Human space flight

Instant Photos (Polaroid)

Insulin

Internet (World Wide Web)

Internet Browser (Netscape, Mozilla,
  Safari)

Iron Lung

Jacuzzi (whirlpool tubs)

Jet ski

Jukebox

Laser

LCD

Machine gun

Microwave oven

Motion Pictures (color)

Motion Pictures (sound or "talkie")

Motor-driven bicycles/motorcycles

MP3/MP3 Players/iPods

Nanotechnology

Pager

Penicillin

Periscope

Photocopier

Polaroid (Instant) Photography

Polyester

Polygraph

Presentation technology (PowerPoint)

Quartz crystal clocks

Radar

Radio

Robotics

Rockets/Space Rockets

Rotor ship

Rotary Phone/Touch Tone Phone

Satellites

Silicon Solar Cells

Smart Speakers (Amazon Echo)

Snow-making Machines

Social Media (Facebook, Twitter,
  Snapchat)

Sonar

Styrofoam

Superconductors

Tablets (iPad)

Teflon

Teletypewriters

Texting

Theory of Relativity (Einstein)

Touch Screen

Trans-Atlantic flight

Transistor

Universal Serial Bus (USB)

Vaccine (tuberculosis, polio)

Video cassettes/video cassette recorders

Video games

Video Conferencing (Zoom)

Video Phone Calls (Skype, Facetime)

Vinyl Record (78/45/331/3 rpm)

Web Streaming (iTunes, Netflix, Hulu)

Wireless Internet/Wi-Fi

Wikipedia

X-rays

YouTube/Vimeo

When we intersect the developmental ("coming of age") perspective discussed in the last chapter with the various technological innovations and advancements that have impacted and influenced wider culture, we begin to see clear "technological generations" emerge. These generations are more fluid and reflect three larger historical phases.

The first phase is **AUDIO**. These generations are defined by motorized wheels, knobs, dials, spindles, and speakers:

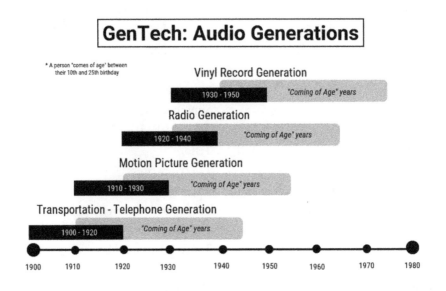

The Transportation-Telephone Generation (b. 1900–1920)
Coming of Age: 1910–1945

The oldest generation, currently in their 100s, is now nearly gone. This generation fought in two World Wars, endured the Great Depression, and led America into the twentieth century through expanding travel (car, plane), entertainment (film, television), and science (space, medicine). They also experienced the emergence of telephone technology. They were the first generation to have home phones, use pay phones, and call long distance. It was a generation of *talk* and *travel*.

The Motion Picture Generation (b. 1910–1930)
Coming of Age: 1920–1955

Those currently in their 90s and 100s are also dying off quickly, but this cohort of kids came of age in an era of motion pictures or film technology. A generation too young to fight in World War I, they nevertheless experienced the Great Depression and fought in World War II and Korea. They were the first generation to grow up attending movies (with sound after 1927). They experienced mass advertising, tabloid journalism, movie stars, and classic Hollywood. It was a generation of *projected visuals.*

The Radio Generation (b. 1920–1940)
Coming of Age: 1930–1965

Currently between 80-100 years old, this generation of American youth experienced a radio world. They grew up listening to music, commentary, entertainment, sports and religious programs through the airwaves. Their first real interaction with a U.S. President was by "fireside" radio chat. They fought wars in World War II, Korea, and Vietnam and participated in the great industrialization of America, from dams to interstates to suburbia. It was a generation of *antennae.*

The Vinyl Record Generation (b. 1930–1950)
Coming of Age: 1940–1975

This generation is in their 70s and 80s and came of age mostly in a post-World War II atomic age. They witnessed the rise of the Berlin Wall, cold war Communism, "duck and cover" survival strategies, the space race, and Vietnam. The predominant entertainment technology of their youth and young adulthood was the vinyl record. They played vinyl records for sock hops, barn dances, and eventually discotheques. Mostly, they dropped their needles at home on portable record players, launching a new form of music known as "rock and roll." It's the generation of Sinatra, Elvis, and the Beatles. It's a generation of *needles* and *speakers.*

The next phase is **VISUAL**. These generations are defined by visual media and satellite technology:

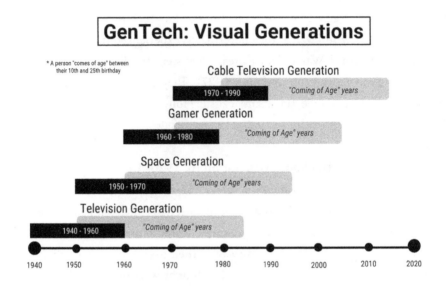

The Television Generation (b. 1940–1960)
Coming of Age: 1950–1985

Currently in their 60s and 70s, this generation is the first American generation to experience television—initially in black and white technology and later in color. They grew up in a rock 'n roll, hippie youth culture that viewed their world through a screen, whether it was Elvis on Ed Sullivan, Vietnam War news updates, Kennedy's assassination, man on the moon, Watergate, or the Reagan revolution. It's a generation of *live news*.

The Space Generation (b. 1950–1970)
Coming of Age: 1960–1995

Now in their 50s and 60s, this generation experienced a number of technologies, particularly related to rockets, satellites, and space exploration, including nuclear missiles, man walking on the moon, Reagan's "star wars," and the Challenger explosion. As kids, they watched *Star Trek* and *Star Wars* and learned of galaxies "far, far away" thanks to Isaac Asimov and Carl Sagan. They dined on meals cooked in microwaves, listened to portable music (cassettes, 8-tracks, and CDs), and were the first to hear (and play on) a "computer." It's a generation of *satellites* and *rockets*.

The Gamer Generation (b. 1960–1980)
Coming of Age: 1970–2005

This generation is currently in their 40s and 50s. As the first pure "gamer generation," they grew up playing arcade (pinball) and video games like Pong, Pac Man, Asteroids, Super Mario Brothers, Mortal Combat, and NBA Jam. They played video games in the arcade, at home, with portable players (GameBoy), and eventually on computers. This generation experienced new media and technology like MTV, VHS/DVD, desktop computers, the web, and cell phones. They are a generation of *consoles* and *controllers*.

The Cable Television Generation (b. 1970–1990)
Coming of Age: 1980–2015

A generation presently in their 30s and 40s, they grew up on cable and satellite television, music videos, video cassette/DVD/DVR recorders, and camcorders. They are defined by certain cable channels like HBO, MTV, ESPN, CNN, Weather Channel, TLC, Discovery, and History. They came of age just as MTV and CNN entered the channel constellation. It's last members witnessed the "beginning of the end" of cable television, as streaming options became prevalent. They are the first time-shift generation, thanks to recording tech (VCR, DVR) that changed television. They are a generation of *the box* and *remote*.

The current phase is **DIGITAL**. These generations are defined by digital, mobile, wireless, and cyber communication:

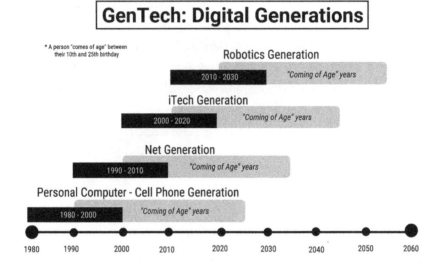

The PC Generation (b. 1980–2000)
Coming of Age: 1990–2025

Currently in their 20s and 30s, this generation grew up with personal computers, home printers, modems, and "windows." It's a generation of the "silver disc" (CD/DVD/Blu-ray) and the first to live completely in a world of email, digital photography, cell phones, and video projection. It's a generation of right and left clicks, the generation of *the mouse*. "PC" also means something else when the letters are flipped to "CP" or *cell phone*. In fact, the flip phone was their first cell phone. The PC/CP generation saw mobile phone technology become mainstream.[46]

The Net Generation (b. 1990–2010)
Coming of Age: 2000–2035

This generation, currently in their preteens to age 30, are the "www" generation. They have experienced and consumed the Internet for most of their coming of age years. They are a fully digital generation thanks to techs like MP3, JPEGs, and MP4s. They prefer laptops and tablets, GPS and DVR. They are the first generation to wholly adopt texting, streaming technology, Google, and a new way to complete an education: e-learning. In fact, it's a *Google* generation.

The iTech Generation (b. 2000–2020)
Coming of Age: 2010–2045

This generation is comprised of teenagers and young adults. Completely wireless and digital, this generation reads digital material on iPads and tablets. They Facetime their grandparents, Snapchat with peers, and watch Netflix, YouTube, and Hulu for entertainment. And they do it primarily on a single device: the smartphone. They are the first purely social media generation (known also to vape and use emojis). It's a generation of *clouds and streams*.

The Robotics Generation (b. 2010–2030)
Coming of Age: 2020–2055

Our youngest generation is currently comprised of children, but the world that they'll experience in their youth will be an "Internet of things" (with practically every device, appliance, clothing, and "thing" you can imagine being wirelessly interactive through the Internet). This will be the first generation to fully experience robotic technology, driverless cars, 3-D printing, genetic engineering, holographic images, and digital money (Bitcoin). This is a generation of *artificial intelligence*.

The world that is on our doorstep is one that anyone over sixty years of age cannot fathom. It's why a clear line must be drawn between those born prior to and after 1960. Modern generations (Transportation, Motion Picture, Radio, Vinyl, Television) are fundamentally *different* from post-modern generations (Gamer, PC, Cable, Net, iTech, Robotics). The only generation that straddles both is the Space Generation (born 1950–1970). It's one of America's most unique generations, living comfortably in the tension between a *Star Trek* universe and a *Star Wars* multiverse.

The generation gap has never been larger. A Television or Space Generation grandparent and an iTech or Robotic Generation grandchild truly struggle to relate to one another.

Generation Blends

A careful examination of these new technological generation frames reveals a blending and overlap. Essentially, depending on the year of birth, every person has a foot in two different generational contexts—*three* if he or she is born in a "0" year—and each context is controlled by defining technologies. That's why I've purposely proposed frames that work within even year formats (00, 10, 20, etc.). We shouldn't focus so much on the year but the emergence of certain technologies within these frames. We must look for patterns. We must be willing to allow for messiness, overlap and fluidity. The telephone, automobile, and motion picture were all invented prior to 1900, but none found cultural traction (tipping points) until after 1900. It's why they frame the Transportation-Telephone (b. 1900–1920) and Motion Picture (b. 1910–1930) generations, respectively.

Perhaps a generational case study will help.

If you were born in 1979, your classic generational frame is "Gen X." But that tag hasn't set well with "Xennials" or those born between 1977 and 1983.[47] Some demographers even push the date range for Xennials to 1985.[48] This "micro-generation" (spanning less than ten years) is a bubble generation, but it fails to meet the wider historical and sociological criteria for a true generation (twenty to twenty-five years in length).

Nevertheless, we can't ignore the tension for those individuals born on the fringes of these traditional generational frames. It's a very real frustration when traditional generational birth frames don't fit. It's why I believe a technological perspective (with fluidity) serves us better. Consider how the tension of "Xennials" is eased when placed within these new "GenTech" technological frames.

For example, someone born in 1979 would be part of two generational contexts: The (late) Gamer Generation (1960–1980) and the Cable Television Generation (1970-1990). This blending makes more sense since these late 1970s kids grew up with video games, from Nintendo to Wii to Xbox. They played video games on portable units at home, in school, and, later, at work. Mattel introduced the first portable video game in 1976, but it was GameBoy (1989) that stole the market.[49] They also were the first kids to insert (and push play) on video cassettes and DVDs. They grew up on HBO, ESPN, CNN, and the

Weather Channel, not to mention Nickelodeon and Disney. They've always had a "box" connected to the television.

And don't forget the "coming of age" factor. Someone born in 1979 came of age between 1989 and 2004. They experienced the dawn of the Internet age.

- Besides the GameBoy, this cohort of kids matured on these "gamer" and television technologies: Super Nintendo (1990), PlayStation (1994), Internet (1995), DISH Satellite television (1996), TiVo (1999), and iTunes streaming video (2001). It's these technologies that mark those born in 1979 and still defines them today.
- They were kids of the '90s. Grunge. Hip Hop. Modern Country. They watched *The Simpsons, Friends, Beverly Hills 90120, Dawson's Creek, The Prince of Bel Air, Full House, Home Improvement, Everybody Loves Raymond,* and *Frasier.*
- They witnessed cultural events like the end of the Cold War (1989–1991), the Gulf War (1990), the Clinton Administration (1992–2001), Waco siege (1993), Oklahoma City bombing (1995), O.J. Simpson trial (1995), Princess Diana death (1997), the Monica Lewinsky scandal and Clinton impeachment (1998-1999), Columbine (1999), Y2K (1999), Bush vs. Gore (2000), New York/DC terrorist attacks (2001), Iraq War (2003), and the Red Sox win their first World Series since 1918 (2004).

If you were born in 1979, you "came of age" during a very unique time and you were clearly walking in two different "generational tech" contexts: video games and cable television.

I believe this dynamic view of generations is superior to the old stiff date frames. The "GenTech" contexts allow the stories, events, and tragedies to emerge. They permit those who live on the fringes to feel more included and valid. They explain why a generation behaves or produces as it does. It's far more fluid and flexible. I will confess that some tags (like "cable television") might not be as culturally "sexy," but they're far more descriptive and helpful. Certain technology (sexy or not) tattoos us—and it matters.

And that's why this book is called *GenTech.*

It's a blending of "generation" and "technology."

The thesis for this book is rather simple: *we are a product of certain technologies that shape us between our tenth and twenty-fifth birthdays.*

Generations do come and go.

And every 500 years a collection of generations experience a larger cultural shifting.

The generations of the twentieth century and early twenty-first century have undergone more technological change in a century than all other historical generations *combined*. In just over a century, we have learned to fly, phone, project, broadcast, film, microwave, refrigerate, televise, text, blog, and surf. We've gone from the Model T to the self-driving car. We moved from silent films to Facebook "Live," from rotary phones to smartphones, from an agricultural economy to e-commerce.

We have migrated from a modern universe to a post-modern multiverse.

It's why we need to dissect the world as it was and as it is, in order to properly understand where it might be headed. We must fearlessly, yet intentionally, march through the halls of history—beginning in the year 1900—to better understand these "tech" generations and their contexts, not to mention our future. This work must be necessarily imperfect. It's not an exhaustive technological history nor a thorough social treatment of each generation, as space and time does not permit. At best, it's a 30,000-foot flyover of America and her people since 1900. It's a story of technology and culture. A tale of life behind wheels and engines, on radios and televisions, through screens and modems.

It will be a most fascinating journey—an exploration from which we will all learn, change, and grow.

So, buckle up.

It's time to fly.

*"Each age tries to form its
own conception of the past.
Each age writes the history of the past
anew with reference to the
conditions uppermost in its own time."*
Frederick Jackson Turner[50]

MODERN GENERATIONS

1900 - 1960

1960

Alaska and Hawaii admitted into the union (1959)
U.S.S.R. launches Sputnik rocket (1957)
Vietnam War begins (1955)
Racial segregation ruled unconstitutional (1954)
Korean War (1950-1953)

Israel created as independent Jewish state (1948)
Jackie Robinson is first black in baseball (1947)

1950 **SPACE**
1950-1970

Atom bomb dropped on Japan (1945)
Roosevelt elected to fourth term (1944)
Japan bombs Pearl Harbor (1941)

TELEVISION **1940**
1940-1960

World War 2 (1939-1945)
Japan invades China (1937)
Hitler rises to power in Germany (1937)

21st Amendment: repeal of prohibition of alcohol (1933)
20th Amendment: Inauguration changed to January (1933)
Franklin D. Roosevelt elected president (1932)

Stock Market Crash (1929)
Charles Lindbergh flies across Atlantic Ocean (1927)

1930 **VINYL RECORDS**
1930-1950

RADIO **1920**
1920-1940

19th Amendment: women's right to vote (1920)

18th Amendment: prohibition of alcohol (1919)
Flu epidemic kills 50 million (1917-1918)
World War I (1914-1918)

17th Amendment: election of U.S. senators (1913)
16th Amendment: income tax authorized (1913)
Titanic sinks in North Atlantic (1912)
Woodrow Wilson elected president (1912)

1910  **MOTION PICTURE**
1910-1930

Panama Canal built (1904-1914)
Theodore Roosevelt becomes president (1901)

TRANSPORTATION
and TELEPHONE **1900**
1900-1920

Chapter Four
Transportation-Telephone

"That's an amazing invention, but who would ever want to use one of them?"
President Rutherford B. Hayes to inventor **Alexander Graham Bell**
about his telephone invention [1876]

BIRTH YEARS: 1900–1920
"Coming of Age" Years: 1910–1945
Primary Tech Event: Telephone
Strauss-Howe Archetype: Hero
Generation Personality: Dominant/Optimistic
Iconic Generation Representatives: Walt Disney and John Wayne

Historical Influencing Events in Youth and Young Adulthood:
San Francisco Quake/Fire, Sinking of the Titanic, World War I, Prohibition,
Charles Lindbergh, Great Depression, World War II

"It is, I believe, the greatest generation any society has ever produced."[51] So says the gospel, according to Tom Brokaw. And he's probably right. From their birth, this generation was anointed with potential. They were the "right stuff" and the "best damned kids in the world."[52] They were the "Superman" generation.[53]

Born at the turn of the twentieth century, this new generation was decidedly *different*. They weren't like their rowdy, fearless, gritty, "Lost Generation" elders. These kids were good, respectful, obedient, and team-oriented. It was the difference between Ty Cobb (b. 1886) and Lou Gehrig (b. 1903), or George Patton (b. 1885) and William Westmoreland (b. 1914), or James Cagney (b. 1899) and Jimmy Stewart (b. 1908). It was a generation that made "Lost" movie directors like Cecille B. DeMille and Frank Capra relish such a "wonderful life."

They were also a generation of *firsts*.

They were the *first* generation born in the twentieth century. They were the *first* boy and girl scouts. The *first* to drink pasteurized milk, eat inspected meat, and consume vitamins.[54] The *first* to be protected by child labor laws. The *first* to collectively attend college. The *first* to have their government give them jobs, welfare and social security. The *first* generation to retire with "senior citizen discounts." They were the *first* to experience automobiles and airplanes. The *first* to view motion pictures, hear radio, and watch television.

They were always *good* kids, but who would have imagined they'd grow up to become "great" Americans too?

They were John Wayne, Charles Lindbergh, Billy Graham, and Ronald Reagan rolled into one. They were tough, persistent, creative, and hardworking. A group of Americans faithful to their fellow man, to country, and God. They liberated Europe twice from German tyranny. They put a man on the moon. They launched fast-food restaurants, built entertainment parks, and led great companies. They produced more U.S. presidents, vice presidents, senators, and congressional leaders than any other American generation.

Social historians Neil Howe and William Strauss notably marked them as a "hero" generation, tagged them as "G.I.'s,"[55] and summarized:

Throughout their lives, these G.I.'s have been America's confident and rational problem-solvers: victorious soldiers and Rosie the Riveters; Nobel laureates, makers of Minuteman missiles, interstate highways, Apollo rockets, battleships, and miracle vaccines; the creators of Disney's Tomorrowland; 'men's men" who have known how to get things done.[56]

In three words: Optimistic. Confident. Influential.

Super men and women.

The G.I. Generation fought World Wars, survived Depression, endured a cold war, engineered rockets, designed suburbs, erected dams, and built the infrastructure that drives America to this day. They guided and guarded America's greatest institutions, from the church house to the movie house to the White House. The G.I. Generation mobilized and moved our nation *forward*, whether on wheels or wings.

In their lifetimes, this generational cohort experienced the greatest mobilization and communication transformation in the history of mankind. They saw the advent of the telephone, automobile, motion picture, radio, vinyl recording, television, and space craft. Those who survived beyond 1990 also witnessed the emergence of personal computers, digital technology, and the Internet. During their lifetimes, humans moved faster, farther, and higher. We conquered great oceans and icy continents. We broke the sound barrier and entered outer space. We communicated instantaneously by voice and video.

Most generations were influenced largely by a singular technology, but not this one. This generation was so grand that twin technologies tattooed their psyches: motorized vehicles and telephones.

They were the powerful TNT generation.

Transportation and telephone.

Born between 1900 and 1920, this cohort of kids is divided by the Roosevelts: The Teddy wave (born 1900–1910) and the FDR wave (born 1911–1920). The former would grow up with a roughrider conservationist, while the latter matured with a New Deal Depression president. In fact, the "transportation and telephone" generation's "coming of age" years—1910 to 1945—coincide with Teddy Roosevelt's launch of the progressive Bull Moose Party (1912) and ends with Franklin D. Roosevelt's death in 1945.

Sunrise, Sunset

The dawn of the twentieth century signaled a sunset.

Only ten years earlier, the great American West was "closed" in a declaration by the 1890 U.S. Census. Americans had finally pushed into every inhabitable nook and cranny west of the Mississippi river, claiming and settling on countless acres of land. Great painters like Frederick Remington and Charles M. Russell hurried to capture what was left of this mighty frontier, particularly the characters who tamed the West. *Cowboys. Indians. Outlaws. Soldiers. Frontiersmen. Wagon train trail bosses.* The Indian wars were over. The westward wagon caravans slowed. Between 1889 and 1912, ten western states joined the Union.[57] It would be nearly half a century before Alaska and Hawaii rounded out our fifty states.

America was changing. A fresh day dawned alongside a new century in time. It proved a period that would change the entire world, shift powers, and elevate the United States to the head of class in international dominance and influence. The twentieth century was dubbed "the American century," according to *Life* magazine publisher Henry Luce, in a February 17, 1941 editorial:

> Throughout the 17th century and the 18th century and the 19th century, this continent teemed with manifold projects and magnificent purposes. Above them all and weaving them all together into the most exciting flag of all the world and of all history was the triumphal purpose of freedom.
>
> It is in this spirit that all of us are called, each to his own measure of capacity, and each in the widest horizon of his vision, to create the first great American Century.[58]

Luce's optimistic and patriotic description of the twentieth century is why we must start here in our journey through American generations. After all, the emergence of America's power is rooted to our ingenuity, perseverance, toughness, and individualism, and it was 20th century American technology that separated us from the rest of the world.

The turn of a new century inaugurated not just a fresh chapter, but also trumpeted an ending. A period was being placed on a period. The end of an era was at hand.

On July 12, 1893, a young historian by the name of Frederick Jackson Turner proposed a compelling thesis at the World's Columbian Exposition in Chicago, IL. Turner argued that "Americans were not simply transplanted Europeans but a people unto themselves and that they were shaped not so much by their history or their institutions as by their *environment* (emphasis added)."[59] Turner theorized that as long as Americans had a "frontier" to explore, we would remain generous, optimistic, self-reliant, and innovative. However, now that the American West was closed, so too was a chapter in America's history.

"And now, four centuries from the discovery of America, at the end of a hundred years of life under the Constitution, the frontier has gone, and with its going has closed the first period of American history."
Frederick Jackson Turner,
The Significance of the Frontier in American History

Turner's thesis that the Americans had no more frontiers to explore proved accurate, at least from a geographical perspective. The land grab that defined the American West for the better part of the nineteenth century was now history. But not every frontier had been fully searched, claimed, or settled. In fact, the American twentieth century dawned with a new generation of children and new technologies that would shape our unique national story for decades. The new "frontiers" would now be in speed, space, nuclear energy, microbiology, and astrophysics. Americans would explore the heavens, from the tops of clouds to the dark side of the moon. Man would create weapons of mass destruction with the ability to destroy our planet several times over. We would break land speed records, sound barriers, gravitational limits, and deep-sea boundaries. Eventually, man would create a vast cyber multiverse that reimagined how we communicate, transact, socialize, commune, worship, learn, fight war, and entertain.

Frederick Jackson Turner believed Americans had to always be moving. *Forward. Upward. Onward.* Without new "frontiers," the American mystique would lose its psychic energy. The "American" century of the 1900s was simply one new frontier after another.

And technology proved the vehicle that fueled progress.

Like Turner, this book's central thesis argues generations are "shaped" more by their *environments* than by "history" or "institutions." Technology, especially in our "coming of age" years (ages ten to twenty-five), guides our collective personalities. It's the environment that interacts with our story and sets us apart from earlier and later generations. More than any historical event or cultural trend, a generation is defined by the technology that impacts the formative years.

The Turn of the Century

For most of human history, the turning of a century was an unheralded event. Centuries came and went, and the dawn of the twentieth century proved no different. Unlike its closing on December 31, 1999, celebrated with massive crowds, fireworks, and global news reports, the twentieth century was greeted with little fanfare. The clock struck midnight and the calendar quietly changed to 01/01/1900.

Of course, few people were awake for that historical turning. In 1900, electricity was just finding a connection. Thomas Edison invented the incandescent light bulb in 1879, but it wouldn't illuminate most homes for decades. In 1925, only half of U.S. houses enjoyed electrical power.[60] Simply put, when it was dark, life naturally slowed. Families consumed supper. Fathers read by candlelight. Children went to bed early. The advent of electrical lighting allowed man to shift time, to stay up later, do more work, entertain guests and operate without sleep.[61]

In 1900, America was an agrarian culture. We were farmers and ranchers. We grew our own gardens and raised our own meat. The more land a person owned, and the greater the produce, the wealthier the lifestyle. Dirt roads and wagons drawn by horses were the norm. Victorian morals, architecture, and fashions ruled. We were mostly country folk, but not for long. By 1920, more than half of all Americans would live in the city and 15 percent of the total population was foreign-born.[62]

Meanwhile, something new and noisy roamed the streets and air. Wheels propelled by engines, powered by a new fuel known as gasoline, rumbled along cobblestone avenues and countryside roads. Iron wagon wheels gave way to rubber automobile tires. In the clouds, a new motorized wheel also appeared: the airplane propeller.

"It was an age of steam, rivets and arrogant grandeur. From 1904 through '14, we built the Panama Canal…carved a foundation for Pennsylvania Station out of stony Manhattan Island and then put up the great station itself, a soaring singing monument to the power of machinery. Machines changed the landscape…they were the landscape."
David Gelernter

The Transportation-Telephone generation was born between 1900 and 1920. In their coming of age years (1910–1945), this cohort of kids experienced the dramatic rise of a motorized culture. This transportation renaissance permitted the populace to travel greater distances at faster speeds. Consequently, people lived further away and ventured to more exotic places. There was no greater explosion of wheels than in the first twenty years of the new century. The wheels of the Transportation-Telephone generation were made not just of rubber, but also metal, plastic, and wood. The wheels were sprockets, gears, rotors, rotary dials, steering wheels, and propellers.

It was motorized wheels that transported almost thirteen million immigrants to America between 1890 and 1910.[63] In 1900, there were seventy-six million Americans, and most were Anglo-Saxon Protestants who migrated from England, Ireland, and Germany. But now, millions of immigrants arrived from places like Russia, Greece, Italy, China, and Poland. America suddenly became more ethnically diverse thanks to the steam engine and "wheels" that moved ships across the ocean at greater speeds.

Motorized wheels propelled an ocean liner named *RMS Titanic* across the Atlantic in the spring of 1912.[64] Motorized wheels carved the "Big Ditch" (Panama Canal) in 1914, opening a new, faster passage from the east to west coasts of America. Motorized wheels transported President Teddy Roosevelt—the first U.S. president to travel abroad—to faraway Panama to inspect the canal's work.[65]

"I am careful and I am thrifty.
At least I was until I became a motorist."
William Ashdown, Confessions of an Automobilist, 1925

Motorized wheels proved the difference in two World Wars. Buses and taxis ferried soldiers to the front, moving them into battle position faster. Wheels and gearings created terrifying new forms of warfare like the machine gun, flame throwers, and mechanized cannons, capable of great human carnage and mass death. The introduction of the tank by the British proved a military game changer, allowing armies to break and crush enemy lines. The American "general purpose" vehicle, or "GP" (jeep), was the transportation of choice in the second World War. Yet, the most omnipotent motorized combat machine of the twentieth century proved the airplane, particularly the B-17 bomber. These planes flew higher and faster than enemy artillery could reach and dropped bombs with greater precision. It's no wonder the Transportation-Telephone generation's youngest members finished coming of age in 1945, just as an atom bomb was dropped by a B-29 (August 6, 1944).

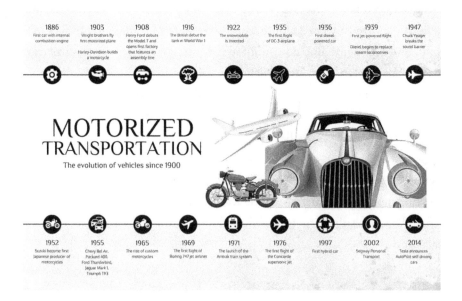

We Auto Know

The 1823 invention of the internal combustion engine by an Englishman named Samuel Brown changed the rules for "wheeled" transportation. For centuries, carts and wagons had carried people and products, pulled by any beast of muscle. Forty years later, Jean-Joseph-Etienne Lenoir developed the first true "horseless carriage"—which traveled at the speed of sloth, or three mph.[66] Consequently, the quest to build a faster "automobile," or a mechanized wheeled machine, was on.[67]

The problem in the 1890s was twofold: the availability of gasoline and the exorbitant price to produce a car. A gas-powered "horseless carriage" was a novelty at best and purely for the rich.[68] That's why, initially, automobiles were found only in the bigger cities. The horse still furnished the true horsepower for most Americans.

But that was about to change.

In 1908, Henry Ford's introduction of the Model T made the automobile accessible. For the next two decades, the Model T (also known as the "Tin Lizzie") was the American car for the common man. It was affordable, durable, dependable, and fun to drive. The car was a symbol of independence, power, innovation, and change—and now, an emerging middle class enjoyed the luxury too.[69] The Model T, unlike other cars of its era, was more reliable (with interchangeable parts) and easier to handle on rough American roads. Furthermore, once Ford began to produce the car on his assembly line in 1913, the cost of production slashed the price of a Model T in half.[70] In nineteen years of production, the Ford Motor Company produced over fifteen million Model T vehicles. By 1925, two-thirds of all cars on American roads were Ford's "Tin Lizzie." It's no wonder that, in 1999, the Model T was named the most influential car of the twentieth century.[71]

However, Henry Ford wasn't the only one making cars. William Durant and General Motors manufactured Buicks, Oldsmobiles, Pontiacs, Cadillacs, and, eventually, Chevrolets.[72] A third major motor company was the Chrysler Corporation, founded by Walter Chrysler in 1925, that produced Dodges, Plymouths, and DeSotos.[73]

———————

According to the *History Channel*, the following are the "Cars that Made America":

1. Oldsmobile Model R
2. Buick Model 10
3. Ford Model T
4. Dodge Brother Model 30
5. 1927 Ford Model A
6. 1931 Chevrolet AE Independence
7. 1932 For Model 18 V-8
8. Duesenberg Model J
9. Chrysler Airflow
10. 1949 Ford
11. 1953 Chevrolet Corvette Roadster
12. 1955 Chrysler C-300 2-Door Hardtop
13. 1955 Chevrolet
14. 1957 DeSoto Adventurer
15. Edsel
16. 1964$^{1/2}$ Ford Mustang
17. Chevrolet Corvair
18. Pontiace Le Mans GTO
19. Chevrolet Vega
20. Ford Pinto
21. Shelby Cobra
22. DeLorean DMC-12
23. 1981 Plymouth/Dodge 'K-Car'
24. 1984 Plymouth/Dodge Voyager/Caravan Minivan

———————

As cars improved in design, they also traveled faster. Europeans had been racing automobiles for years on open country roads, but Americans made car racing a destination experience. The Indianapolis 500 (established in 1911) allowed people to watch a car race from beginning to end inside an enclosed arena.

The motorcycle also moved the Transportation generation. With the emergence of internal combustion engines, bicycles were the first fitted for motorized travel.[74] The French, Germans, and English all worked to improve motorized bicycle technology. In America, two highly-competitive companies led the way: the Indian Motorcycle Manufacturing company (1901) and Harley-Davidson Motorcycles (1903).[75] World War I introduced both the motorcycle and the automobile to combat, but the size, durability, and flexibility of the smaller motorized bike proved invaluable in wartime, handling reconnaissance, message transport, and policing.[76] And when these G.I.s came home from war—especially World War II—they brought with them a passion for Harley-Davidson (who produced tens of thousands of motorcycles for the military).

The Transportation-Telephone generation drove wartime jeeps and tanks, gangster getaway cars, and "grapes of wrath" trucks to California during the Great Depression. They established a new "vacation" (recreational vehicle) and "road" (Route 66) culture. They flocked to movie drive-ins (1933) and enjoyed restaurant drive-throughs (1947).[77] In middle age, the Transportation generation designed, built and traveled the U.S. interstate system. They also forged the American car culture of the 1950s, including the most famous "car year" of all: 1955.[78] They pioneered the "biker gang" culture in a post-World War II America.[79] In late adulthood, this car generation retired to sunbelt destinations in Florida, California, and Arizona, many refusing to give up their car keys until family, law enforcement, or government officials wrested the privilege away.

The Transportation generation loved its wheels. Wheels were *their* symbol of autonomy and freedom.

The Friendly Skies

Another motorized "wheel" technology for this generation flew overhead. The TNT Generation was the first cohort of kids to grow up with mechanical beasts flying in the sky, buzzing the tree line, disappearing in the clouds, and dusting the crops. These aviation beasts included zeppelin airships, gliders, airplanes, and helicopters.

The introduction of the internal combustion engine was, once again, the decisive moment in the evolution of aeronautical transportation. For most of the nineteenth century, the experimental flights of gliders, balloons, and zeppelins graced the skies. In World War I, the German army employed zeppelins for reconnaissance and bombing. However, with the emergence of airplanes that were faster and more dependable, the zeppelin airship quickly lost influence after the Great War. The infamous 1937 Hindenburg disaster—which killed thirty-six people in Manchester Township, New Jersey—proved the end of the line for these mechanical balloons.

The origin of the motorized propeller airplane is debatable.[80] Nevertheless, Wilbur and Orville Wright have long been credited with the first sustained flight of a powered and controlled aircraft at Kitty Hawk, North Carolina on December 7, 1903. Orville's brief, twelve-second flight traveled a mere forty yards. Wilbur would best his brother on the fourth flight of the day, staying aloft for nearly one minute and three football fields. Two years later, with improvements in engine and plane design, Wilbur flew an amazing twenty-four miles in thirty-nine minutes.[81]

The age of airplanes had dawned.

Initially used for reconnaissance during World War I, planes were eventually fitted with guns and bombs that created a whole new way to fight. Some planes flew only at night. Some were used for attacks or "trench strafing." Some simply scouted.[82] The air wars also introduced a new war hero: the "ace" fighter pilot. America's Eddie Rickenbacker and Germany's "Red Baron" were among the most notable, legendary and decorated aviators of their day.[83] These war pilots were helped by fighter planes that were better designed and built from steel. Consequently, these new war planes flew higher, farther and carried more bombs.[84]

War was never the same again.

———————

"For heaven's sake, if you have any influence, with that wild-eyed, hallucinated young man, call him off before he is killed. Have him devote his energies to substantial, feasible and profitable pursuits, leaving dreaming to the professional dreamers."
Postcard from the family doctor to the mother of Glen Martin, an experimental aviator, dated September 30, 1910

———————

After World War I, the airplane continued to improve in design and use.[85] Barnstorming pilots grandstanded their skills for adoring crowds. Crop dusters served farmers. Postal messages were carried by airmail. In 1927, Charles "Lucky Lindy" Lindbergh became the first person to fly solo across the Atlantic (later duplicated by Amelia Earhart). He was just twenty-five years old and one of the first heroes and celebrities of the Transportation-Telephone generation. Lindbergh's feat sparked interest in commercial aviation, as numerous regional airlines were started to carry passengers from city to city.[86]

The first U.S. commercial (scheduled) flight carried one passenger across Tampa Bay twice a day in 1914. Five years later, K.L.M. Royal Dutch Airlines first offered flights between Amsterdam and London. Several major U.S. airlines were established in the 1920s, including Delta (1924), United and American Airlines (1926). The first American coast-to-coast flight service was offered by Trans World Airlines between New York and Los Angeles (1930). Unfortunately, it wasn't non-stop. The planes needed a layover in Kansas City due to the dangers of night flying.

The Great Depression dampened flight in the 1930s, although air travel continued to improve and expand. A Pan America flight from California to China was a three-day journey (with stops on various Pacific islands, including Hawaii and Wake). It only cost a whopping $1,438 (or $21,702 in today's dollars)! It's no wonder commercial air travel was limited to the uber-rich.

World War II revived the use of airplanes for military use. It was airplanes that bombed Pearl Harbor. It was airplanes that helped Allies drop thousands of soldiers behind enemy lines at Normandy. It was airplanes that took off from huge naval carriers to strafe Japanese-occupied Pacific islands. It was an airplane that dropped the atom bomb on Hiroshima and Nagasaki. For the Transportation generation, the airplane was a historical "savior." It was always there (and overhead) when you needed it. This generation even added airplane features (like tail fins) to their automobiles to create aerodynamic bodies and wore bomber jackets to ride their motorcycles.

Commercial aviation exploded after World War II, particularly in America.[87] The large B-29 bomber was considered a prototype for transporting great numbers of people long distances. However, again, the price of air travel was out of reach for most Americans until 1969. That's when Boeing introduced the 747—an aircraft able to transport 350 passengers in economical comfort. Finally, the middle class could afford to fly.[88]

THE TELEPHONE

The history and growth of phone technology since 1900

95%
of U.S. adults

own a cellphone in 2018.
U.S. homes with a landline:
43%

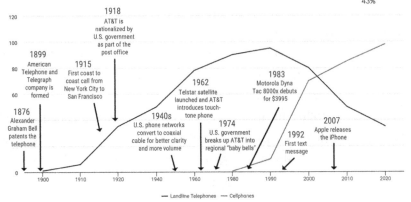

1918
AT&T is nationalized by U.S. government as part of the post office

1899
American Telephone and Telegraph company is formed

1915
First coast to coast call from New York City to San Francisco

1962
Telstar satellite launched and AT&T introduces touch-tone phone

1983
Motorola Dyna Tac 8000x debuts for $3995

1876
Alexander Graham Bell patents the telephone

1940s
U.S. phone networks convert to coaxial cable for better clarity and more volume

1974
U.S. government breaks up AT&T into regional "baby bells"

1992
First text message

2007
Apple releases the iPhone

— Landline Telephones — Cellphones

Everybody's Talking

As significant as flight and motors were to the emerging American psyche, no technology proved more influential than the telephone. In fact, arguably, the telephone might be bested only by the printing press, television and Internet for its impact upon mankind. Certainly, its later incarnation as mobile technology proved a watershed cultural shift. The ability to communicate anytime and anywhere flattened communication and revolutionized social boundaries.

The true inventor of the telephone is hotly contested. There were dozens of early prototypes as far back as 1854.[89] The first to legally patent a device was Alexander Graham Bell on March 7, 1876. Three days later, the famous first telephone message was heard: "Mr. Watson, come here. I want you."[90] The problem was nobody knew what exactly to do *with* the telephone. What use was it? Bell offered Western Union an opportunity to purchase his patent, but they refused with this curt response:

> We do not see that this device will be ever capable of sending recognizable speech over a distance of several miles. Messer Hubbard and Bell want to install one of their 'telephone devices' in every city. The idea is idiotic on the face of it. Furthermore, why would any person want to use this ungainly and impractical device when he can send a messenger to the

telegraph office and have a clear written message sent to any large city in the United States?…Mr. G.G. Hubbard's fanciful predictions, while they sound rosy, are based on wild-eyed imagination and lack of understanding of the technical and economic facts of the situation, and a posture of ignoring the obvious limitations of his device, which is hardly more than a toy…This device is inherently of no use to us. We do not recommend its purchase.[91]

Western Union's conclusion proved myopic. In 1900, there were 600,000 telephones (less than 1 percent of American households), but by the final birth year for the Transportation-Telephone generation in 1920, over a third of American homes—37.2 million—were wired for conversation. By the sunset of the twentieth century, over 95 percent of American households either owned a landline or cell phone.

For most of the twentieth century, America communicated through the Bell system, also known as the American Telephone and Telegraph company (founded in 1899). AT&T was nationalized as a public utility in 1918. Only three years earlier, it connected the east and west coast through a transcontinental line. Until the 1920s, the famous "candle stick" phone was the norm. The receiver was hung on a switch hook to end a call. It's why we called it "hanging up" the phone. Eventually, the ear and mouth piece were wedded into a single handset. In the 1930s, a rotary dial was added and remained standard until the touch tone phone landed in 1962. Telephones went from old-fashioned "clicks" to modern "beeps" overnight. Between 1949 and 1983, AT&T sold its most popular phone (the 500 series) in different colors from black to red to tan.

In the 1940s, telephone cabling was converted from copper wires to coaxial cables that could be laid underwater, overhead, or beneath ground. This was a game changer in telephone technology, producing the ability in the mid-1950s to make calls from the U.S. to Europe or the mainland to Hawaii. In the late 1980s, fiber-optic cables replaced coaxial to open up more space for data relays. In 1962, the Telstar satellite created a new frontier for telephone technology. It was now possible for calls to connect via satellites.

The Bell System (AT&T) was a rock star business in the early 1970s, controlling over 80 percent of the U.S. market. In 1974, the Justice Department finally ended the monopoly and divided the Bell system into several "baby bell" regions. AT&T focused on long-distance, while these regional "bells" handled local service. Ultimately, it paved the way for national cell service carriers like Sprint, Verizon, T-Mobile, and Cingular to enter the market.

Ironically, it would be another "hero" generation born in the last two decades of the twentieth century who were influenced by the emergence of *mobile* phone technology. This generation—commonly known as the Millennials—grew up with a cell phone that eventually morphed into a personal computer or "smartphone." Like the Transportation and Telephone (TNT) generation, these Millennials also enjoyed twin "flip" technologies of PC/CP: personal computers and cell phones.

Even still, it would be their great grandfathers and great grandmothers who first experienced telephone technology, not to mention motorized wheels and flight.

The Transportation-Telephone generation moved America forward, with wheels beneath and another one to turn. They even fingered a rotary "wheel" dial to make phone calls. At the advent of the nineteenth century, a "new" world with fresh technologies dawned. Power shifted from steam and coal towards oil and electricity (created through nuclear, water, and wind energy).

The sky was now the limit. Or maybe it was the moon.

It wouldn't matter.

The Transportation-Telephone generation led the way.

A TIMELINE OF TECHNOLOGICAL EVENTS (1900–1910):

- 1900: New York subway system is started. F.E. Dorn discovers radon and Max Planck formulates quantum theory. Browning revolver gun is introduced. R.A. Fessenden transmits voice over radio waves. First flight of a Zeppelin air ship.
- 1901: The first wireless transmission sent by Marconi between England and Canada. Hubert C. Booth invents vacuum cleaner. Willis Carrier dehumidifies ("air conditions") a room. First motor-driven bicycles.
- 1903: Harley-Davidson builds their first motorcycle. Orville and Wilbur Wright take flight. King C. Gillette introduces disposable razor. R.A. Zsigmondy invents ultramicroscope. Wilhelm Einthoven invents electrocardiograph. Henry Ford starts the Ford Motor Company.

- 1904: Ultraviolet lamps introduced. Work begins on the Panama Canal. Rolls-Royce founded. First telegraphic transmission of photographs. Carl Lindstrom Company begins producing phonographs and needles.
- 1905: The Nickelodeon theater shows first motion picture in the U.S: *The Great Train Robbery*. Einstein formulates Special Theory of Relativity. First neon lights appear.
- 1906: First run of the French Grand Prix motorcar race. Clemens von Pirquet introduces the term "allergy" to medicine. First radio program of voice and music broadcast in America. Morse code SOS adopted.
- 1907: Louis Lumiere develops a process for color photography. S.S. Lusitania breaks transatlantic record from Ireland to New York in five days, forty-five minutes.
- 1908: The first Model T automobile rolls out of production ($850) at Henry Ford's Motor Company. Fritz Haber synthesizes ammonia. General Motors Corporation founded.
- 1909: The first fingerprint evidence is used to solve a murder case. An automobile serves as a hearse for the first time, replacing traditional horse and carriage. First commercial manufacturing of Bakelite begins the Age of Plastic.
- 1910: Murray and Hjort commence the first deep-sea research expedition. Halley's Comet observed.

INFLUENTIAL PERSONS IN THE TRANSPORTATION GENERATION:
Presidents:
- Lyndon B. Johnson (1908–1973), thirty-sixth U.S. President
- Richard Nixon (1913–1994), thirty-seventh U.S. President
- Gerald Ford (1913–2006), thirty-eighth U.S. President
- John F. Kennedy (1917–1963), thirty-fifth U.S. President

Business, Education, Athletes and Other Leaders:
- Walt Disney (1901–1966), cartoon and film producer
- Charles Lindbergh (1902–1974), aviator
- Ray Kroc (1902–1984), businessman
- Lou Gehrig (1903–1941), baseball player
- J. Robert Oppenheimer (1904–1967), scientist

- Howard Hughes (1905–1976), businessman
- William Levitt (1907–1994), creator of the modern suburb
- Thurgood Marshall (1908–1993), First African American Supreme Court Justice
- Billy Graham (1918–2018), evangelist

Entertainers:
- Clark Gable (1901–1960), actor
- Louis Armstrong (1901–1971), jazz musician
- Ed Sullivan (1901–1974), television host
- Bob Hope (1903–2003), comedian and actor
- Henry Fonda (1905–1982), actor
- John Wayne (1907–1979), actor
- James Stewart (1908–1997), actor
- Walter Cronkite (1916–2009), news anchor

Authors:
- John Steinbeck (1902–1968), novelist
- George Orwell (1903–1950), novelist
- Dr. Seuss (1904–1991), poet

Chapter Five

Motion Pictures

"There are two mechanical contrivances.... [that will] revolutionize entertainment, doing for it what the printing press did for books. They are the talking motion picture and the electric vision apparatus with telephone. Either one will enable millions of people to see and hear the same performance simultaneously."
S.C. Gilfillan, writing in 1912

BIRTH YEARS: 1910–1930
"Coming of Age" Years: 1920–1955
Primary Tech Event: Talkie Movies
Strauss-Howe Archetype: Hero-Artist
Generation Personality: Dominant/Optimistic
Iconic Generation Representatives: Ronald Reagan and Joe DiMaggio

Historical Influencing Events in Youth and Young Adulthood:
*World War I, Prohibition, Charles Lindbergh, Great Depression,
Rise of Nazi Germany, World War II, Atom Bomb, Korean War*

The motion picture story begins on a bet.

In the late 1800s, a Californian tycoon named Leland Stanford—who later founded Stanford University—was in a pickle. He had to prove a wager. The bet was simple: Does a horse's four hooves completely leave the ground in full gallop or not? Stanford hired photographer Eadweard Muybridge to settle the bet. By 1878, camera technology had greatly improved. Faster apertures meant less blurring of things in motion.[92] Muybridge set up a series of cameras along a race track, with wires that tripped each camera's aperture when the horse ran by. The experiment worked flawlessly, collecting a series of photographs of a running horse and rider.

If Muybridge had stopped there, so would the story.

After all, the bet was confirmed for Leland Stanford. Indeed, there was a brief moment when a horse's four legs were completely suspended in the air. But Muybridge wasn't done. He decided to compile his photographs into a seamless brief animation. The result was magical, and Muybridge knew it. He took his horse show on the lecture circuit to rousing success. Audiences couldn't get enough of that running horse.[93]

It was the first time a photograph of something living had been animated.

And it changed the world.

Every Picture Tells a Story

Since the dawn of time, man has captured pictures of his world.

"The cinema is an invention without any future."
Auguste and **Louis Lumière**, inventors of motion pictures

Cavemen scrawled pictographs on rock walls. Egyptians painted portraits of pharaohs, gods, and temples on ancient papyri.[94] Centuries later, Greeks and Romans drew pictures, some even pornographic, to leave stories of tyrants, aristocrats, philosophers, and statesmen.[95] During the Renaissance, artists like Michelangelo, Leonardo da Vinci, and Raphael painted inspirational masterpieces to communicate divine ideas to the common man.

MOTION PICTURES

A History of the Movies

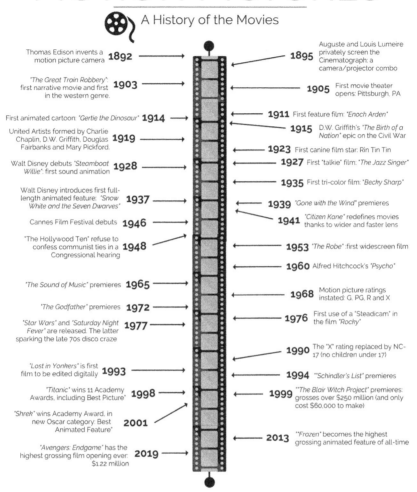

Thomas Edison invents a motion picture camera **1892**

1895 Auguste and Louis Lumeire privately screen the Cinematograph: a camera/projector combo

"The Great Train Robbery": first narrative movie and first in the western genre. **1903**

1905 First movie theater opens: Pittsburgh, PA

First animated cartoon: *"Gertie the Dinosaur"* **1914**

1911 First feature film: *"Enoch Arden"*

United Artists formed by Charlie Chaplin, D.W. Griffith, Douglas Fairbanks and Mary Pickford. **1919**

1915 D.W. Griffith's *"The Birth of a Nation"* epic on the Civil War

1923 First canine film star: Rin Tin Tin

Walt Disney debuts *"Steamboat Willie"*: first sound animation **1928**

1927 First 'talkie' film: *"The Jazz Singer"*

1935 First tri-color film: *"Becky Sharp"*

Walt Disney introduces first full-length animated feature: *"Snow White and the Seven Dwarves"* **1937**

1939 *"Gone with the Wind"* premieres

Cannes Film Festival debuts **1946**

1941 *"Citizen Kane"* redefines movies thanks to wider and faster lens

"The Hollywood Ten" refuse to confess communist ties in a Congressional hearing **1948**

1953 *"The Robe"*: first widescreen film

1960 Alfred Hitchcock's *"Psycho"*

"The Sound of Music" premieres **1965**

1968 Motion picture ratings instated: G, PG, R and X

"The Godfather" premieres **1972**

1976 First use of a "Steadicam" in the film *"Rocky"*

"Star Wars" and *"Saturday Night Fever"* are released. The latter sparking the late 70s disco craze **1977**

1990 The "X" rating replaced by NC-17 (no children under 17)

"Lost in Yonkers" is first film to be edited digitally **1993**

1994 *"Schindler's List"* premieres

"Titanic" wins 11 Academy Awards, including Best Picture" **1998**

1999 *"The Blair Witch Project"* premieres: grosses over $250 million (and only cost $60,000 to make)

"Shrek" wins Academy Award, in new Oscar category: Best Animated Feature" **2001**

2013 *"Frozen"* becomes the highest grossing animated feature of all-time

"Avengers: Endgame" has the highest grossing film opening ever: $1.22 million **2019**

Photography was a nineteenth-century innovation that quickly became a cultural phenomenon.[96] The history of America, particularly the Civil War and westward expansion, was brilliantly captured through "real" pictures.[97] For the first time, we saw life as it was, not as some artist painted it to be. The photograph gave us an authentic snapshot of life in the moment.

For most of the 1800s, motion pictures were depictions and representations, nothing more than a series of sketches rapidly flipped for the viewer's enjoyment.[98] It wasn't until Muybridge's horse animation that the possibility of "motion pictures" posed a serious reality.

Thankfully, a certain wizard from Menlo Park was also on the job.

Thomas Edison invented the phonograph (1877), microphone (1878), and incandescent light bulb (1879). By the late 1800s, he was an American brand and cultural icon. For years Edison envisioned "moving pictures" and so when he learned of Muybridge's horse animation, the inventor sought an audience. Inspired by what he witnessed, Edison hired W.K.L. Dickson, a talented young photographer, to invent a "moving pictures" camera and viewer. In 1892, they finally succeeded: a movie camera and Kinetoscope were released. The film age was born.[99] Edison had made motion pictures, but he still wasn't satisfied. His real vision was to marry his phonograph (sound) to film.[100] The wizard wanted movies to *talk*.

But the bigger problem was projection. At the time, motion pictures were for single-viewer use only. Across the Atlantic, two French brothers—Auguste and Louis Lumière—solved that dilemma when they invented a motion picture projector (1895).[101] Now it was possible for audiences to collectively view a film. Yes, it was exciting, visual magic, but generally uninteresting material. Early films were brief, silent, and focused on routine topics. *Two people boxing. A person dancing. A group of people leaving a building.* Consequently, it didn't take long for audiences to bore, even when multiple films were patched together in a new type of theater called a "Nickelodeon."[102]

What motion pictures needed was a story.

"[From movies] we learned how tennis was played and golf,
what a swimming pool was…and of course we learned about
Love, a very foreign country like maybe China or Connecticut."
Kates Simons, writer

Consequently, a new form of filmmaking emerged: the narrative motion picture. One of the earliest narrative films was the twelve-minute western *The Great Bank Robbery* (1903).[103] Within a few years, most films featured a story line that amused audiences. These "moving" images "moved" people and, subsequently, the "movies" were born.

It was into this brave new cinematic world the Motion Picture generation (1910-1930) was born. They grew up on films that entertained, inspired, comforted, and informed. It's not surprising that the "Golden Age of Classical Hollywood Cinema" (1910 to early 1960s) matches the birth and "coming of age" years for the "Motion Picture" generation.[104] It's an era of silent pictures, "talkies," Disney animation, and the greatest movies (and movie stars) in Hollywood history.

The Birth of a Film Nation

The first birth year of the Motion Picture generation was equally significant in film history.

In 1910, the cinema industry started to credit actors for their roles. It was also the year that newsreels became an innovative way to receive "news" and the horror movie *Frankenstein* premiered. More importantly, a new theater chain opened in New York City by a business magnate named Marcus Loew.[105] Within three years, Loew's film houses debuted in Boston, Philadelphia, and Washington, D.C. He later acquired Metro Pictures and Goldwyn Picture Corporation, which eventually merged into Metro-Goldwyn-Mayer or MGM. MGM was now a major film company (featuring a "roaring lion" mascot to introduce every film).[106]

The Motion Picture generation "came of age" (1920–1955) in movie houses like Loew's Theaters, idolizing stars such as Charlie Chaplin, Rudolph Valentino, Joan Crawford, Shirley Temple, Gene Autrey, John Wayne, and Marilyn Monroe. In their teens, they were influenced by new fads introduced by their elder Transportation generation siblings. *Flappers and vamps. Sheiks and shebas.* A post-Victorian age morality emerged in urban centers that challenged the status quo.[107] A new type of journalism also appeared: "fan magazines" or tabloid journalism. As a generation, they primarily viewed black and white "talkies." But by the end of the 1950s, their final "coming of age" years, "technicolor" films were dominant.

On February 8, 1915, the first blockbuster movie was released: D.W Griffith's *The Birth of a Nation*. This silent picture drama of post-Civil War Reconstruction featured early screen star Lillian Gish and was originally titled *The Clansman*.[108] It was the first motion picture screened at the White House. President Woodrow Wilson, a Southern Democrat, reportedly reacted, "It's like writing history with lightning. And my only regret is that it is all terribly true."[109] The movie was controversial.[110] It's heroic depiction of the Ku Klux Klan actually revived the violent, racist fraternity,[111] and re-opened wounds between blacks and whites.[112]

Race relations became a generational theme for the Motion Picture generation. They witnessed Jim Crow laws, Southern segregation, and civil rights legislation. In fact, it was two Motion Picture members—Jackie Robinson (1919) and Martin Luther King, Jr. (1929)—who were figureheads in the civil rights movement for black Americans.

In the 1920s, the heart of black America found it's beat in New York City. Between 1920 and 1930, the city of Harlem population shifted from 32 percent to 70 percent black. Referred to as the "Harlem Renaissance" and the rise of the "new negro," Harlem became a cultural capital for black literature, music, and art.[113] A new music also emerged. Known as "jazz," it featured artists like Billie Holiday, Louis Armstrong and Duke Ellington.

Throughout their youth and young adulthood years, the Motion Picture generation experienced live-action pictures that shaped their generational personality. They attended theaters that were "ornate, gilded places" for palatial, cinematic experiences.[114] They watched current events via "Movietone" news reels (which ran in movie houses between 1928 and 1963). Newsreels created awareness of global events unknown to previous generations. The events that defined the Motion Pictures generation were visually experienced inside theaters: the stock market crash (1929),[115] repeal of Prohibition (1933),[116] Hindenburg disaster (1937),[117] Japanese attack on Pearl Harbor (1941),[118] the death of Franklin D. Roosevelt,[119] and the Korean War (1950).[120]

And the Babe Will Lead Them

The Motion Picture generation also experienced the dawn of modern advertising and mass marketing. From Burma Shave roadway signage to radio jingles to 1960s corporate culture *Mad Men*, this cohort thrived in the context of the commercial. Coca-Cola reinvented Christmas with its depictions of Santa Claus.[121] Advertising in the 1920s also pushed and promoted "stars."

And no star was bigger than the "Babe."

Babe Ruth emerged as America's first sports superstar at a time when baseball was mired in a sad, tragic mess. The 1919 World Series had been fixed by gamblers and eight White Sox players, including the popular Shoeless Joe Jackson, were thrown out of baseball for life. The fact that it happened wasn't shocking, as rumors of gambling in baseball were well-known, but the integrity of the game was deeply challenged.

The 1920 major league baseball season also signaled a new day for the old ball game. The "dead ball" era for pitchers was over. No longer could hurlers "dirty up a new ball" with "dirt, licorice, tobacco juice" nor soften it with spikes, nor scar or sandpaper it into a "misshapen, earth-colored ball that traveled through the air erratically."[122] The baseball was now manufactured to be "livelier." The result was more home runs.

And nobody smashed baseballs farther than George Herman "Babe" Ruth.

The Babe single-handedly changed the game and inspired America—particularly Motion Picture kids—as the King of Swing. Ruth might've had more nicknames than homers. *The Bambino. The Sultan of Swat. The Wali of Wallop. The Wazir of Wham. The Maharajah of Mash. The Rajah of Rap. The Caliph of Clout. The Behemoth of Bust.*[123] In 1920, just as first-year Motion Picture children were coming of age, a desperate Red Sox owner sold Babe Ruth to the Yankees hoping to finance yet another Broadway show.[124] It proved a box office smash for the Yanks. The Babe slugged fifty-four homers in 1920 (more than double his total in 1919). To put that in perspective: only one team in 1920 had that many homers *combined!*[125]

"Sometimes I still can't believe what I saw. This 19-year-old kid, crude, poorly educated, only lightly brushed by the social veneer we call civilization, gradually transformed into the idol of American youth and the symbol of baseball the world over—a man loved by more people and with an intensity of feeling that perhaps has never been equaled before or since."
Harry Hooper, teammate

Babe Ruth quickly became a publicist's dream. His cherub face was everywhere, from chocolate to soap to breakfast cereal. He drove expensive cars, drank like a fish, sported with whores, dined with celebrities, and loved the kids. Everywhere the Babe went, a story followed. Newspapers around the nation started to run a call-out section titled "What Babe Ruth Did Today." The Babe's personality sparked a new type of journalism known as sports writing (with plenty of flowery language). Ruth starred in motion pictures and was featured on magazine covers. Banks and stores closed when he played. In 1930, as most Americans financially struggled in the Great Depression, the Babe made more money than President Herbert Hoover. When Ruth was asked if such an exorbitant salary was proper and deserved, the Babe quipped, "Why not? I had a better year than [Hoover] did."[126]

Between 1920 and 1960, baseball experienced its glory years and the Motion Picture generation enjoyed a front row seat. They grew up cheering for Giants and Yankees, Cardinals and Dodgers. Other professional sports, including football, basketball, golf, and boxing, also gained in popularity, but baseball remained America's favorite game. Indeed, it was the soundtrack to the twentieth-century American story.

Hail to the Chief

If there's a single person who represents the positive, winsome, and charismatic personality of the Motion Picture generation, it was Ronald Wilson Reagan.

Reagan was born February 6, 1911 in Tampico, Illinois and grew up in nearby Dixon. After graduation from college, Reagan found work in radio, but eventually moved to films. Reagan was the quintessential film star of the Motion Picture generation. He had rugged good looks, broad shoulders, chiseled facial features, and styled locks. A smooth and persuasive voice and a killer smile rounded out his repertoire. In his first two years of filming, Reagan starred in nineteen movies. He was nicknamed "The Gipper"—a moniker that stuck his entire life—for his role as George Gipp in the 1940 film *Knute Rockne, All American*.

"I never thought it was my style or the words I used that made a difference; it was the content. I wasn't a great communicator, but I communicated great things, and they didn't spring full bloom from my brow, they came from the heart of a great nation—from our experience, our wisdom and our belief in the principles that have guided us for two centuries."
Ronald Reagan (farewell address, 1989)

Although a Democrat in his youth and young adult years, Reagan converted to right-wing conservatism in 1952. He was elected governor of California (1967–1975) and eventually U.S. President (1980–1989). Reagan's popularity and political clout was rooted to his Motion Picture generation personality. He was as tough as John Wayne and as handsome as Clark Gable. He was funny like Chaplin and told stories like Disney. He reported it "the way it is" like Cronkite. Reagan preached a messianic new vision for America in the vein of Charlton Heston (as Moses). After all, Cecil B. DeMille's *The Ten Commandments* was an epic technicolor masterpiece for his generation. And it was released in 1956, just as the last Motion Picture members came of age.

Ronald Reagan's "morning in America" vision—the theme of his presidency—proved to be a sunset for the Motion Picture generation. By 1990, the world had changed again, and the cinema generation was now dying off. With exception to Lyndon B. Johnson, every President between 1960 and 1989 was born in the Motion Picture cohort, more than any other U.S. generation. The charismatic John F. Kennedy (1917–1963)—helped into office by his "Jack Pack" of Hollywood celebrities—carved an inspirational "technicolor" vision for America in the 1960s.[127] Kennedy also married Hollywood with the presidency, a symbiotic relationship enjoyed by other administrations—most notably, Reagan, Bill Clinton, and Barack Obama.

Color Me Hollywood

In the 1920s, Hollywood, CA emerged as ground zero for the film industry. Four out of every five motion pictures were Tinseltown films.

The Motion Picture generation is framed by two Hollywood hunks who were critically acclaimed actors: Rudolph Valentino (1895–1926) and James Dean (1931–1955). Both died young and tragically. Valentino was a cinematic heartthrob who passed unexpectedly at the age of thirty-one due to complications related to appendicitis.[128] Valentino's death set off riots at the local New York funeral parlor when thousands of people (mostly female) gathered to see his body. Similarly, James Dean (1931–1955) was killed in a car accident on September 30, 1955. Dean, like his character in *Rebel Without A Cause* (released the same month as his death) was a tortured, complicated soul.[129] Comparisons to Valentino's untimely death and legendary status were immediate. The era of classical Hollywood began with Valentino and ended with James Dean.[130]

The year 1927 was a notable year for motion pictures. On May 11, the Academy of Motion Picture Arts and Sciences was founded in Los Angeles by Douglas Fairbanks.[131] But, more importantly, it was the year of the first "talkie." *The Jazz Singer*, starring Al Jolson, was a box office smash and sound motion pictures—the dream of Thomas Edison—were now reality. By 1929, nearly all films were "talkies." With sound tracks, Hollywood began to spin new stars like Shirley Temple and Gene Autry, not to mention blockbusters like *King Kong* (1933).

But there was a mouse in the theater house, too.

Mickey Mouse.

On November 18, 1928, Walt Disney released an animated short film with a soundtrack that included special effects, music, and dialogue. Theater patrons loved Mickey Mouse and *Steamboat Willie* single-handedly launched the Disney brand.[132] Disney films pioneered new ways to tell old stories through feature films like *Snow White and the Seven Dwarfs* (1937), *Pinocchio* (1940), *Bambi* (1942), *Cinderella* (1950), *Alice in Wonderland* (1951), *Peter Pan* (1953), and *Sleeping Beauty* (1959). These fanciful feature animations arrived just in time to suckle the children of the Motion Picture generation during their childbearing years. Later, these grandkids, now also grown up parents, would revive the Disney cartoon in the late 1980s (*Who Framed Roger Rabbit, Little Mermaid*) and 1990s (*Beauty and the Beast, Aladdin, The Lion King, Toy Story*) for their own children.

If there was a year that defined the Motion Picture generation, it might be the twelve months that spanned 1939–1940, dubbed "the greatest year in the history of Hollywood."[133] At the time, the youngest of the generation was nine and the oldest was twenty-nine, so it fits those "coming of age" years perfectly. Between March 1939 and February 1940, several classic Tinseltown films premiered, including *The Hound of the Baskervilles* (March 31), *The Wizard of Oz* (August 25), *Mr. Smith Goes to Washington* (October 19), *Gone with the Wind* (December 15), and *Pinocchio* (February 7).[134] These five non-comedy movies encompass the most popular film genres: fantasy, drama, mystery, historical fiction, and animation.

After World War II, Hollywood and the film industry buzzed with communist innuendos, allegations, and finger-pointing. Eventually, the rumors produced blacklists and a new word for the American lexicon: *McCarthyism*. In the 1950s, theater attendances also began to decline, thanks to a new form of family entertainment known as "television." To win back audiences, movies were increasingly released in color, widescreen, and 3-D.

On July 18, 1955, Walt Disney opened the gates to a new American destination location known as "Disneyland." The amusement park featured new worlds like "Adventureland," "Frontierland," "Fantasyland," and "Tomorrowland."[135] Disneyland gave Motion Picture parents and their kids an opportunity to rediscover the American ideal (or the Disney *vision* of that American ideal).

Wheels in Motion

The Motion Picture generation, like its Transportation elder siblings, was influenced by motorized wheels. It's just that their wheel was a *reel*…on a projector. The rapid clicking of a motion picture spool would be an iconic sound for the movie-goer's experience during most of the twentieth century, as would the slap-slap-slap noise when a film finished its course through the projector.

Just as automobiles and airplanes transported people to new locations, the motion picture carried audiences into the past or future, to faraway lands, or to places familiar. In an hour or two, a movie became an escape from reality, a place of relaxation, serendipity, magic, and beauty.

And one generation experienced every enchanted moment.

A TIMELINE OF TECHNOLOGICAL EVENTS (1911–1920):

- 1911: General Motors installs the first electric self-start in a Cadillac automobile. First Indianapolis 500 held (average speed: 74.59 mph). Rutherford formulates his theory of atomic structure. A flight from Munich to Berlin reaches record height of 12,800 feet.
- 1912: The Titanic sinks in the north Atlantic Ocean drowning 1,513 people. Edwin Bradenberger invents a process for manufacturing cellophane. Wilson's cloud-chamber photographs lead to the detection of protons and electrons. Viktor F. Hess discovers cosmic radiation. First successful parachute jump.

- 1913: Henry Ford Motor Company introduces the assembly line. Stainless steel is invented. H. Geiger invents an electrical device for counting individual alpha rays. Rene Lorin states the basic ideas of jet propulsion.
- 1914: World War I begins. Panama Canal opens. Robert H. Goddard begins his rocketry experiments. Dr. Alexis Carrel performs first successful heart surgery on a dog.
- 1915: Germans use poison gas in trench warfare. First transcontinental telephone call between New York City and San Francisco. Einstein creates General Theory of Relativity. Ford produces one millionth car. Automobile speed record: 102.6 mph.
- 1916: Ford's Model T's now cost $368 per car, allowing the general public to purchase.
- Thompson ("Tommy Gun") submachine gun invented by General John T. Thompson. Blood for transfusion is refrigerated.
- 1918: United States first use of aircraft in war. American airmail service begins.
- 1919: Rotary dial telephone and pop-up toaster invented. F.W. Aston builds mass- spectrograph and establishes the phenomena of isotopy. First experiments with shortwave radio. J.W. Alcock and A. Whiten Brown make first nonstop transatlantic flight from Newfoundland to Ireland in 16 hours, 27 minutes. Radio Corporation of America founded.
- 1920: Surgeon Harvey Cushing develops new techniques in brain surgery. German engineer Anton Flettner invents the rotor ship. Marconi opens first public broadcasting station in Britain at Writtle.

INFLUENTIAL PERSONS IN THE MOTION PICTURE GENERATION:

Presidents:
- Ronald Reagan (1911–2004), fortieth U.S. President
- John F. Kennedy (1917–1963), thirty-fifth U.S. President

Business, Education, Athletes and Other Leaders:
- Jesse Owens (1913–1980), track and field athlete
- Joe DiMaggio (1914-1999), baseball player
- Jackie Robinson (1919–1972), baseball player
- John Glenn (1921–2016), astronaut

- Hugh Hefner (1926–2017), founder/publisher of *Playboy* magazine
- Martin Luther King, Jr. (1929–1968), civil rights leader

Entertainers:

- Robert Johnson (1911–1938), blues singer and guitarist
- Lucille Ball (1911–1989), actress
- Gene Kelly (1912–1996), actor
- Frank Sinatra (1915–1998), singer
- Leonard Bernstein (1918–1990), composer
- Judy Garland (1922–1969), actress
- Hank Williams, Sr. (1923–1953), country music artist
- Charlton Heston (1923–2008), actor
- Marlon Brando (1924–2004), actor
- Johnny Carson (1925–2005), television host
- Marilyn Monroe (1926–1962), actress
- Vin Scully (1927–present), sportscaster
- Fred Rogers (1928–2003), television actor
- Dick Clark (1929–2012), television host
- Barbara Walters (1929–present), journalist

Authors/Artists:

- Chuck Jones (1912–2002), animator
- J. D. Salinger (1919–2010), novelist and critic
- Ray Bradbury (1920–2012), novelist
- Isaac Asimov (1920–1992), novelist
- Gene Roddenberry (1921–1991), novelist
- Stan Lee (1922–1918), comic book author
- Charles Schultz (1922–2000), cartoonist
- Jack Kerouac (1922–1969), novelist
- Maya Angelou (1928–2014), poet

Chapter Six
Radio

"Radio is the most intimate and socially personal medium in the world."
Harvey von Zell

BIRTH YEARS: 1920–1940
"Coming of Age" Years: 1930–1965
Primary Tech Event: Roosevelt Fireside Chats
Strauss-Howe Archetype: Artist
Generation Personality: Dominant/Pessimistic
Iconic Generation Representatives: John Glenn and Johnny Cash

Historical Influencing Events in Youth and Young Adulthood:
Great Depression, Rise of Nazi Germany, World War II, Atom Bomb, Korean War, rock and roll, Space Race, JFK's assassination

---

He was the biggest name in radio for six decades.

Between 1952 and 2008, Paul Harvey's news and commentary was a weekly broadcast on twelve hundred stations that reached nearly a quarter of a million people. Harvey was a true airwaves rock star and a pioneer in conservative news radio.[136]

His silky, baritone voice was unmistakable, particularly the way it lifted like a rocket on certain syllables or words. He started every broadcast the same: "Hello Americans, this is Paul Harvey…and now the *news!*" Harvey was known for his gentle, inspiring stories, particularly a "history mystery" segment called "The Rest of the Story"—a clever re-telling of a forgotten or overlooked storyline that concluded with a surprising twist. Harvey was old-school. His right-wing views were often out of touch with the new post-1960s counterculture. A *Salon* writer once opined that Harvey is "an astute dissector of current events, cultural phenomena and middle-American minutiae. But more than that, he is perhaps the finest huckster ever to roam the airwaves."[137]

Paul Harvey certainly had some "huckster" in him. It's why countless businesses—from *Bose* radios to *Select Comfort* mattresses—paid him big bucks to pitch their products. Harvey was cut from the cloth of the Great Depression. He pushed a broom in his first radio job but eventually his golden voice landed him a lifelong communications career. In 2009, the *New York Times* eulogized his down-home influence on America:

> [Harvey] personalized the radio news with his right-wing opinions, but laced them with his own trademarks: a hypnotic timbre, extended pauses for effect, heart-warming tales of average Americans and folksy observations that evoked the heartland, family values and the old-fashioned plain talk one heard around the dinner table on Sunday.

Paul Harvey was born in 1918. Though two years shy of the Radio generation (1920–1940), in many ways, he's cohort model number one; the original mold and the unique voice for the entire generation. He told stories of the Radio generation, for the Radio generation…on the radio. For those born after 1920, Paul Harvey was the man behind the mike.

However, Harvey wasn't the only radio star of his generation. The king of talk radio (and later television) was the incomparable Larry King (b. 1933). King's interviews with celebrities, world leaders, and other cultural leaders made him a household name.

But now you need to know the *rest* of the story.

Radio was born in the roaring 1920s and found its footing during the Great Depression. It served a struggling nation that was doing its best to hang together. In the wake of the stock market crash of 1929, America was in a financial funk. Consumer spending dived. Hurricanes and droughts decimated the land.[138] Farms went belly-up. Unemployment soared. Half of the nation's banks failed. The entertainment venues of the 1920s fell on hard times. Baseball attendance plummeted. Motion picture theaters closed. Few could afford anything of *luxury*...except the radio. It was the one thing Americans couldn't live without. By 1933, most American homes sported a radio and millions found comfort in it.[139] The radio gathered the nation (like a church or classroom) to transport Americans to faraway places. Radio made the world smaller and imaginable. Sometimes we listened to the President. Sometimes we tuned into a baseball game. Sometimes we were entertained by a comedy act or soap opera.

The Radio generation was born just after the Great War and during the Great Depression. The oldest members were the troops who stormed Normandy and the youngest fought communists in Vietnam rice paddies. It's a group of American kids who grew up with their heads inside headphones or ears glued to radio speakers. Later, they'd buy muscle cars with radio consoles and boogie at the beach to transistor portables. They'd pioneer a new musical genre (perfect for radio) known as "rock and roll."

Radio was how Americans got their news, entertainment, sports, and religion. But not everyone saw this Radio generation as productive—or even interesting. This generation also lived in the shadow of the great Transportation-Telephone and Motion Picture generations. One historian zinged his own peers as "withdrawn, cautious, unimaginative, indifferent, unadventurous—silent."[140] It's a description that became a label in Strauss and Howe's *Generations*, who officially dubbed those born between 1924 and 1942 as the "Silent Generation."[141]

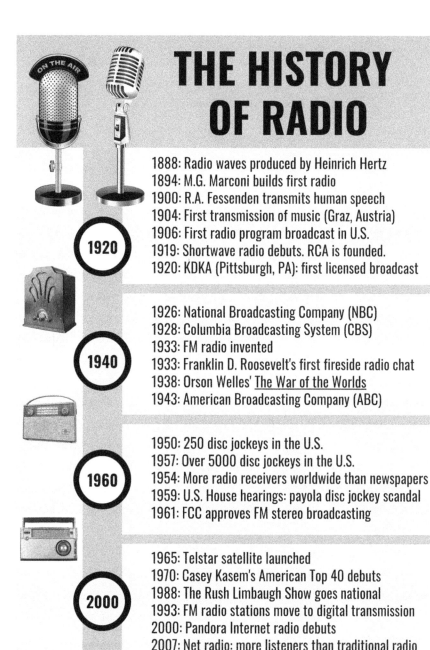

THE HISTORY OF RADIO

1888: Radio waves produced by Heinrich Hertz
1894: M.G. Marconi builds first radio
1900: R.A. Fessenden transmits human speech
1904: First transmission of music (Graz, Austria)
1906: First radio program broadcast in U.S.
1919: Shortwave radio debuts. RCA is founded.
1920: KDKA (Pittsburgh, PA): first licensed broadcast

1920

1926: National Broadcasting Company (NBC)
1928: Columbia Broadcasting System (CBS)
1933: FM radio invented
1933: Franklin D. Roosevelt's first fireside radio chat
1938: Orson Welles' The War of the Worlds
1943: American Broadcasting Company (ABC)

1940

1950: 250 disc jockeys in the U.S.
1957: Over 5000 disc jockeys in the U.S.
1954: More radio receivers worldwide than newspapers
1959: U.S. House hearings: payola disc jockey scandal
1961: FCC approves FM stereo broadcasting

1960

1965: Telstar satellite launched
1970: Casey Kasem's American Top 40 debuts
1988: The Rush Limbaugh Show goes national
1993: FM radio stations move to digital transmission
2000: Pandora Internet radio debuts
2007: Net radio: more listeners than traditional radio

2000

"It's no exaggeration to say that radio brought the whole country together, all at the same instant, everyone listening to the same things."
Bob Trout, radio/television broadcaster

And yet, most of this "silent generation" cohort is the "Radio generation." Which is a far more accurate and *positive* moniker.

After all, the "Silent Generation" wasn't all that *quiet* nor *"cautious."* The Radio generation" produced great aviators and astronauts like John Glenn, Buzz Aldrin, Neil Armstrong, and Chuck Yeager (who broke the sound barrier). This generation wasn't "unimaginative" nor "unadventurous" either. Many groundbreaking business leaders come from its ranks, from Ted Turner and Rupert Murdoch, to Warren Buffett and S. Truett Cathy. This generation pioneered rock and roll (Elvis Presley, Buddy Holly, Chuck Berry) and modern country music (Johnny Cash, Waylon Jennings, Loretta Lynn). The civil rights movement was led by a Radio generation voice: Martin Luther King, Jr.

And while it's true this generation produced no U.S. Presidents; it wasn't without serious influence at the highest levels of government. Every principal Presidential advisor from Kennedy to H.W. Bush was born between 1925 and 1942, in the heart of the Radio generation.[142] Indeed, this generation produced many presidential contenders (Walter Mondale, Michael Dukakis, John McCain) and notable first ladies (Jacqueline Kennedy, Rosalynn Carter, Nancy Reagan, and Barbara Bush).

If there was anything "silent" about the Radio generation, it was birth rates. The Great Depression put a lid on live births in the United States. Consequently, the Radio generation is the smallest U.S. generation in history. Between 1925 and 1935, live birth rates dipped to 2.4 million births, the lowest number of babies born in America since 1900.[143]

Don't Touch That Dial!

Italian Guglielmo Marconi is often credited with inventing radio, and that's mostly true. He was the first to transmit a sound via electromagnetic waves in 1894, but Marconi had some help. The concept of radio originated in the theoretical calculations of a physicist named James Maxwell. He was the first person to create a working formula for electromagnetic waves in 1864. Twenty years later, Henrich Hertz proved Maxwell's theory and built the first transmitter and receiver.[144] Marconi relied upon Maxwell's theory, and the work of Hertz to transmit sounds to greater distances (using antennae). And don't forget Nikola Tesla. His ideas—particularly the "Wardenclyffe Tower Project"—also contributed significantly to wireless communications.[145]

"Nothing I guess."
Heinrich Hertz, on any potential applications
for his transmitter and receiver

But let's be honest, primitive radio was just pushing "clicks" for communication purposes.

Essentially it was Morse code through the air (also known as "wireless" telegraphy). The development of amplitude modulation (AM radio) was necessary to eventually produce *voice* transmission. On December 20, 1900, Reginald Fessenden became the first person to transmit his voice via electronic waves—a significant step forward in radio communication.[146] The invention of the vacuum tube (1906) and amplification (1912) further evolved radio technology. Nevertheless, at the time, most people who tinkered in radio communications were mere amateurs employing homemade sets. It wasn't until World War I that radio transmissions of the voice got truly serious. Radio allowed for immediate military maneuvers to occur and that made radio particularly *useful* in the Great War.

And when that war was over, radio turned its transmissions to the home front. In 1920 the commercial age of radio began.

That's the year RCA (Radio Corporation of America) launched its initial AM broadcast and the first radio station was licensed to Pittsburgh's KDKA. During the 1920s and 1930s, radio stations, radio programming, and radio set sales soared. Everybody and anybody went on the air, including farmers, hardware store owners, school teachers, and the police. "Radio was to the air," wrote Peter Jennings, "as the automobile was to the earth, an agent of transport to a world as wide open as the imagination."[147]

"People who weren't around in the Twenties when radio exploded can't know what it meant, this milestone for mankind. Suddenly, with radio, there was instant human communication. No longer were our homes isolated and lonely and silent. The world came into our homes for the first time. Music came pouring in. Laughter came in. News came in. The world shrank, with radio."

Red Barber, sportscaster

For the next twenty years, the Golden Age of Radio ruled America, and it perfectly matches the birth range of the Radio generation (1920–1940), who "came of age" between 1930 and 1965. The front end of the generation grew up with Franklin D. Roosevelt "fireside chats," while the back end of the generation witnessed television's marginalization of radio. By the mid-1960s, television was the preferred medium for news and entertainment. The assassination of Kennedy, Beatlemania, sitcoms, dramas, and westerns were all *visual* events. Radio was forced to adopt music, news, and talk as its primary programming format.

Nevertheless, radio's impact upon American culture is significant.

Mostly because it radically reinvented modern entertainment.

Radio brought the world into the home. You didn't have to go to church to hear a preacher. You didn't have to buy a newspaper to get the news. You didn't have to go to a movie house to enjoy a show. During the "Golden Age of Radio," a whole host of new broadcasting entertainment flooded into American households, including variety hours, children's shows, quiz games, situation comedies, plays, soap operas, and mystery theater. Radio stars like Jack Armstrong, Jimmy Durante, Charlie McCarthy, Jack Benny, and Bob Hope were America's newest sensations.

And then there was Orson Welles' legendary 1938 adaptation of H.G. Wells' *The War of the Worlds*.[148] It sounded so much like a live news broadcast of an alien Martian invasion of America that the listening audience broke into bedlam. Only a year earlier, Herbert Morrison's radio report of the fiery Hindenburg catastrophe showed the power of the medium as a "live" observer of catastrophic events.[149] Orson's report of aliens was so well performed that many Americans couldn't tell the difference. It was "fake news" radio-style. Welles was even forced the next-day to offer an apology.[150]

Baseball and radio have been friendly partners since the sport's first broadcast on August 5, 1921. Baseball play-by-play was something special. It was picturesque, inspiring, informative, and creative. Some early sportscasters actually concocted the action. Radio reached a wider sports community than those who physically attended games. Stations like WGN (Chicago), KMOX (St. Louis), and WMGM (New York) were baseball juggernauts for their respective teams.

"The biggest kick I get is to communicate with those who are exiled from the game—in hospitals, homes and prisons—those who have seldom seen a game, who can't travel to a game, those who are blind."
Jack Buck, sportscaster

Radio created a new celebrity in the sportscaster. The most famous was the "Ol' Red Head," or Red Barber.[151] Barber's career spanned four decades and three iconic teams: Reds, Dodgers, and Yankees. He generated a new lexicon of baseball lingo with celebrated, Southern-influenced catchphrases like "walkin' in tall cotton" (a team on a winning roll), "rhubarb" (controversy on the field), or "can of corn" (easily caught fly ball). Red Barber joined other great sportscasters like Mel Allen, Harry Caray, Russ Hodges, and Ernie Harwell. The Radio generation also fielded its own team of great play callers, including Jack Buck, Vin Scully, Bob Uecker, Joe Garagiola, and Skip Caray.

Radio consoled the American public. It changed how we were entertained, informed, and educated. Eventually, radio conditioned Americans to buy a different, bigger box for their living rooms: *television*. In the 1950s, radio shows transformed into television programming. Radio laid the groundwork necessary for television to thrive. It even carved the broadcast day, including the prime-time family hours of 7 to 10 p.m.

We Interrupt This Broadcast

The Radio generation experienced some of America's greatest industrial achievements.

In 1928, a dam was authorized by Congress on the Arizona-Nevada state line to serve Southwest residents with hydroelectric power, flood control, water, and recreation. Between 1931 and 1936, thousands of workers—most of them unemployed due to the Great Depression—built a concrete dam to block the Colorado river. The dam was 726 feet tall, 1,233 feet across, and 660 feet thick at the base. More than 3.2 million cubic yards of concrete composed the dam. It was an architectural wonder that not only created Lake Mead but a new American hot spot: Las Vegas. Prior to dam construction, Vegas was a small, dusty, desert oasis at best, but with the influx of dam workers, its population tripled overnight.[152] Legalized gambling, speakeasies (for drinking during Prohibition), and prostitution gave dam workers plenty of vices and venues to spend their hard-earned paychecks. Essentially, a dam in the desert birthed an entertainment capitol, with some help from eastern mobsters. Initially, the project was called "Boulder Dam," but was renamed "Hoover Dam" in 1947 to honor the late U.S. President.

In the Black Hills of western South Dakota, another wall of rock proved equally attractive to a Danish sculptor named Gutzon Borglum. He was commissioned in 1927 to carve images of people from the hard granite of Mount Rushmore.[153] Originally, the subjects proposed were western heroes like Lewis and Clark, Red Cloud, and Buffalo Bill Cody. However, Borglum suggested subjects with wider attraction: U.S. Presidents. Between 1927 and 1941, the sixty-foot faces of George Washington, Thomas Jefferson, Theodore Roosevelt, and Abraham Lincoln were blasted, carved, and chiseled from the southeast face of Mount Rushmore. Initially, the sculptures were to be head to waist, but Borglum's death in March 1941 halted federal funding for the project and further carving ceased. In the end, the four faces and their story were enough to inspire.[154] Today, over two million visitors annually journey to Mount Rushmore to experience these patriotic sculptures.[155]

The Radio generation witnessed many other modern marvels in construction, including Eisenhower's massive interstate highway project, the Golden Gate bridge, and the St. Louis arch. They also grew up in an increasingly unionized workplace. During the Great Depression, Americans needed employment security, inspirational stories and monuments of glory. But, more importantly, Americans needed a voice of reason, encouragement, and vision.

And nobody did that better than Franklin D. Roosevelt.

Roosevelt understood the persuasive power of the new radio medium and masterfully used it to update America through a series of thirty "fireside chats" between 1933 and 1944. These informal addresses, which redefined how a U.S. President interacted with the American public, focused on various national issues, crises, and struggles—from the failure of banks to the nation's role in World War II.

"When Roosevelt came to power, that voice...that brilliant, ringing, uplifting voice which we all heard on the radio made an almost immediate philosophical difference."
Marty Glickman, 1936 U.S. Olympic athlete

Roosevelt had delivered radio chats since 1929, when he served as governor of New York and recognized the new medium's ability to persuade. Consequently, only days after his inauguration as president, Roosevelt turned to radio to fix a national financial mess that seemed insurmountable. Across America, banks continued to fail in 1933.[156] Many shut down due to nervous patrons cashing out their accounts. One of Roosevelt's first acts as president was to close every American bank under a "bank holiday." Congress then passed the Emergency Banking Act that guaranteed deposits through federal insurance. The entire nation was now on edge. The recession had already sucked the life out of the economy for years and continued bank failures only exasperated the issue. Trust was desperately low in financial institutions (not to mention politicians).

On Sunday night at 10 p.m. eastern standard time on March 12, 1933, Roosevelt took to the airwaves to explain the situation to over sixty million Americans. In a fatherly, reassuring tone, he outlined how it happened, why it was necessary to close every bank, and the process for reopening these financial institutions. His "chat" worked.[157] The public's confidence was restored. When the stock market opened on Monday morning, trading skyrocketed. Even more helpful, most of those patrons who had cashed out accounts now returned their money to the banks.

Radio saved the day.

The Radio generation, still children and early teenagers, watched the confidence of their parents grow with every "fireside chat" by the president. Roosevelt's "New Deal" put their fathers back to work through federal programs like the Civil Conservation Corps, Civil Works, and the Farm Security Administration. Social Security offered safety nets for vulnerable Americans. During the 1930s, America struggled to escape the Great Depression and Roosevelt's radio conversations eased fears and raised hopes. It was Roosevelt's radio message regarding the bombing of Pearl Harbor that continues to "live in infamy."[158] If there was trouble, Roosevelt was on the job—and on the radio.

After all, economic depression and war weren't the only worries.

From 1930 to 1940, major droughts baked the country. The great southern drought of 1930 was catastrophic, but so were the Great Plains droughts later in the decade. Though mostly concentrated in western Kansas, Oklahoma, and north Texas, these Dust Bowl droughts also clipped Nebraska, Colorado, and New Mexico. Poor midwestern farming practices combined with these severe droughts created a perfect storm of dust that raced across the plains with a fury. Some "black blizzards" carried Midwest topsoil as far as the east coast. Over 100 million acres of farmland were impacted, and tens of thousands of impoverished families from America's breadbasket packed up and moved out, many hoping to find better lives in faraway places like California.[159]

But the promise of wealth for these migrants only produced grapes of wrath. Things were no better in the Golden State. They were just Hollywood dreams for the Radio generation.

And Now A Word From Our Sponsors

In the early days of radio, many radio stations were financed by power manufacturers (Westinghouse Electric, General Electric) and department stores that sold radio sets (Gimbels). The American Telephone and Telegraph (AT&T) company launched a new controversial trend in 1922: establishing stations that sold airtime to advertisers. New York's WEAF was the first to broadcast a paid radio commercial on August 28, 1922 for a new apartment complex. By the end of the decade, nearly every radio station used paid advertising to fund the cost of programming, equipment, and staff.[160]

*"Rock and roll saved radio. You're talking about a
wonderful part of our culture that is primarily in the
automobile…the car is the savior of radio."*
Larry King, radio personality

Over the years, radio ads ranged from on-air ad-libs to well-produced commercials, from ten seconds to one minute in length. Certain times of the day became coveted space for advertisers, most notably "drive time" (when motorists commuted to and from work). In fact, the addition of a radio to an automobile proved a match made in heaven. The Radio generation never really knew a day when automobiles didn't have radios, as Motorola installed the first car radios in 1930. Throughout their lifetimes, car stereo equipment—with various high-tech features, mixers, cassettes/CDs, speakers—has been must-own technology for adolescent males. Americans loved their driving music, not to mention access to news, sports, and religion via the radio.[161]

Pilot of the Airwaves

Frequency modulation (FM) was invented in 1933 by engineer Edwin Armstrong. It immediately found favor among music broadcast enthusiasts. FM radio's sound quality was far superior to AM, and that mattered as radio stations began to lose their audience with the advent of television.

In the 1950s and 1960s, when the Radio generation was in young adulthood, television emerged as the new media darling. Most radio programs migrated to television, and the only thing left on the AM dial was news, talk, and music. The problem? AM radio was stacked with stations and that caused "bleeding" (when one station's signal mixed with another). AM music radio didn't sound as good either. It was built for the voice, not the rich timbres and varying percussions of music. Finally, at night, the Federal Communications Commission forced AM stations to cut their power to avoid interference. Even during the day, AM had interference problems with power lines, motors, and electronic equipment.

None of this was good for music-formatted stations. And that's what the listeners now wanted in radio. In the early 1950s, television was winning the entertainment war.

Radio needed a new direction and new stars.

"TV probably did radio a favor. Look at radio today and look at radio in the 'Golden Age.' In the 'Golden Age'—the thirties and forties—it thrived. There were shows on radio. All of a sudden those shows moved to television. And when that happened, radio didn't know what to fall back on. And then along came a guy named Elvis Presley and rock and roll, and all of a sudden radio found itself. It knew exactly the direction it should take. Radio became local and radio became music and radio thrived."

Casey Kasem, radio personality

Radio needed someone like Robert Weston Smith. A disc jockey sporting radio nicknames like *Daddy Jules, Roger Gordon*, and *Big Smith*.

But his final persona was his most renown: *Wolfman Jack*.

This raspy voice disc jockey from Brooklyn developed his own clever canine alter ego for radio station KCIJ in Shreveport, LA. He got his inspiration for the moniker from Alan Freed, the celebrated Cleveland DJ who coined the term "rock and roll" and used a recorded howl to punctuate his "Moondog" broadcasts of black rhythm and blues.[162] Smith liked the touch. The name "Wolfman Jack" combined Smith's love of horror shows with common street slang (as in "hit the road, jack" or "jack of all trades"). He was now the Wolfman, jack.

Or, *Wolfman Jack*.

In the early 1960s, a Mexican border station hired Wolfman to jockey music for its 250,000-watt station (the U.S. legal limit is 50,000 watts). Essentially, that ensured the Wolfman's rock 'n roll show could be heard nearly coast to coast in America. "We had the most powerful signal in North America," Wolfman Jack recalled, "Birds dropped dead when they flew too close to the tower. A car driving from New York to L.A. would never lose the station."[163] During his shows, Wolfman Jack pitched dozens of products, from dog food to baby chicks to sex drive pills.

He often punctuated his persona with growls and howls, not to mention sexual innuendos.[164]

Now *that's* rock 'n roll.

At his peak, Wolfman Jack was heard on over 2000 radio stations in fifty-three countries. He eventually landed at Los Angeles' KRLA in 1984 doing a syndicated show. Several years earlier, Jack scored a minor role as the disc jockey in the 1973 cult classic *American Graffiti*, a movie chronicling 1950s teen escapades. That's when Wolfman Jack became a household name. The success of the movie, and subsequent television appearances in shows like *Emergency!* and *Hollywood Squares*, paid his bills for life. The Guess Who even penned a 1974 tribute to him titled *Clap for the Wolfman*.

Wolfman Jack, like many of his peers, was born in the Radio generation.

He spun the wax alongside other local jockeys like Philadelphia's Hy Lit, New York's Bruce Morrow, L.A.'s Robert W. Morgan, and San Francisco's "Big Daddy" Tom Donahue. In the 1970s, Casey Kasem created and hosted the *American Top 40* countdown show, broadcast every weekend from 1970 to 1988. At its zenith, *AT40* was heard on over 1000 stations in fifty countries. Kasem concluded every broadcast with a visionary blessing: "Keep your feet on the ground and keep reaching for the stars."[165]

No Static at All

The concluding bookend for the Radio generation happened in the early 1960s when the youngest members of the generation were in their early 20s.

A series of tragedies, scandals, and unique events—between 1957 and 1963—muffled "rock and roll" radio. First, Little Richard found religion and became a preacher.[166] Then, in 1958, Elvis joined the military.[167] Both situations shocked fans. In 1958, it was discovered that Jerry Lee Lewis had married his thirteen-year-old cousin—a scandal that canceled concerts and blacklisted Lewis.[168] Then Buddy Holly, J.P. "Big Bopper" Richardson and Ritchie Valens were killed in an Iowa plane crash on February 3, 1959.[169] In 1962 Chuck Berry went to prison for sex with a minor.[170]

And finally, famed disc jockey Alan Freed fell from grace.

Freed's troubles started in Boston when he was arrested and fired for inciting a 1958 riot on the radio. A year later, he was embroiled in the payola scandal. Payola was the illegal practice of accepting money from record publishers to play certain records in order to increase a song's popularity. Chicago WAIT's disc jockey Phil Lind confessed in a Congressional hearing he once pocketed $22,000 to play a certain record.[171] Freed was fired from WABC radio in 1959 and eventually pled guilty to payola charges in 1962. The scandal rendered him mostly unemployable. He bounced from job to job and eventually died at forty-three on January 20, 1965 from uremia and cirrhosis due to alcoholism.[172]

It was the end of an era.

Radio was changing. News, Top 40 pop, and sports dominated AM. The FM dial was splintered into various genres from rock to blues to country. In the late 1970s, a television comedy named *WKRP in Cincinnati* satirized radio's troubled times. Despite the hire of a new program director, Andy Travis, and disc jockeys Venus Flytrap and Dr. Johnny Fever, the new talent struggled to fix a local station experiencing ratings decline. The sitcom found an audience, but many radio stations in the 1980s did not. Television changed the market. By the 1990s, most music stations were fully automated. Nobody was physically flipping a record, twisting the knobs, or reading the news. It was all outsourced. Today, the music playlist is computer-generated.

In the early 1990s, AM radio found its renaissance in talk radio—particularly conservative, political commentary. Right-wing talk show host Rush Limbaugh claimed to be "talent on loan from God" behind his "golden EIB microphone." His conservative "Rush is Right" talk attracted millions of listeners known as "dittoheads." Limbaugh re-energized the Reagan base and paved the way for Newt Gingrich's 1994 "Contract with America" that produced a red wave Republican majority in Congress. Limbaugh's talk radio nation inspired other right-leaning media outlets, including The Drudge Report (1995) and Fox News (1996).

Satellite and Internet radio further democratized and decentralized the medium in the new millennium. New subscription services like Sirius emerged in 2008. SiriusXM features entertainment, news, talk and sports channels. Shock jock Howard Stern reinvented his daily local New York City radio show—a haven for strippers, crass humor and obnoxious conversation—into a Sirius satellite radio juggernaut that now attracts A-list celebrities like Paul McCartney and Ben Stiller. By 2010, Sirius boasted over 32 million listeners every week.[173]

For the Radio generation, from AM to FM, from Roosevelt to rock 'n roll, from Friday night radio soap operas to Saturday afternoon baseball games, from Paul Harvey to Alan Freed to Wolfman Jack to Rush Limbaugh, it didn't matter what was *on the radio* as long as *the radio was on*:

These Depression era children just wanted to tune in.

With as little static as possible.

A TIMELINE OF TECHNOLOGICAL EVENTS (1921–1930):

- 1921: First radio broadcast of a baseball game. British Broadcasting Company formed. Pittsburgh radio station KDKA transmits first regular radio program in U.S.
- 1922: John Harwood invents a self-winding wristwatch. Insulin first administered to diabetic patients. Dr. Alexis Carrel discovers white corpuscles. 500 commercial radio stations in operation in America.
- 1923: First birth control clinic opens in New York. First portable radio developed. Notable invention: hearing aid.
- 1924: Ford Motor Company produces ten-millionth car. Insecticides used for first time. 2.5 million radios in use in America. IBM Corporation founded. Notable invention: frozen food.
- 1925: Scottish inventor John Logie Baird transmits recognizable human features by television. Synthetic oil developed. A copy of the Bible costs $3 (it was $100 in the seventeenth century). The Chrysler Corporation founded by Walter Chrysler. Calvin Coolidge is first U.S. president to broadcast inauguration via radio. Notable invention: Scotch tape.
- 1926: Richard E. Byrd and Floyd Bennet fly from Spitsbergen to North Pole and back. "Electrola," a new electric recording technique, is developed. First liquid rocket fuel is fired. Lufthansa airlines founded. Aerosol sprays developed in Norway.
- 1927: Airplanes first used to dust crops with insecticide. Deepest well in the world (8,000 ft) sunk in Orange County, CA. Ford ceases Model T after fifteen-millionth car is produced. "Iron Lung" developed by P. Drinker and L.A. Shaw. Holland Tunnel opens as first vehicular tunnel linking New York and New Jersey. Pan American Airways formed. First transatlantic telephone call.

- 1928: J.L. Baird demonstrates color television. Alexander Fleming discovers penicillin. Teleprinters and teletypewriters have restricted use in U.S., Britain, and Germany. First scheduled television broadcasts by WGY (Schenectady, NY). *New York Times* installs moving electric sign around *Times* building. Notable inventions: sliced bread maker, bubble gum.
- 1929: W.A. Morrison introduces quartz-crystal clocks for precise timekeeping. Robert E Byrd flies over the South Pole. Bell Laboratories experiments with color television. Kodak introduces 16mm movie film. First car radio created by Motorola. Public phone booths appear in London. Notable inventions: chain saw, sunglasses.
- 1930: The planet Pluto is discovered. Photoflash bulb comes into use. "Technocracy" (the absolute domination of technology) becomes a popular conversation. Yellow fever vaccine created. Notable invention: jet engine.

INFLUENTIAL BIRTHS IN THE RADIO GENERATION:

Presidents: None

Business, Education, Athletes and Other Leaders:

- Stan Musial (1920–2013), baseball player
- John Glenn (1921–2016), astronaut
- S. Truett Cathy (1921–2014), businessman
- Chuck Yeager (1923–present), pilot
- Robert Kennedy (1925–1968), politician
- Neil Armstrong (1930–2012), astronaut
- Warren Buffett (1930–present), entrepreneur
- Mohammed Ali (1931–2006), boxer
- Ruth Bader Ginsburg (1933–present), Supreme Court justice
- Ted Turner (1938–present), entrepreneur

Entertainers:

- Dick Van Dyke (1925–present), actor
- Paul Newman (1925–2008), actor
- David Attenborough (1926–present), television host
- Andy Williams (1927–2012), pop singer
- Audrey Hepburn (1929–1993), movie actress
- Pat Summerall (1930–2013), sportscaster

- Dan Rather (1931–present), newsman
- Johnny Cash (1932–2003), country singer
- Casey Kasem (1932–2014), radio/TV host

Authors/Artists:

- Ray Bradbury (1920–2012), novelist
- Alex Haley (1921–1992), autobiographer
- Neil Simon (1927–2018), playwright

Chapter Seven
Vinyl

"The four building blocks of the universe are fire, water, gravel and vinyl."
Dave Barry

BIRTH YEARS: 1930–1950
"Coming of Age" Years: 1940–1975
Primary Tech Event: Atom Bomb
Strauss-Howe Archetype: Artist-Prophet
Generation Personality: Dominant/Pessimistic
Iconic Generation Representative: Elvis Presley

Historical Influencing Events in Youth and Young Adulthood:
Great Depression, World War II, Atom Bomb, Korean War, Space Race,
Vietnam War, John F. Kennedy's Assassination, Woodstock, Watergate

---

The sound of a needle dropping on a vinyl record is unmistakably *groovy*. The buzzed hum and click that happens when a needle first contacts vinyl is magical. Then the series of snaps and pops that follows, as the stylus works its way toward the first song, grows anticipation with every crackle. Every album is *different*. The pops are *different*. The silence until the first song is *different*. The imperfections of vinyl create a uniqueness, dare I say, "humanness."

Unlike digital formats today, vinyl recordings are like most human beings: they have issues, faults, and shortcomings.

"Somebody was trying to tell me that CDs are better than vinyl because they don't have any surface noise. I said, 'Listen, mate, life has surface noise.'"
John Peel

Needles got stuck and repeated over and over and over and over and over and over and over and over…until a bump of the record player or a nudge of the tone arm gently pushed it beyond its failed groove. Records skipped, sometimes gleefully, across the vinyl, ruining both song and experience. And then there were those "rice krispies" (snaps, crackles, and pops) of well-worn, much-loved (or greatly abused) vinyl. These imperfections, amplified with volume, soured the listening experience. Finally, records warped. If stored in the wrong place, such as direct sunlight in a bedroom window, the vinyl bent and twisted, which didn't exactly help the stylus remain grounded to the groove.

Maybe that's why "virgin" vinyl—a record still in its shrink wrap—was so coveted.

Every album was specially wrapped in plastic to protect the cover sleeve and communicate that this recording was *new* and never played. Some record aficionados deftly sliced the edge of the shrink wrap to release a record, leaving the plastic to guard the cardboard sleeve from damage. Others inserted their records in sturdier sleeves for storage protection. Most people didn't care. They ripped off the shrink wrap, wrote their names on the cover, and even tacked the sleeve to their walls as art. Vinyl records had other applications, too. Vinyl has been cut, shaped, worked, and glued into chandeliers, clocks, bowls, coffee tables, bottle holders, and even Christmas trees.[174] Sometimes record covers were used for writing desks, leaving behind indentations of recognizable lines of letters.

The *cool* advantage to vinyl was that if you didn't like a song, you merely lifted the tone arm and moved it to the next recording. When the songs on Side A were finished, the turntable was stopped, the record lifted and flipped, then the needle dropped on Side B. You didn't just listen to vinyl. You personally participated. You experienced it. Other technology—like cassettes and 8-tracks—sounded too good and were less interactive. Tape didn't skip when you danced to it. It didn't jump when you accidentally bumped the stereo. And it didn't snap, crackle, or pop. Vinyl was naturally *imperfect*, and it made music naturally imperfect.

"The history of the music industry is inevitably also the story of the development of technology. From the player piano to the vinyl disc, from reel-to-reel tape to the cassette, from the CD to the digital download, these formats and devices changed not only the way music was consumed, but the very way artists created it."
Edgar Bronfman, Jr.

Maybe that's why we loved it.

The first generation of Americans to fully experience the rise of vinyl recordings was born between 1930 and 1950. They came of age between 1940 and 1975, the golden age of vinyl that spans the birth of rock and roll to the inception of corporate rock. In the mid-70s the cassette also stole sales and the introduction of the Sony Walkman (1979) signaled a death knell for vinyl records. By 1983 cassettes finally dethroned vinyl's long supremacy.[175] The early wave in the Vinyl generation listened to crooners like Bing Crosby, Andy Williams, and Frank Sinatra. They danced the swing, rumba, and jitterbug.[176] The second wave grooved to rock 'n roll (Elvis, Beatles), psychedelic rock (Jefferson Airplane), folk (Bob Dylan), rhythm and blues (Supremes), soul (James Brown), and classic country (Hank Williams, Johnny Cash). They didn't just drop the needle; they also dropped acid and dropped out. They were '50s hipsters and '60s hippies. True to their vinyl heritage, one of their favored slang words was "groovy."[177]

The Vinyl generation was born during the Depression and came of age in three wars (World War II, Korea, and Vietnam). They initially faced Nazi fascism, but the Cold War of Soviet communism proved the more difficult adversary. In their youth, they enjoyed postwar prosperity in the suburbs, "I Like Ike" conservative politics, and "Father Knows Best" parenting. Two 1946 films, *It's A Wonderful Life* and *The Best Years of Our Lives*, portrayed a generational personality that persevered

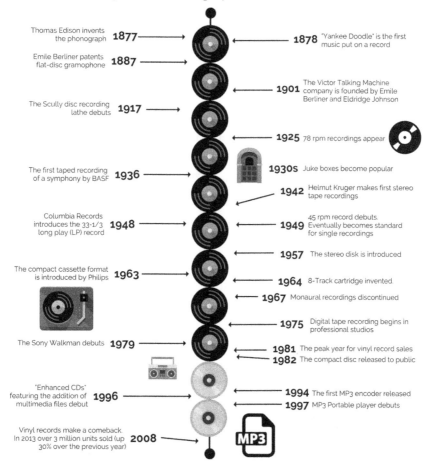

VINYL RECORDS
A History of the Phonograph and Audio Formats

Thomas Edison invents the phonograph **1877**

1878 "Yankee Doodle" is the first music put on a record

Emile Berliner patents flat-disc gramophone **1887**

1901 The Victor Talking Machine company is founded by Emile Berliner and Eldridge Johnson

The Scully disc recording lathe debuts **1917**

1925 78 rpm recordings appear

1930s Juke boxes become popular

The first taped recording of a symphony by BASF **1936**

1942 Helmut Kruger makes first stereo tape recordings

Columbia Records introduces the 33-1/3 long play (LP) record **1948**

1949 45 rpm record debuts. Eventually becomes standard for single recordings

1957 The stereo disk is introduced

The compact cassette format is introduced by Philips **1963**

1964 8-Track cartridge invented.

1967 Monaural recordings discontinued

1975 Digital tape recording begins in professional studios

The Sony Walkman debuts **1979**

1981 The peak year for vinyl record sales

1982 The compact disc released to public

"Enhanced CDs" featuring the addition of multimedia files debut **1996**

1994 The first MP3 encoder released

1997 MP3 Portable player debuts

Vinyl records make a comeback. In 2013 over 3 million units sold (up 30% over the previous year) **2008** in combat, built a nation's infrastructure, launched space rockets, and initiated various social revolutions (civil rights,[178] women's equality,[179] gay rights,[180] Jesus movement[181]).

And thanks to vinyl, every movement had its own music.

Dropping The Needle

Thomas Edison invented the phonograph in 1877. Initially, it could both record and replay sounds, but other than novelty uses, the phonograph "proved too crude to be put to any practical use."[182] Twelve years later, Emile Berliner was the first to develop "lateral cut disc records" to play on his device known as a "gramophone" but, again, the applications were limited only to the curious.

In the early 1900s, ten-inch and twelve-inch discs were introduced that allowed for longer, two-minute recordings. Various format skirmishes ensued—such as Edison's *Amberol* cylinder—but eventually the disc format won the day. Speed was also an issue. Early disc recordings ranged from 60 to 130 rpms, but by 1925, the 78 rpm recording was standard.

Most recordings until the early 1920s were acoustic in nature. It wasn't until the invention of the microphone by Orlando Marsh that sound recordings greatly improved. Another help was sound amplification through speakers. A classical recording of Chopin's "Impromptus" and Schubert's "Litanei" on Victor records were the first true electronic recordings.[183] Records suddenly started to receive critical notice, but it would take five more years for a tipping point to occur. A *New York Times* music critic wrote in 1930:

> ...the time has come for serious musical criticism to take account of performances of great music reproduced by means of the records. To claim that the records have succeeded in exact and complete reproduction of all details of symphonic or operatic performances...would be extravagant... [but] the article of today is so far in advance of the old machines as hardly to admit classification under the same name.[184]

It was the genesis of sound recordings.

In 1931, RCA Victor sold the first commercial $33^{1/3}$, long-playing vinyl record. By the end of the decade, vinyl recordings were the dominant format.[185] Between

1930 and 1950, Americans grooved to records. *78s. 33¹/³s. 45s.* The ability to put music on wax and vinyl was a sea change in home entertainment. Prior to records, music had to be accessed or attended. It was on stage and in theaters, schools, or churches. You had to go *somewhere* to hear the band play. Jazz clubs were popular music getaways in the 1920s.[186]

The record brought the music *home.*

It was purely American technology that "we the people" controlled. We decided on the song, format, and style we wanted to hear. Records democratized music and that democracy was something to share with the world, whether to oppressed Europeans under Hitler fascism or Korean and Vietnamese people imprisoned by communism.

————————

"Vinyl is democratic, as surely as the iPod is fascist. Vinyl is representational: it has a face. Two faces, in fact, to represent the dualism of human nature. Vinyl occupies physical space honestly, proud as a fat woman dancing."
Adam Mansbach

————————

Radio technology quickly found records helpful to their programming formats. Until vinyl records emerged, radio stations used live performances to broadcast music. Now, music stations popped up all over America as sound recordings became more abundant. *Jazz. Swing. Blues. Country and Western. Pop.* And, eventually, *rock and roll.* In many ways, without the innovation of records, the technology of radio might've stagnated. It's no wonder the Ramones asked in their seminal hit song the serious question: *do you remember rock and roll radio?* Vinyl is what made radio famous. Records even created a new cult hero: the local disc jockey. These jockeys spun the wax on Saturday nights as the soundtrack for countless adolescent adventures, from cruising main street to bedroom bull sessions to backyard barbecues.

Swingtown

The first cultural hero of the Vinyl generation was a blue-eyed, handsome, Italian crooner from immigrant parents in Hoboken, New Jersey.

His name was Frank Sinatra.

Sinatra sold more records (150 million globally) than any other music artist in history, including Elvis Presley. His first record thrilled young females (also known as "bobby soxers") and catapulted him to superstardom as "The Voice."[187] He crooned his way through the 1940s and 1950s, eventually landing a permanent stage in Las Vegas where he gathered a group of pals known as the "Rat Pack."[188] Sinatra was a film star in classic movies like *From Here to Eternity* (1953), *The Man with the Golden Arm* (1955), and *The Manchurian Candidate* (1962). He even hosted his own short-lived, self-titled television show.

Sinatra helped the Vinyl generation dance again after the Great Depression and find comfort in a post-atomic bomb culture. He recorded fifty-nine albums and released 297 singles in his career, including memorable songs like "Young at Heart," "Love and Marriage," "Strangers in the Night," and "My Way." Sinatra did do it *his way*. Despite a slump in the early 1950s that nearly ended his career, Frank found resurrection in the Nevada desert singing to sold-out Vegas shows. He was the "Chairman of the Board" with "style, swing and swagger."[189] "Ol' Blue Eyes" personified the Vinyl generation who, as one biographer penned, was "cocky, eye on the main chance, optimistic, and full of the sense of possibility."[190]

That was the Vinyl generation in a sentence.

But Sinatra wasn't alone. He participated in a company of crooners during this period, including Bing Crosby, Nat King Cole, Perry Como, Dean Martin, Sammy Davis, Jr., Bobby Darin, Tom Jones, Johnny Mathis, and Andy Williams. Their distinctive vocal styles can still be heard today through the music of Harry Connick, Jr. and Michael Buble.

I Love Rock 'N Roll

Rock 'n roll's "big bang" happened in 1956—but not without some luck, or maybe a dose of Divine intervention.

That's the year a Memphis studio on 706 Union Avenue assembled a who's who of musical talent that forever changed modern music. The studio was Sun Records and the record producer was Sam Phillips. In 1951, Phillips recorded what many credit was the first true "rock 'n roll" single: "Rocket 88" by Jackie Brenston and his Delta Cats.[191] Phillips also produced blues artists like B.B. King, Howlin' Wolf, and James Cotton. However, Sam Phillip's greatest pioneering contribution might be his keen sense of talent, particularly in gathering a group of legendary white singers and songwriters who sang country, gospel, and blues music.

Charlie Rich. Roy Orbison. Johnny Cash. Carl Perkins. Jerry Lee Lewis. Elvis Presley.

The last four artists orchestrated in an impromptu 1956 jam session that forever marked them with a golden nickname: "The Million Dollar Quartet."[192]

But let's not get ahead of the story.

The Vinyl generation knows full well that "rock 'n roll"—a sexually-loaded term coined by Cleveland disc jockey Alan Freed in 1951—had plenty of other players to light the fuse for what eventually happened in 1956.

Ever since World War II, music had evolved from older stylistic forms. Black gospel birthed the blues. Jazz generated "rhythm" music. Hillbilly music launched country and western. In the 1930s and 1940s, music was segregated to particular ethnic styles. *Black gospel and jazz. White urban pop and dance. White rural hillbilly.* Radio stations catered to these ethnic tastes and never crossed those lines. However, in a post-war America, these genres began to mix and blend. *Boogie woogie. Rhythm and blues. Bluegrass. Western swing. Folk.* For the most part, these styles remained black and white, urban and rural. The blues were earthy and sensual. Honky-tonk was wild and backwoods. Gospel was for religious folk. If you wanted to hear these styles, you had to go to church, the other side of the tracks, back in the holler, or to "that" part of town.

Country music evolved primarily behind the influence of Hank Williams' honky-tonk blues. Williams was born in the south and grew up during the Depression. He was to country music what Frank Sinatra was to pop or Mississippi John Hurt was to the blues. He laid the foundation for modern country with songs like "Lovesick Blues," "Cold Cold Heart," "Hey Good Lookin'," and "Your Cheatin' Heart."

Unfortunately, Hank Williams was also one of the first celebrity tragedies of the Vinyl generation. On New Year's Day in 1953, he headed to a performance in Charleston, WV but never arrived. Williams died of heart failure due to prescription drug abuse and alcoholism. He was only twenty-nine years old. In the years that followed, his legend only grew. In a career that spanned a mere six years, Williams scored twenty-nine top ten hits (including eight number ones). After his death, posthumous releases earned him seven more top ten hits (of which, three went to number one).[193]

Significant changes also happened in black music. After World War II, a major migration of blacks brought southern blues and gospel to northern cities like Chicago, Detroit, Cleveland, Philadelphia, St. Louis, and Memphis. Thanks to radio technology, white adolescents now tuned into these black stations. With vinyl record technology, they also brought the music *home*. This black rhythm and blues sound—also known as "race music"—significantly influenced the evolution of "rock and roll" music, as did gospel, boogie woogie, and swing. With the "Rocket 88" record, other black musicians started to emerge. *Lloyd Price. Fats Domino. Johnnie Johnson. Little Richard and Chuck Berry.*

In fact, many purists argue Little Richard and Chuck Berry are the true original "kings" of rock and roll—and for good reason. Little Richard's legendary show-stopping songs and piano-pounding performance antics built a formidable audience across the southern U.S. in the early 1950s. Meanwhile, Berry's guitar licks and stage personality—including his famous "duck walk"[194]—energized audiences around his hometown of St. Louis. Most contemporary rock guitarists still cite Berry as an influence upon their own styles.

Everything broke for Little Richard and Chuck Berry in 1955.

That's the year Berry met Muddy Waters in Chicago, who introduced him to Leonard Chess, the founder of Chess Records. Berry recorded the chart-topping single "Maybelline" and his guitar-slinging career shot into the stratosphere. In the next decade, he'd post seven top ten records, including "Roll Over Beethoven," "Rock and Roll Music," and "Johnny B. Goode."[195] Berry would be the first artist elected in the inaugural, ten-member class of the Rock and Roll Hall of Fame (1986).[196] Outside of Elvis Presley, according to a tribute at the Cleveland shrine, only Chuck Berry "had more influence on the formation and development of rock and roll."[197]

Little Richard might disagree with that opinion. And he would have good reason.

Originally known as Richard Penniman, Little Richard also found success in 1955 with his release of "Tutti Frutti." Between 1955 and 1958, Richard charted fourteen legendary top ten hits on the American R&B charts, including "Long Tall Sally," "Ready Teddy," "Lucille," and "Good Golly, Miss Molly." Whereas white charts weren't as kind to Richard as they were to Berry, it's clear that Richard was equally prolific and significant. *Time* magazine cited 1957's *Here's Little Richard* as one of the most influential albums ever recorded. It was only one of four albums from the 1950s to make this prestigious list.[198] Richard would depart his rock and roll ways after a religious experience in 1957. For the next three decades, he'd float between the secular and sacred, often blending the two. He was often a lightning rod for controversy, particularly his androgynous look that sparked criticism and rumors about his sexuality.

Initially, "rock and roll" was too edgy and uncouth for white audiences. Consequently, tamed covers of rock 'n roll hits were suitable pacifiers. Pat Boone's restrained copy of Fats Domino's "Ain't That a Shame" went to number one (while Fats original only rose to number ten).[199] In 1955, the first year of Billboard's charts, the only rock 'n roll song to reach number one was Bill Haley's "Rock Around the Clock." Haley was white and his western, swing-infused, boogie woogie rockabilly was easier to swallow.[200]

What rock and roll needed was a *white* guy who sounded *black*.

----

*"All the white disc jockeys thought Elvis sounded too black, and
all the black disc jockeys thought he sounded too hillbilly."*
Sam Phillips, record producer

And they found their "king" in Memphis and a kid named Elvis Presley.

Presley literally changed the world in 1956. In that year, there were seventeen number one songs. Three of those songs were by Elvis and two of those songs were unabashed, raw "rock and roll": "Heartbreak Hotel" and "Hound Dog."[201] The latter tune was a revised cover of Big Mama Thornton's classic R&B hit.[202] But Elvis wasn't the only artist scoring rock 'n roll hits in 1956. There was a tsunami wave of rock and roll. "Long Tall Sally" by Little Richard. "Roll Over Beethoven" by Chuck Berry. "Blueberry Hill" by Fats Domino. "Blue Suede Shoes" by Carl Perkins. "Be-Bop-A-Lula" by Gene Vincent and the Blue Caps. Even Sam Phillip's country artist Johnny Cash crossed over with "I Walk the Line."[203]

Rock and roll was here to stay.

Sam Phillips took a greasy-haired, hip-swinging, curled-lip, rock 'n roll messiah from Tupelo and managed to do what no one else could: make black rhythm and blues cool to white audiences. Elvis "the Pelvis" Presley was a white guy singing black songs and that didn't sit well with the status quo. He gyrated like Chuck Berry and put censors in a tizzy, forcing television producers to broadcast Presley from the waist up.[204] And yet everything Elvis did in the late 1950s turned to gold. Later, he starred in movie musicals like *G.I. Blues* and *Blue Hawaii.* He even recorded what many believe to be the first modern "contemporary Christian music" record in 1960.[205]

Elvis was handsome, talented, and *cool.* The Vinyl generation, now in their teens and 20s, made him a superstar. He was the icon of their generation.

In his musical wake followed other rock 'n roll legends.

Jerry Lee "The Killer" Lewis was rock 'n roll's first true "wild child." His raucous piano playing, long golden locks, and bawdy lyrics frightened the establishment through songs like "Great Balls of Fire" and "Whole Lotta Shakin' Goin' On." He continually pushed the envelope. Lewis was kicked out of Bible college for playing a boogie-woogie version of a gospel standard. He married his thirteen-year-old cousin (the first of seven marriages). He had troubles with the Internal Revenue Service. He carried a gun and once allegedly attempted to shoot Elvis.[206]

Rock and roll!

Buddy Holly hit the charts in 1957. His Texas swing rockabilly produced three top ten hits that year, including "That'll Be the Day," "Peggy Sue," and "Oh Boy!" Holly would chart five more Top 40 hits in his abbreviated career. At twenty-two years old, he was tragically killed in a plane crash on February 3, 1959. Buddy had chartered the plane to avoid a long, cold bus ride to Minnesota. In a strange twist of fate, one of his band members, Waylon Jennings, volunteered his seat to J.P. "Big Bopper" Richardson, who was nursing the flu. Another rising star was also on the plane: Ritchie Valens, a rising Chicano rock 'n roller with hits like "Donna" and "LaBamba."

They say it's the day the music died.

But that obituary proved premature.

After 1960, there was a second wave of fresh sounds and legendary artists rooted to particular American cities. In Detroit, there was Berry Gordy and Motown (starring *Diana Ross and the Supremes, The Temptations, Four Tops, Isley Brothers, Gladys Knight and the Pips, Marvelettes, Wilson Pickett,* and *Little Stevie Wonder*).

In Los Angeles, Phil Spector created a "Wall of Sound" (featuring the *Righteous Brothers, Ronettes, The Crystals, Ike and Tina Turner*). In Philadelphia, soul artists like the *O'Jays, Spinners*, and *Patti LaBelle* joined other soul singers like *Ray Charles, Ben E. King*, and *Aretha Franklin*. And then there was *James Brown*, the godfather of soul and pioneer of funk.

In the early 1960s, folk music found cultural traction. *Peter, Paul and Mary. The Kingston Trio. The New Christy Minstrels. Joan Baez. Joni Mitchell. Phil Ochs. Arlo Guthrie. Richie Havens.* And then there was the legendary *Bob Dylan*, the poet of the Vinyl generation. Dylan prophesied the "times were a'changin'" and then plugged in his electric guitar at the 1965 Newport Folk Festival to prove he wasn't kidding. Dylan always surprised his audiences, including a 1979 conversion to Christianity and gospel rock recordings that temporarily alienated his hardcore fans.

California was ground zero for American rock music in the 1960s. First the *Beach Boys* pioneered surf music. Then the *Byrds* and the *Mamas and Papas* laid the foundation for a summer of love. The psychedelic rock of the *Jefferson Airplane* and *Grateful Dead* paved the way for protest, peace, and flower power. Beat poets, hallucinogenic drugs, Human Be-Ins, and hippies drew a "California dreaming" map to San Francisco...and eventually to a farmer's field near Woodstock, New York. It was music—sometimes angry and sometimes philosophical—that challenged conventional wisdom. The music questioned parental rules. It attacked educational norms, Judeo-Christian ethics, and establishment politics. It was the soundtrack for civil rights, free love, drug exploration, war protest, communal lifestyles, and spirituality. Artists like *Buffalo Springfield, Janis Joplin, The Doors, Crosby, Stills, and Nash and Young* unveiled a new counterculture.

However, the most significant sea change in popular music happened across the pond.

In the early 1960s, four lads from Liverpool created a fresh sound, with original songwriting, that changed all the rules for how music was penned, produced and performed. The Beatles wrote a cultural hymnbook that still plays well today. In their wake, other English bands invaded America. *The Rolling Stones. The Animals. The Yardbirds. The Who. The Kinks. Pink Floyd. Cream.* Later in the decade, the Brits forged a guitar-driven edgy type of music known as hard rock. No doubt drawing inspiration from Seattle's *Jimi Hendrix*, groups like *Led Zeppelin, Deep*

Purple, and *Black Sabbath* pounded their way into the psyche (and pocketbook) of American youth.

"The genius of vinyl is that it allows—commands—us to put our fingerprints all over that history: to blend and chop and reconfigure it, mock and muse upon it, backspin and skip through it."
Adam Mansbach

By the early 1970s, the Vinyl generation had fully come of age, the last of the cohort maturing mid-decade. Most of the generation was over thirty. It was time to grow up, and by 1975, American music clearly showed maturity and diversity. Yes, there were still the old frames of soul, blues, R&B, rock, gospel, and country. But now those genres were shattered into countless sub-categories. *Funk. Dance. Disco. Reggae. Southern Rock. Outlaw Country. Truck Driving Country. Heavy Metal. Shock rock. Glam rock. Prog Rock. Industrial Rock. Theater Rock. Synth Rock. Jazz rock. Roots Rock. Soft Rock. Pop Rock. Blues Rock. Stadium Rock. Jesus Rock. Punk Rock. Singer-Songwriter.*

And all of it was carved into vinyl.

Vinyl Is Final

The Vinyl generation birthed the majority of the 1950s and 1960s rock and roll artists. This generation bought their records, attended their concerts, sported their t-shirts, created fan clubs, and tuned in on the radio. As other music formats—8-track, cassette, CD, and MP3—emerged, this generation always retained their affection for vinyl. In their garages, closets, and spare bedrooms, they stored their vinyl legacy.

This shouldn't be surprising. It's how they experienced life. It could be said the Vinyl generation played out their generational existence like a record.

Their story started in the snaps, crackles, and pops of economic Depression and World War. However, as the needle of time worked through the first half of their lives, there was a post-war peace and rock and roll energy that flavored their careers, achievements, and homes. The Vinyl generation enjoyed countless modern conveniences previously unavailable to older generations. Their kitchens featured ice machines, microwaves, blenders, and dishwashers. Their living rooms boasted televisions, high-fi record players, and radios. They slept on better beds in bigger master bedrooms and enjoyed additional bathrooms featuring showers and "his 'n her" sinks.

"My record collection probably tells the story of my life better than I could in words."
Colleen Murphy

In the Side B of their lives, the Vinyl generation became dutiful grandparents to struggling Gen X kids surviving their parents' divorces. They went to church and joined service clubs. They were loyal to jobs that produced increasingly better pay over their lifetimes. Consequently, once the house was paid off, they bought campers, boats, motorcycles, and snowmobiles. The Vinyl generation created retirement nests that allowed them to purchase second homes in new fifty-five and up retirement communities in such places as Palm Beach and Sun City. They were the original "snowbirds." Their love for old-time rock 'n roll created a nostalgia craze that re-launched careers for fading stars like Chuck Berry, The Beach Boys, and the Monkees. These artists and bands performed on summer fair circuits, in smoke-filled casinos, on cruise ships, and in micro-entertainment meccas like Branson and Reno.

The Vinyl generation has shown that no generation finishes without a scuff, scratch or scar. We all get stuck in a moment or occasionally skip a beat. But they also remind us of the music. Good times rock and roll that forever plays gentle on our minds.

Maybe that's why vinyl is final. As a format, it's *perfectly* imperfect. It's limited. It has liabilities. It's easily scuffed and scratched. But it always carries a song and story. Songs, like the Vinyl generation, that leave a mark.

And a smile.

A TIMELINE OF TECHNOLOGICAL EVENTS (1931–1940):

- 1931: Synthetic rubber invented. Spicer-Dufay process of natural color photography. Heavy hydrogen discovered. Notable inventions: electric razor, nylon, aerosol can.
- 1932: James Chadwick discovers the neutron. Vitamin D discovered. Parking meter invented. Notable inventions: radio telescope, Polaroid camera.
- 1933: Electron microscope invented. Drive-in movie theater developed.
- 1934: A refrigeration process for meat cargos is developed. Notable invention: trampoline.
- 1935: Radar equipment to detect aircraft built by Robert Watson Watt. Germany releases the Volkswagon Beetle. Toyota car company forms in Japan. General Electric begins selling fluorescent tubes for lighting. Notable invention: helicopter.
- 1936: Hoover Dam completed on Nevada-Arizona border. Dr. Alexis Carrel invents artificial heart. Notable invention: Zippo lighter.
- 1937: Nylon is patented. First jet engine built by Frank Whittle. Amelia Earhart disappears on Pacific flight. Hindenburg dirigible crash is described in first transcontinental radio broadcast. Golden Gate Bridge in San Francisco, CA opens. First blood bank opens in Chicago.
- 1938: Ballpoint pen invented. Oil discovered in Saudi Arabia. 20,000 television sets are in service in New York City. Howard Hughes flies around the globe in 3 days, 19 hours, 17 minutes. Notable inventions: photocopier, freeze-dried coffee.
- 1939: Joliot-Curie demonstrates possibility of splitting the atom. First baseball game televised in U.S. Radar stations used in Britain for early warning of approaching enemy aircraft. Frequency modulation (FM) invented. First air-conditioned car (Packard).
- 1940: Cavity magnetron invented.

INFLUENTIAL BIRTHS IN THE VINYL GENERATION:

Presidents:
- Bill Clinton (1946)
- George W. Bush (1946)

Business, Education, Athletes and Other Leaders:
- Mickey Mantle (1931–1995), baseball player
- Carl Sagan (1934–1996), astronomer
- Jimmy Swaggart (1935–present), preacher
- Jesse Jackson (1941), civil rights leader
- Stephen Hawking (1942–2018), physicist
- Hillary Clinton (1947), politician

Entertainers:
- Clint Eastwood (1930–present), actor
- Carol Burnett (1933–present), actress
- Elvis Presley (1935–1977), singer
- Bill Cosby (1937–present), actor
- Evel Knievel (1938–2007), daredevil
- John Lennon (1940–1980), rock singer
- Bob Dylan (1941), folk-rock singer
- Paul McCartney (1942), pop-rock singer
- Mick Jagger (1943), rock singer
- George Harrison (1943), pop-rock singer
- George Lucas (1944), director
- Bob Marley (1945–1981), reggae singer
- Eric Clapton (1945), guitarist
- Freddy Mercury (1946–1991), rock singer
- Dolly Parton (1946), country singer
- Elton John (1947), pop-rock singer
- Bruce Springsteen (1949), rock singer

Authors/Artists:
- Tom Clancy (1947), novelist

Chapter Eight

Television

"Television is a medium because anything well done is rare."
Fred Allen

_____

BIRTH YEARS: 1940–1960
"Coming of Age" Years: 1950–1985
Primary Tech Event: Color television
Strauss-Howe Archetype: Prophet
Generation Personality: Recessive/Optimistic
Iconic Generation Representative: Oprah Winfrey

Historical Influencing Events in Youth and Young Adulthood:
Korean War, Space Race, Vietnam, John F. Kennedy's assassination, man on the moon, Woodstock, Kent State, Watergate, Iran hostages, Ronald Reagan

_____

I t was a made-for-television moment.

The type of drama you can't script. True reality television.

The new chair for the Federal Communications Commission was set to address the powerful National Association of Broadcasters on the future of television. This was the chairman's first speech in his newly appointed post, and he leaned into the microphone with passion and purpose. As a former attorney, he minced no words.

"When it works, television conveys impressions and evokes memories. When it works well, television makes us feel."
Paul Newman

Television, he bluntly summarized, with all the fervor of a fire and brimstone preacher, was a "vast wasteland." To be fair, his indictment of the medium's evils stopped short of complete condemnation. The FCC chairman conceded that "when television is good…nothing is better." Nevertheless, the chairman criticized how televised entertainment had failed the American public:

> You will see a procession of game shows, formula comedies about totally unbelievable families, blood and thunder, mayhem, violence, sadism, murder, western bad men, western good men, private eyes, gangsters, more violence, and cartoons. And endlessly, commercials—many screaming, cajoling, and offending. And most of all, boredom.[207]

It's a speech that could've been given in 1971, or 1991, or 2011.

But it wasn't.

Newton N. Minow delivered this scathing rebuke in *1961*, when television was still juvenile, still maturing into what we know today.

He gave this speech before "formula comedies" like *Gilligan's Island, The Brady Bunch*, and *Alf* existed. He made his remarks before the broadcast of "murder" dramas like *Hawaii Five-O, NYPD Blue*, and *C.S.I.*. He leveled his criticism before reality television and controversial, edgy programs like *The Smothers Brothers, All in the Family*, and *Saturday Night Live*.

Years later, Minow reflected further on his rebuke of early television and uncompromisingly confessed that the medium's "vast wasteland" was now a "toxic dump."[208]

"Television is chewing gum for the eyes."
Frank Lloyd Wright

Whether that's true or not is one man's opinion, but one thing is certain: a particular American generation experienced it all.

Born between 1940 and 1960, the Television generation was uniquely positioned to witness the greatest *televised* show on earth. Their "coming of age" years span the golden age of television, from 1950 to 1985. In their youth, they were portrayed as "Beaver and Wally," "Gidget," and "Greg and Marcia Brady." In young adulthood, they were "Rob and Laura Petrie," "Mike and Gloria Stivic," and *thirtysomething* yuppies. Today, they are patriarchs of a diverse *Modern Family*. They've evolved from "Ray and Debra Barone" to the opinionated *Last Man Standing* in *The Middle*.

The Television generation is aging fast, but you wouldn't know it. They're grandparents and great grandparents. They're silver surfers with golden park passes and active Facebook accounts. They live in Del Webb fifty-five and up retirement communities, work as superstore greeters, and participate in community clubs like Toastmasters, Rotary, and Kiwanis. They're a "Peter Pan" generation seeking to stay forever young. And they still love to rock and roll.

Traditionally, we've tagged this generational cohort as "baby boomers," but they've collected other nicknames along the way: yuppies,[209] Generation Jones,[210] and zoomers. They're the Woodstock and Protest Generation. They were hippies, yippies, Black Panthers, Jesus freaks, draft dodgers, and flower children. These post-war "Spock" babies were born in a time of rising prosperity and birth rates. In 1948, four million babies were born (one every eight seconds). A decade later, nearly one-third of the U.S. population was under fourteen years of age.[211] No one denies this birth demographic was huge, but its size is far less significant than the mega-tech technology that shaped its personality.

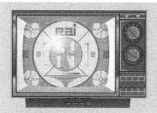

THE HISTORY OF TELEVISION

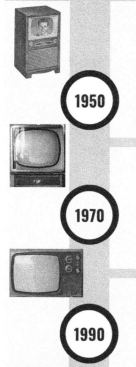

1950

1907: Jenkins/Baird experiment with mechanical TV
1924: Vladimir Zworykin invents television color tube
1927: Philo T. Farnsworth patents his electronic TV
1928: First television set is sold
1938: Berlin Olympics are televised
1939: Television spotlighted at New York's World's Fair
1944: John Logie Baird demonstrates color TV system

1970

1954: Tournament of Roses parade broadcast in color
1962: Telstar satellite launched to beam TV worldwide
1967: Beatles globally televise "All We Need Is Love"
1969: Over 600 million view televised moon landing
1970: Over half of U.S. homes own a color television set
1976: Sony Betamax debuts: first home recording unit

1990

1980: CNN debuts
1981: Music Television debuts
1982: Dolby surround sound premieres
1986: Super VHS is introduced
1988: 98% of U.S. homes have a television set
1994: DirectTV satellite service begins

2010

1997: Panasonic releases flat screen television
2006: Amazon announces video on demand service
2007: Netflix begins streaming content
2009: Digital television becomes standard
2013: Blockbuster Video closes all stores
2015: Sling TV launches

They aren't just "boomers." That's just another sub-category nickname.

In general, they're the *Television* generation.

Collectively, their birth years begin when Americans first witnessed television at the New York City's 1939 World's Fair and NBC announced the start of television broadcasting. For the next two decades, this new media matured and evolved within American culture. By 1960, the final year of birth for this generation, nine in ten households owned a television set (52 million).

Now there was no hiding the truth—or the camera.

On November 2, 1959, for example, television experienced its first scandal, just as the first members of the Television generation became young adults. That's when Charles Van Doren shocked the nation with his confession to a U.S. Senate subcommittee that he conspired to rig matches in a popular television quiz show named *Twenty-One*.[212] The nation was shocked. Television was suddenly no longer innocent or fair. It could manipulate, seduce, and even lie.

A year later, the first broadcast of a presidential debate on September 26, 1960 was equally historic. John F. Kennedy squared off against Richard Nixon, but Nixon clearly proved he wasn't ready for prime time television. Don Hewitt, founder of *60 Minutes*, commented how Kennedy appeared "tan and fit...a matinee idol," while Nixon, who perspired and seemed uncomfortable, looked "like death warmed over."[213] Nixon's television failure handed Kennedy both the debate and the election. Ultimately, television create a new reality: *visual* public persona. Good ideas meant nothing if you *looked* bad on television.

As The World Turns

Television "came of age" as a medium in 1960.

In the next two decades, its programs, news, sports, and coverage of live entertainment events radically shifted and shaped not just the Television generation but a new, emerging post-modern society. That's why 1960 is the epicenter year for a cultural earthquake that produced the post-modern world we know today.

Television is on par with other historical mega-techs like Gutenberg's printing press or the mechanical clock, possessing a unique power to evolve cultural languages. After 1960, television reinvented every social institution it touched, moving us from words to images, from print to visual. We began to process information *visually*—or better, audio-visually. Television killed the radio star. In fact, all generations born since 1960 inherited this new post-modern landscape. It's why we *see* things differently than pre-1960 generations.

In my speaking and consultations, nearly always there are individual who are unsettled by this idea (that those born after 1960 are more "post-modern" in their perspectives). It's because they don't feel "post-modern" even though they were born after 1960…and they're right to feel that way. And yet, in most cases these individuals also grew up in unique situations where television was *outside* their "coming of age" experience. They grew up rural, poor or environments that prohibited television. In such cases, even though born after 1960, these individuals still lived in a *modern* world. It still happens today, most notably in religious cultures like the Amish.

Nevertheless, the emergence of television is so influential that two different generations in our narrative bear its name: The Television Generation (b. 1940–1960) and The *Cable* Television Generation (b. 1970–1990). Even other post-1960 technological generations (like the Gamer, PC, and iTech) employ television technology. Television wasn't like the airplane or motion picture or even radio, as great as those technologies were. Television was *different*. Walter Cronkite mused that "probably nothing since the printing press has been as much of an influence on…the mindset of the peoples of the world."[214]

And that's the way it is.

———

"You could turn on a machine and be somewhere else. Television changed absolutely everything."
Tom Hanks

———

In The Beginning

The story of electronic television originated in remote eastern Idaho with a Mormon farm boy named Philo T. Farnsworth. As a kid, Farnsworth tinkered with motors and electric gadgets but excelled in physics and chemistry.

---

*"TV will never be a serious competitor for radio
because people must sit and keep their eyes glued on the
screen; the average American family hasn't time for it."*
Unknown, New York Times, 1939

In the spring of 1921, the adolescent Farnsworth engineered an equation for projecting images just like a radio transmits sounds. In his enthusiasm, the teenager showed his sketches to his Rigby, Idaho high school science teacher. The young Farnsworth was on to something, but it would be years before his dream materialized. Then his father's unexpected death forced the young Mormon inventor to focus on the family farm, delaying further his tele*vision*. Farnsworth eventually attended Brigham Young University and settled in the Salt Lake City area. But his television ideas continued to bubble.

The only problem is Farnsworth wasn't alone in that aspiration.

A Russian inventor named Vladimir Zworykin was noodling the same concept. His mentor was the famed Boris Rosing, who demonstrated a crude television model in 1911. After World War I, Zworykin migrated to the United States and found employment at Westinghouse laboratories in Pittsburgh. His task was simple: invent *electronic* television. Zworykin eventually applied for a television patent in 1923 but struggled to create a working model.

The race was heating up to invent "television."

In 1926, a newly married and freshly financed Philo T. Farnsworth moved to California, eventually landing in San Francisco. A year later, he transmitted an actual electronic image, but not without his own problems. Meanwhile, other inventors— particularly John Logie Baird—were developing television through old-fashioned "mechanized" formats, considered by many the medium's future structure.[215] But not Farnsworth and Zworykin. They envisioned *electronic* television. In 1928, Farnsworth finally improved his design sufficiently to introduce his invention to the press. It *worked*. Philo was the first inventor to produce a working electronic television.

Unfortunately, he'd get little credit for it, thanks to David Sarnoff.

Like Zworykin, David Sarnoff was born in Russia. His Jewish family emigrated to the United States in 1900 and, to help his family survive, the young Sarnoff found work with the Marconi Wireless Telegraph Company. Sarnoff idolized Marconi (even dressed like him) and quickly proved a promotional genius. In 1919, Sarnoff was included in a deal that created the Radio Corporation of America. For the next half-century, he passionately led RCA in various ventures that pioneered radio and television programming.

One of those ventures included luring Vladimir Zworykin away from Westinghouse in 1930. Sarnoff saw the future in electronic television and Zworykin's ideas persuaded the young RCA executive to hire him on the spot. Sarnoff was the visionary and Zworykin built the vision…or in this case, tele*vision*.

But Sarnoff still had a serious problem.

"Television is a medium of entertainment which permits millions of people to listen to the same joke at the same time, and yet remain lonesome."
T.S. Eliot

Philo T. Farnsworth already owned several electronic television patents that stood in his way. Sarnoff pressed the Idaho farm boy, even intimidated him, to acquire those patents. He offered to buy him out and employ him like Zworykin. Nothing worked. Farnsworth refused to relinquish his patents without ongoing royalties. RCA eventually sued, arguing that Zworykin's 1923 patent superseded Farnsworth. However, a 1934 U.S. Patents ruling gave Philo the final credit. His crude 1921 adolescent sketches of electronic television, the ones he shared with his science teacher, proved he was *first*. Farnsworth was *the* inventor of television and deserved his royalties.

Unfortunately, David Sarnoff saw things differently and he was used to getting his own way. After all, Sarnoff was the undisputed king of radio in the mid-1930s. His RCA empire included the National Broadcasting Corporation (NBC), founded in 1926. Sarnoff's chief competitor was William S. Paley, the founder of the Columbia Broadcast Company (1928). During the 1930s, NBC and CBS battled for radio supremacy, but behind closed doors, Sarnoff hatched a different plan. He knew television had more of a future than radio. Vladimir Zworykin was his key to that vision becoming reality.

Sarnoff's dream of broadcast *television* led him to design a television studio. On July 7, 1936, Sarnoff launched an experimental televised broadcast featuring dancers, speeches, and military maneuvers. Few saw the broadcast, but it proved a moderate success. Sarnoff then started televising programs to a limited New York City audience, but, again, not without issues. Late 1930s television had an image problem: few "saw" it. *Weak signals. Expensive sets. Intermittent programming.* And don't forget radio. Sarnoff's myopic dream for television was eroding his radio empire status. CBS started to pull ahead of NBC.

Sarnoff needed a big, promotional event.

Thankfully, the 1939 World's Fair theme focused on the "future," and television took center stage. Sarnoff, the consummate self-promoter and marketer, used the fair to unveil televised programmed broadcasting. Sarnoff declared a "birth" of a "new art" that was "so important in its implications that it [was] bound to affect all society."[216] At the time, his prediction for television seemed ostentatiously bold, but time eventually confirmed Sarnoff's ideas. Without a doubt, television influenced every person born after 1940.

It's when the Television generation began.

But the 1939 World's Fair equally proved equally tragic for Philo T. Farnsworth. He had invented electronic television, but the RCA television exhibit scrubbed his name as a pioneering influence. In fact, Sarnoff took the credit as the "father of television." Farnsworth had beat Sarnoff in court for the original patent, but Sarnoff would do his best to erase Philo from television history. And Sarnoff pretty much accomplished that objective. In the coming decades, Farnsworth secured 300 patents for his various inventions, including the incubator, but his claim to television was mostly forgotten. He once appeared as a "mystery" television game show contestant in 1957.

Farnsworth won when he stumped the panel as the "inventor of television."

He's still mostly an obscure footnote in technology history.[217]

The Tube Takes Off

Originally, Sarnoff's NBC scant television programming—a few shows a week—reached a couple hundred people in New York City. Nevertheless, his new venture was gaining ground and getting noticed. In 1934, the Federal Communications Commission formed and, in 1940, introduced a federal antitrust law to bust Sarnoff's RCA/NBC monopoly. The result produced the sale of an NBC network to Edward J. Noble in 1943, who renamed it the American Broadcasting Company. The "big three" networks were now in place.

By the mid-1940s, American post-war prosperity infused everything. People wanted to relax and recreate. The vibrant economy meant there was money to spend. Unfortunately, television remained too expensive for most Americans.[218] In 1945, fewer than 10,000 television sets existed, and they were generally in local taverns. It would take the first broadcast of a live sports event (the 1947 World Series) to unleash television's true star power. That October contest between two New York juggernauts—the Yankees and the Dodgers (featuring rookie sensation Jackie Robinson)—packed drinking establishments. Many others congregated outside store windows to watch the baseball games. Suddenly, television was cool.

Enter Los Angeles car dealer and huckster Earl "Madman" Muntz.

Muntz knew people would buy television if they could *afford* television. He developed a low-cost, stripped-down television set—known as the Muntz television—that undersold competitors by hundreds of dollars. It proved an instant hit.[219] The Muntz television set off a sales war that finally made television affordable. In 1948, 35,000 televisions were sold in the U.S, but just a year later, there were four million sets in American homes.

The golden age of television had dawned.

Between 1948 and 1951, several significant television shows debuted. *The Milton Berle Show* (NBC).[220] *The Ed Sullivan Show* (CBS).[221] *The Lone Ranger* (ABC).[222] *The Howdy Doody Show* (NBC).[223] And the landmark *I Love Lucy* (CBS), the first to feature a female lead.[224] By 1951, just as the first members of the Television generation came of age, one in three U.S. homes owned a television. The "family hours" created by radio shifted quickly to television, as people turned their eyes (and ears) to a new box in the corner. Even the White House saw the power of the tube. In 1952, President Harry Truman offered Americans the first televised tour of the White House.[225]

———————

"I must say I find television very educational. The minute somebody turns it on, I go to the library and read a good book."
Groucho Marx

———————

But there remained frontiers. With the emergence of technicolor motion pictures, why not color television? Once again, David Sarnoff and RCA won the day, producing the first color set in 1954. Unfortunately, it would take a decade for color programming to catch up.

By mid-decade, the tipping point for television occurred, as two-thirds of U.S. households now owned a television set.[226] Between 1954 and 1960, there were debuts of memorable family dramas (*Father Knows Best,*[227] *Lassie,*[228] *The Donna Reed Show,*[229] *The Andy Griffith Show*[230]), westerns (*Gunsmoke,*[231] *Have Gun Will Travel,*[232] *Bonanza*[233]), mysteries (*Alfred Hitchcock Presents*[234]), science fiction (*The Twilight Zone*[235]), and special kid's programs (*Mickey Mouse Club*[236]).

However, one show proved truly ground breaking.

The Honeymooners' brief, thirty-nine-episode run (1957–1958) rightfully garnered critical reviews.[237] Jackie Gleason's portrayal of Ralph Kramden as a gritty, loud-mouthed, middle-class New York City bus driver was must-see television. Perhaps more important, the show produced a boilerplate for future middle-class, married couple sitcoms from *All in the Family* to *Roseanne* to *Everybody Loves Raymond.* Even cartoons like *The Flintstones*[238] seemed to parody this trailblazing show.

Music also played a *televised* role for this generation. From Ed Sullivan's promotion of Elvis Presley and the Beatles (among many other emerging pop, R&B, and rock acts) to Dick Clark's *American Bandstand, Soul Train,* and, eventually, music television or MTV.[239] The Television generation came of age on musical images.

Commercial Breaks

From the beginning, the sheer birth size of the Television generation was a marketer's dream. As television sales climbed, so did the plethora of ads. During the 1950s, advertising money was poured into television commercials to entice a prosperity culture. From cigarettes to Chevrolets and beer to bread, advertisements pitched a "better" life, often with memorable musical jingles that hooked both mind and pocketbook. These primitive commercials significantly shaped a generation of American kids.

The Television generation cut their teeth on *Heinz* baby foods and suckled *Pet* evaporated milk. They drank *Ovaltine*, munched on *Fritos* chips, and ate *Zoom* hot cereal. They feasted on *Jiffy Pop* popcorn, *Jell-O* instant pudding, and *Cracker Jack*. They painted pictures with *Daffy Drops* and drew cartoons with *MouseKartooners*. Early members played with *Mattel toy guns* and *Remco magic kits*, while later members enjoyed *Barbies*, *Chatty Cathys*, *G.I. Joes*, and *Rock'em Sock'em Robots*. They played with *Play-Doh* and *Silly Putty*, *Matchbox cars*, and *Slinkies*. They collected *Topps* baseball cards and animal cards inside *Sugar Daddy* caramels. They washed their hair with *White Rain* shampoo, soothed stomach aches with *Alka Seltzer*, brushed with *Pepsodent*, and patched wounds with *Band-Aids*. They wore *Keds* shoes, *Davy Crockett* coonskin caps, and *Annette Funicello* poodle skirts.

"I hate television. I hate it as much as peanuts.
But I can't stop eating peanuts."
Orson Welles

From *Howdy Doody* to *Mister Rogers*, the Television generation found a home on *Sesame Street*. It's been estimated that this cohort of kids watched over 500 hours of televised advertisements before leaving kindergarten and by their twenty-first birthday had ingested over 300,000 television commercials.[240] This new focus upon kid culture in the 1950s—raised under the tutelage of child psychologist Dr. Benjamin Spock—created a distinct and segregated subculture from previous generations. The Television generation had different music, celebrities, foods, fashions, cars, toys, technology, and morality than their parents. Televised programming in the 1950s presented a homogeneous, middle-income, white culture. However, the Television generation, especially those who lived in more metropolitan contexts, saw through that facade. Father didn't always know best and families weren't all wholesome—or even white. Mothers weren't always perfect housewives and homemakers. People weren't all well-to-do nor always clothed in suits, ties and dresses.

Television also rearranged social habits. People switched from radio to television (consuming nearly five viewing hours per day). Consequently, fewer books, journals, magazines, and newspapers were read. Children could recall television and commercial jingles—such as the ingredients to a Big Mac[241]—but struggled to remember Bible verses, science facts, and historical figures.[242]

Television created fads in fashion that shaped a generation. *Mouseketeer ears. Greased-back hair* (thanks, Elvis). *Afros. Bell bottom jeans. Bouffant hairdos* (thanks, Jackie Kennedy). *Go-Go boots. Granny glasses. Miniskirts. Mood rings. Platform shoes. Tie-Dyed shirts. Turtlenecks. Daisy Dukes. Earth shoes. Black leather jackets* (thanks, Fonzie).

It also created dance crazes like *the Bop, Stroll, Twist, and Loco-Motion.*[243] And let's not forget the 1970s sport of streaking. Without television to broadcast the naked truth, who "nude" what might've happened. From bikinis to skinny dipping, skin was *in* with the Television generation.

Generation Ideal

The Television generation grew up surprisingly idealistic, despite the tragedies that marked their youth. The morality of the *Lone Ranger* mixed with *Father Knows Best* integrity and Walt Disney "wish upon a star" optimism gave the Television generation a sense of principled, positive social responsibility in the face of cultural collapse and social revolution. According to Tom Brokaw, a Television generation member, the "Sixties blindsided us with mind-bending swiftness, challenging and changing almost everything that had gone before."[244]

"Television brought the brutality of war into the comfort of the living room. Vietnam was lost in the living rooms of America—not on the battlefields of Vietnam."
Marshall McLuhan

This generation watched blacks get beaten, hosed, and lynched for their skin color, unleashing marches in Selma and riots in Watts. From Rosa Parks to Malcolm X, the Television generation saw a "black and white" culture, mostly through a television screen, that demanded civil rights, equality justice and social change. Then, they watched in horror as the voices of cultural leaders John F. Kennedy, Martin Luther King, Jr., and Bobby Kennedy were silenced in assassination.

Their answer?

Black power salutes. Love ins. Peace marches.

"All we need is love." And *"we shall overcome."*

The Television generation witnessed their brothers and friends sent to fight in Vietnam—the first *televised* war—to save the world from the "Red Menace" of communism. They watched a *televised* Tet Offensive, Viet Cong guerillas, and napalm bombs bring these brothers and friends home in body bags. They listened to their leaders propagate falsehoods about the war.

Their solution?

"Flower power" protests, student strikes, and two-fingered "peace" signs.

"All we are saying is give peace a chance."

They observed once-trusted authority figures—parents, preachers, teachers, cops, and politicians—fabricate the "truth." Their reaction was a countercultural "consciousness" movement, sprinkled with "days of rage" that threatened every institution. It was *burn, baby, burn*, including draft notices, bras, and joints. The Television generation chose to light up, sit down, flip off, tune in, turn on, and drop out. They escaped through mind-altering drugs, free love, psychedelic rock, communal living, Summer of Love/Woodstock experiences, eastern mysticism, Dianetics, Jesus Movement evangelicalism, and pop psychology.

Their ideals on race, gender, and sex sparked multiple social movements in the 1960s. *Women's liberation. Environmentalism. Gay rights.* They also influenced religion, especially in the 1980s as they entered mid-life. The Television generation consulted new-age gurus and followed megachurch pastors. The youngest members of the cohort uniquely experienced the fall and resignation of a U.S. President, rising divorce rates, falling SAT scores, legalized abortion, 1970s culture wars, a coarsening in moral decencies, energy crises, pollution, and disco (from which some have never fully recovered).

None of these real-world problems detoured the Television generation's social idealism. Strauss and Howe rightly noted they "have always seen their mission not as constructing a society, but of justifying, purifying, even *sanctifying* it."[245] Deep in this generation's psyche clearly lies the Kennedy admonition to "ask not what your country can do for you, but what you can do for your country."

Consequently, it's not surprising the "coming of age" years for the Television generation are framed by U.S. Presidents with classic television style. The oldest members of this cohort turned twenty in 1960 to John F. Kennedy's "Camelot" mystique, while the youngest members left adolescence during Ronald Reagan's "Morning in America" vision. The similarity between both the Kennedy and Reagan administrations is fascinating. They are like political mirrors of different eras and parties. Both presidents used compromise to get things done. Both used tax cuts to guide their economic policies. Both dealt with Cold War communism and Russian aggressions. Both were criticized for their religion. Both were "great communicators"—able to inspire, persuade, comfort, and inform. Both faced an assassin's bullet. Additionally, both Kennedy and Reagan uniquely used the power of television to communicate their vision for America.

And That's The Way It Is

NBC and CBS pioneered network news in the 1940s. On May 3, 1948, the first nightly news segment aired with CBS's Douglas Edwards. Two years later, CBS was the first news network to broadcast nationally. Edwin R. Murrow's *See It Now* (CBS) was a groundbreaking news show that aired between 1951 and 1958. Murrow covered hard-hitting issues with insightful commentary.[246]

"Well, of course, it is the most impressive medium of all.
It's the medium that's going to either save America or send
it down into demise. There's no question about it."
Ralph Nader on *The Dick Cavett Show*

Initially, most newscasts were fifteen minutes long. And, for most of the 1950s and 1960s, news belonged to CBS's Walter Cronkite and NBC's tag team of Chet Huntley and David Brinkley. However, in early September 1963, both networks converted to half-hour newscasts. In 1970, Huntley's retirement was rechristened *NBC Nightly News* featuring three anchors: Brinkley, John Chancellor, and Frank McGee. Chancellor eventually assumed full anchor in 1971, and Brinkley moved to commentary.

ABC Evening News first aired in 1953 (with John Charles Daly) but didn't expand to the half-hour format until 1968. By then, Frank Reynolds anchored the news with Howard K. Smith joining a year later. In 1975, Harry Reasoner left CBS for ABC and Smith slid into a commentary role. Barbara Walters joined Reasoner a year later.

For the rest of the decade, it was Cronkite vs. Reasoner-Walters vs. Chancellor. However, as the Television generation fully embraced adulthood, the anchors all changed again. CBS's Cronkite retired in 1981 and left his newscast to Dan Rather. ABC and NBC News turned their anchor keys over to Peter Jennings and Tom Brokaw, respectfully, in 1983.[247]

It was the end of an era for the Television generation.

After all, if there was a single trusted voice for this generation, it was "Uncle Walter Cronkite." Each night, Cronkite ended his broadcast with his trustworthy signature statement: *"that's the way it is."*[248] Cronkite reported the news, and nothing but the news, for two decades. His first newscast with CBS Television was on April 16, 1962. Eighteen months later, his somber, on-air, announcement of Kennedy's assassination cemented his familial appeal. He was trusted for journalistic depth and accuracy.[249] He also took broadcasting risks. In 1968, Cronkite traveled to

Vietnam to weigh the situation. His conclusion was contrary to what the American government had long reported. Cronkite recognized that America would not win the war and stated we should "negotiate, not as victors, but as an honorable people."[250] Cronkite's assessment lit a match under anti-war protests. A year later, his reporting on the space mission to the moon rocketed CBS News to top ratings.

NBC's introduction of *The Today Show* on January 14, 1952 was another transformational moment that pioneered a new genre: morning news television. Host Dave Garroway and his sidekick monkey J. Fred Muggs launched a two-hour show that featured headline news, interviews with newsmakers and celebrities, plus other lifestyle stories.[251] The format proved a hit and *The Today Show* became a popular "wake up" call for the Television generation. A who's who of American journalists have hosted *The Today Show*, including Hugh Downs, Barbara Walters, Tom Brokaw, Jane Pauley, Bryant Gumbel, Deborah Norville, Katie Couric, Matt Lauer, Meredith Vieira, and Ann Curry. A dedicated weather reporter joined the morning roster in the late 1970s. The lovable Willard Scott, who created and played the fast-food clown Ronald McDonald, quickly became a fan favorite.

ABC's *Good Morning America* debuted on November 3, 1975 and has been the only strong competitor to *The Today Show*, which is the fifth longest running television series.[252]

Don't Change That Channel

The Television generation recollects a day when broadcasts began and ended with the national anthem. They recall an age of television theme songs and commercial jingles (and can still sing them). They remember afternoon soap operas, Friday night fights, Saturday morning cartoons, and Sunday night Disney. They experienced the rise of televised religion. *Billy Graham crusades. The PTL Club. CBN.* And television news commentary. *Meet the Press. 60 Minutes. 20/20. Nightline.* And televised sports. *The Super Bowl. Monday Night Football. The Olympics. Wide World of Sports. The NFL Today. This Week in Baseball.*

"Television is the most perfect democracy.
You sit there with your remote control and vote."
Aaron Brown

Television shaped their generational psyche.

Since their birth, the Television generation has seen much ink spilled to describe its unique personality. Countless books, magazine articles, doctoral dissertations, and research journals were penned to explain this "booming" American generation. From my view, its clear television shaped these birth years from 1940 to 1960 *distinctly*. And I'm not alone in that assessment. As one historian penned:

Television—along with the marketers who used it—and music gave Boomers a common language and created the first integrated national culture…Television separated the Boomer from every previous generation…Starting in the 1950s Americans across the country watched the same shows, laughed at the same jokes, and watched the same news stories unfold…Television transformed American social habits.[253]

It's why I think "Television generation" is the most accurate moniker for this cohort. A group that includes pitchman athletes (*O.J. Simpson, Dick Butkus, "Mean" Joe Greene*), child stars (*Jerry Mathers, Ron Howard, Maureen McCormick, David Cassidy*), television music artists (*Cher, Donny Osmond, Michael Jackson*), television journalists (*Geraldo Rivera, Diane Sawyer, Bill O'Reilly*), talk show hosts (*Jay Leno, David Letterman, Oprah W*infrey), megachurch preachers (*Bill Hybels, Rick Warren, TD Jakes*), and three U.S. Presidents (*Bill Clinton, George W. Bush, Donald Trump*).

From *Ozzie and Harriet* to Ozzy Osbourne reality shows, television happily shared this generation's stories. From the Beatles on *Sullivan* to a white bronco chase through Los Angeles, television captured every groove and move. From a chimp on *The Today Show* to Bill Clinton blowing his sax on *Arsenio*, television inspired and entertained.

Television changed the world.

And it still does.

A TIMELINE OF TECHNOLOGICAL EVENTS (1941–1950):

- 1941: Hans Haas begins underwater photography. "Manhattan Project" of intensive atomic research begins. Dacron invented. Plutonium discovered. Grand Coulee dam in Washington opens.

- 1942: Enrico Fermi splits the atom. The first electronic brain or computer is developed. Magnetic recording tape invented. First jet airplane tested. Instant coffee introduced. Notable inventions: duct tape, napalm, guided missile.
- 1943: Penicillin successfully used to treat disease. Aqualung invented for underwater breathing. Colossus computer developed by British. Notable invention: Slinky.
- 1944: First nonstop flight from London to Canada. Kidney dialysis invented in Netherlands. Sunscreen created to protect soldiers.
- 1945: First atomic bomb detonated near Alamogordo, New Mexico. Later dropped on Hiroshima and Nagasaki to end World War II. 5,000 U.S. homes have television sets. First general-purpose computer assembled and used for calculations. Notable invention: microwave oven.
- 1946: The discovery that sun spots emit radio waves. Isotope Carbon-13 discovered. Pilotless rocket constructed. Xerography process created by Chester Carlson. AT&T announces first car phones. The Vespa scooter produced.
- 1947: Airplane flies at supersonic speeds. Bell Labs invents the transistor. First instant camera developed. Goodrich manufactures first tubeless tire. Sound barrier broken. Notable inventions: Frisbee, hologram.
- 1948: Long-playing record invented. Studies by Charlotte Auerbach commence the science of chemogenetics. First port radar system introduced. A rocket missile reaches seventy-eight miles in altitude and 3000 miles per hour. Porshe is founded. One million televisions in U.S. Notable invention: random access storage device,
- 1949: Cortisone is discovered. U.S. Air Force jet crosses the country in three hours, forty-six minutes. A guide missile travels 250 miles in altitude. First automatic street lights installed in New Milford, CT. The world's first commercial computer released (Ferranti Mark 1).
- 1950: Antihistamines become popular remedy for allergies and colds. Diners Club issues first credit card. Eight million U.S. homes have television. First television remote control released by Zenith.

INFLUENTIAL BIRTHS IN THE TELEVISION GENERATION:

Presidents:

- Donald Trump (1946)

Business, Education, Athletes and Other Leaders:

- Robert Kraft (1941), entrepreneur
- Stephen Hawking (1942–2018), physicist
- Newt Gingrich (1943), politician
- O.J. Simpson (1947), football player
- Steve Wozniak (1950), entrepreneur
- Ben Carson (1951), doctor
- Walter Payton (1954–1999), football player
- T.D. Jakes (1957), religious leader

Entertainers:

- Tom Brokaw (1940–present), news anchor
- Stephen Spielberg (1946), director
- Meryl Streep (1949), actress
- John Belushi (1949–1982), actor
- Robin Williams (1951–2014), actor
- Tim Allen (1952), actor
- Oprah Winfrey (1954), TV show host
- Jerry Seinfeld (1954), actor
- Ron Howard (1954), actor/director
- Maureen McCormick (1956), actress
- Katie Couric (1957), TV host
- Michael Jackson (1958–2009), pop singer
- Prince (1958–2016), pop singer
- Bono (1960), rock singer

Authors/Artists:

- Stephen King (1947), novelist
- Matt Groening (1954), cartoonist

Chapter Nine
Space

"Space, the final frontier…
To boldly go where no man has gone before"
Star Trek intro

BIRTH YEARS: 1950–1970
"Coming of Age" Years: 1960–1995
Primary Tech Event: The moon landing
Strauss-Howe Archetype: Prophet-Nomad
Generation Personality: Recessive/Optimistic
Iconic Generation Representatives: Tom Hanks and Bono

Historical Influencing Events in Youth and Young Adulthood:
Space Race, Vietnam, John F. Kennedy's assassination, man on the moon,
Kent State, Watergate, Iran hostages, Ronald Reagan, Challenger explosion,
end of Cold War, O.J. Simpson

Americans reached a summit in human history on July 20, 1969.

The landing of astronauts on the moon was, as Neil Armstrong so eloquently stated, "one small step for man, one giant leap for mankind."[254] In a single moment, humans boldly went where none had traveled before. And we've gone many places. Since the dawn of time, we've explored the canvas of our own terra firma, but this was our first exploration of a different rock in space.

That's why nothing compares to that historic moment. When Americans stepped foot on the moon, it was bigger than Columbus discovering the western world. It was grander than Lewis and Clark charting a path to the Pacific Ocean. It was greater than any exploration of earth's ocean's depths, polar landscapes, and desolate desert regions.

And only Americans did it.

But not without sacrifice, hard work, and ingenuity.

Our story in space is a tale for the ages.

Rocket Man

The technological history of space exploration originates a thousand years ago when the Chinese first used gunpowder to propel primitive rockets. Two centuries later, the Mongols introduced powder-fueled rockets to Europe. Ever since, propelled rockets have been in the military arsenal (even if crude by today's standards). In fact, it was the "rocket's red glare" that inspired Francis Scott Key's famed "Star-Spangled Banner" lyric about an 1814 British battle against Fort McHenry.[255]

At the turn of the twentieth century, the idea of space exploration was on everyone's mind. The first narrative motion picture ever released—the 1902 French film *A Trip to the Moon*—used space travel as its topic.[256] Men and women had long dreamt of outer space…and schemed to get there.

The story of space travel originates with a Russian scientist named Konstantin Tsiolkovsky (himself inspired by the science fiction writings of Jules Verne). Tsiolkovsky was the first to theoretically map how to put man into space.[257] His classic 1903 book about space travel, *Exploration of Outer Space by Means of Rocket Devices*, was a landmark work.[258] Tsiolkovsky didn't just inspire Russians, but also French, American, and German rocketeers. More significantly, his ideas and

SPACE EXPLORATION

A History of Rockets and Man's Journey into Space

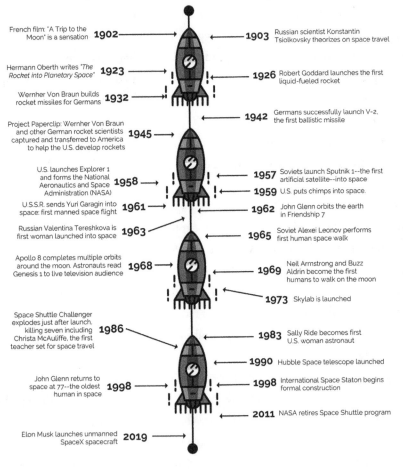

French film: "A Trip to the Moon" is a sensation **1902**

1903 Russian scientist Konstantin Tsiolkovsky theorizes on space travel

Hermann Oberth writes *The Rocket into Planetary Space* **1923**

1926 Robert Goddard launches the first liquid-fueled rocket

Wernher Von Braun builds rocket missiles for Germans **1932**

1942 Germans successfully launch V-2, the first ballistic missile

Project Paperclip: Wernher Von Braun and other German rocket scientists captured and transferred to America to help the U.S. develop rockets **1945**

U.S. launches Explorer 1 and forms the National Aeronautics and Space Administration (NASA) **1958**

1957 Soviets launch Sputnik 1--the first artificial satellite--into space

1959 U.S. puts chimps into space.

U.S.S.R. sends Yuri Garagin into space: first manned space flight **1961**

1962 John Glenn orbits the earth in Friendship 7

Russian Valentina Tereshkova is first woman launched into space **1963**

1965 Soviet Alexei Leonov performs first human space walk

Apollo 8 completes multiple orbits around the moon. Astronauts read Genesis 1 to live television audience **1968**

1969 Neil Armstrong and Buzz Aldrin become the first humans to walk on the moon

1973 Skylab is launched

Space Shuttle Challenger explodes just after launch, killing seven including Christa McAuliffe, the first teacher set for space travel **1986**

1983 Sally Ride becomes first U.S. woman astronaut

1990 Hubble Space telescope launched

John Glenn returns to space at 77--the oldest human in space **1998**

1998 International Space Staton begins formal construction

2011 NASA retires Space Shuttle program

Elon Musk launches unmanned SpaceX spacecraft **2019**

writing forged the foundation of the highly-successful Russian space program in the 1950s and 1960s.

"Earth is the cradle of humanity, but one cannot live in a cradle forever."
Konstantin Tsiolkovsky

The American space story originates with a young man named Robert H. Goddard. On one October day in 1899, as Goddard pruned cherry trees and fantasized about space, he found his life's purpose:

On this day I climbed a tall cherry tree at the back of the barn…and as I looked toward the fields at the east, I imagined how wonderful it would be to make some device which had even the possibility of ascending to Mars, and how it would look on a small scale, if sent up from the meadow at my feet…I was a different boy when I descended the tree from when I ascended. Existence at last seemed very purposive.[259]

Goddard spent the next two decades getting a higher education in physics and feverishly worked to make rockets more than just amateur play. Despite criticism and ridicule—and a reputation as the "lone rocket man"—Goddard continued to light fuses.

On March 16, 1926, Goddard launched the first liquid-fueled rocket. Three years later, he sent a rocket into the atmosphere carrying scientific tools—including a barometer and camera. Goddard pioneered not just rocketry—launching thirty-five rockets over fifteen years—but he also laid foundational theories for space travel. Unfortunately, at the time, American interest in rocketry was minimal and funding was sporadic. Consequently, the work of Goddard, which included 214 patents, enjoyed mediocre success at best. He once tried to convince the U.S. military to consider long-range rockets in warfare but got nowhere. Just prior to his death in 1945, Goddard happened upon a recovered German V-2 military rocket. The V-2 had elements of his own rocket design—a revelation that surprised Goddard because he meticulously guarded his rocketry secrets.

"Don't you know about your own rocket pioneer?
Dr. Goddard was ahead of us all."
Wernher von Braun

The fact that Germans might've stolen his work—something Goddard passionately believed—is debatable but entirely plausible. After all, the story of American space travel is also tethered to Germany, the rise of the Third Reich, and a collection of scientists and engineers known as the "German Society for Space Travel." This brain trust was formed by famed German physicist Hermann Oberth, considered one of the founding fathers of astronautics.[260] Among the individuals in this space society was a German adolescent that Oberth took under his wing—a kid who became a giant in *American* space exploration: Wernher von Braun. Years later, von Braun reverently remembered his mentor's influence:

> Hermann Oberth was the first, who when thinking about the possibility of spaceships grabbed a slide-rule and presented mathematically analyzed concepts and designs… I, myself, owe to him not only the guiding-star of my life, but also my first contact with the theoretical and practical aspects of rocketry and space travel. A place of honor should be reserved in the history of science and technology for his ground-breaking contributions in the field of astronautics.[261]

Oberth and von Braun, funded by Hitler's war machine, built missile rockets for Germany during World War II. They enjoyed limited success until they developed the first ballistic missile known as "Vengeance 2," or V-2. This missile eventually caught the attention of the U.S. military. Consequently, as the second World War mopped up, American commanders launched "Operation Paperclip" to scour Germany and locate Oberth and von Braun. Americans had already recovered their rockets and shipped them home for study, but now we wanted the brains behind the missiles. Naturally, this secret deportation of Nazis to the home front was highly controversial.[262] In time, though, these German rocket scientists proved their worth.

The Right Stuff

In 1946, the war was finally over. America was ready to relax. After a decade of Depression and years of war, the nation needed a breather.

Unfortunately, we'd soon learn Russia took no such siesta.

Even though America got the German rocket brain trust, Russia possessed the motivation. The Soviets initiated a dedicated rocket testing program, including rounding up over two thousand German rocket scientists and engineers of their own. The Russians were highly secretive, sometimes resorting to propaganda and false reports.[263] The Soviet space program was masterminded by Sergei Korolev, who found inspiration in the great Konstantin Tsiolkovsky. Korolev's identity and job was a highly-classified state secret until his death in 1966. Even his own mother didn't know what he did.

Back in America, the highly esteemed von Braun relocated to Fort Bliss, Texas to mostly sit on his hands and criticize his new Lone Star state living conditions. Meanwhile the American military showed little interest in rockets. It was far more fun to fly planes as fast and high as possible. One of their finest pilots was Chuck Yeager, who broke the sound barrier on October 14, 1947. As a result, the Soviets started to lead the world in rocket development. Even after Soviet premier Nikita Khrushchev announced Russian plans for intercontinental missiles and satellites in 1956, most of the world didn't believe it. The idea still seemed ludicrous, especially to Americans enjoying post-war peace and prosperity.[264] With the horror of Hiroshima still fresh in our minds, Americans desired to move on and let the rest of the world rebuild and recover.

Consequently, when the Soviets launched an earth satellite named Sputnik on October 4, 1957, it shocked the world. Shooting rockets into the sky was one thing but putting a satellite into orbit was something altogether different. With radio beacon signals, the Sputnik satellite circled the globe every ninety minutes as an alarming reminder the Soviets had done something new and *amazing*. Americans suddenly realized a chilling reality: if the Russians could put a rocket into space or create missiles capable of reaching America, what stopped them from attaching nuclear bombs to these devices? After all, since 1949, the Russians had engineered their own atomic bombs. It created a new, terrifying reality.

It's why the Space generation's first birth year is 1950.

Americans weren't just inhabiting a "space age" but also a new *nuclear* age. Beginning in 1951, civil defense authorities initiated public service announcements to prepare Americans to "duck and cover" for "the blast."[265] Many U.S. homeowners even built their own backyard bomb shelters.

Sputnik proved a national wake-up call for anyone still snoozing. For the budding Space generation, its oldest members in early elementary school when Sputnik was launched, the era of Cold War politics, nuclear war fearmongering, and the "space race" had only begun.

Unfortunately, America was way behind.[266] Thousands of scientists, engineers, and technicians feverishly went to work in various locations from Huntsville, Alabama to Fort Bliss, Texas to build an operational rocket. On January 31, 1958, we finally succeeded. Explorer 1—America's first satellite—found flight, but not without the genius of a former Nazi named Wernher von Braun. As a result of this achievement, a new civilian space agency was created: The National Aeronautics and Space Administration (NASA).

America was in space.

The Mercury Project was initiated as America's first step towards space travel. Between 1958 and 1963, the finest fighter pilots trained for space exploration. A month after the Soviets launched the Sputnik satellite, they sent a dog on a rocket ride. The canine didn't survive, but Russian intention was clear: they were working to put a man in space. NASA recruited seven of America's finest aviators—including John Glenn, Alan Shepard, and Virgil Grissom—to pilot the Mercury Project. In 1959, NASA launched America's first spy satellite, but even more importantly, successfully put two chimps into space. Suddenly, space travel for humans seemed a possibility.

"Across the sea of space, the stars are other suns."
Carl Sagan

Unfortunately, the Russians once again beat America to that prize.

At the midway point of the Space generation birth years—April 12, 1961—the Soviets sent Yuri Garagin 200 miles into the atmosphere for a 108-minute flight.

America answered a month later, when Alan Sheppard was launched into space.[267] America was energized by Sheppard's feat. Space travel was no longer conjecture and fancy; it was becoming *reality*. John F. Kennedy seized the moment to address Congress and the American people with a bold, fresh national vision:

> I believe that this nation should commit itself to achieving the goal, before this decade is out, of landing a man on the moon and returning him safely to the Earth. No single space project in this period will be more impressive to mankind, or more important for the long-range exploration of space; and none will be so difficult or expensive to accomplish.[268]

Less than a year later—February 20, 1962—John Glenn orbited the earth in Friendship 7. America started to win the space race…with a little help. An early proponent of space exploration was national newsman and favorite son Walter Cronkite. He enthusiastically promoted NASA exploits, reporting regularly on the program. America trusted "Uncle Walter."

Lost In Space

In the mid 1960s, American television caught the space bug and televised several shows with outer space themes and characters.[269]

"Since that dark day in 1969 when NBC brought the programming hammer down on Star Trek, there probably hasn't been a 24-hour period when the original program, one of the original episodes, wasn't being aired somewhere."
Chicago Tribune, 1987

However, no space exploration show was more influential than *Star Trek: The Original Series*, which debuted in 1966. Its three-year run surprisingly ended on June 3, 1969—one month shy of man actually stepping on the moon. *Star Trek* shaped the Space generation to "boldly go where no one has gone before." The "voyages of the starship Enterprise"—captained by James T. Kirk and his sidekicks named Spock, "Bones," Scotty, Sulu, and Uhuru—enthused television audiences.

Star Trek routinely pushed societal boundaries, from human equality to the controversial, historic first televised kiss between a white man (Kirk) and black woman (Uhuru).[270] It also created new cultural idioms like "Beam me up, Scotty." But most importantly, *Star Trek* provided the Space generation with a template for the future. Talking computers. Interactive screens. Information at your fingertips. Wireless communication. Multi-ethnic contexts. The future portrayed in *Star Trek* wasn't dark or desperate, but magical and promising.

Perhaps that's why NBC's decision to end *Star Trek* proved woefully short-sighted.[271] The Space generation loved the show and kept it alive as a syndication juggernaut. Eventually, this generation would help re-launch "Next Generation" sequels, feature films, collectibles, and conventions for "trekkies." *Star Trek* is the iconic cultural television show for the Space generation, but it wasn't alone in the universe. The *Star Wars* trilogy (1977–1983) also tapped into the existential, spiritual force of this generational cohort. The saga of Luke Skywalker, Princess Leia, and Han Solo "in a galaxy far, far, away" thrilled audiences through the Zen wisdom of Jedi masters, death matches with dark lords, and memorable characters like wookiees, droids, and other galactic citizens.

The launch of satellites allowed television to also reach a global audience. On June 25, 1967, hundreds of millions of people viewed the Beatles perform as the closing act on the premiere broadcast of "Our World"—a live two-and-a-half-hour variety show featuring performers from nineteen different countries.[272] The Beatles invited the Rolling Stones and Eric Clapton to join in their global "all you need is love" message of love, peace, and unity.

Satellite technology would later wire the Space generation for international events like the Vietnam War and Apollo moon mission coverage, the Olympics, and Live Aid concerts. Furthermore, the earliest adopters of satellite television (Dish Network, DirecTV) were Space Generation members. Television generation kids born in the 1960s never knew a world without global visual connection, thanks to television and satellites.

The Eagle Has Landed

The race to space was a two-nation, cold war, winner-take-all battle: U.S.A. versus U.S.S.R.

The Soviets were certainly faster off the blocks. Besides launching the first satellite and man into space, they also sent the first woman: cosmonaut Valentina Tereshkova (June 16, 1963). Tereshkova orbited the earth forty-eight times during her three days in space. America wouldn't send a woman into space for two more decades when the aptly named Space generation member Sally Ride (b. 1951) rode into orbit nearly twenty years to the day later on *The Challenger* (June 18, 1983).

Kennedy's assassination on November 22, 1963 dealt a major blow to America's space vision. It was Kennedy's vision and charisma that sparked our venture into space.[273] His death was potentially lethal to the young program, but fortunately that fear was never realized. Texan Lyndon B. Johnson picked up the mantle and kept NASA on track. Johnson actually proved an enthusiastic supporter for space exploration. Houston's Space Center (which housed Mission Control) would eventually bear his name.

The space race, once again, yielded to the Russians on March 18, 1965 when Soviet Alexei Leonov performed the first human spacewalk. American astronaut Ed White accomplished the same feat three months later (June 3, 1965). Six months after that historic moment, Gemini 7 completed a difficult space rendezvous with another craft. It was a significant step to getting humans completely to the moon.

For the next three years, space exploration continued to improve techniques and draw closer to a lunar landing. However, neither the U.S. nor Soviet space programs escaped without deep sacrifice. On January 27, 1967, the Apollo 1 capsule exploded and burned alive three U.S. astronauts trapped inside. The terrible tragedy forced many Americans to question the cost to beat the Russians to the moon. Even if we made it, what ultimate purpose would it serve? And is it worth the human lives we expend to get there? Any failure or tragedy in the American space program re-surfaced these doubts.

"We are now approaching lunar sunrise and, for all the people back on Earth, the crew of Apollo 8 has a message that we would like to send to you: 'In the beginning God created the heaven and the earth…'"
William Anders, astronaut

But American grief for the Apollo 1 tragedy proved short-lived, as did the skepticism. It wasn't long before the spacecraft Apollo 7 gave U.S. audiences their first live look at humans in space. And then, in late December 1968, Apollo 8 completed multiple orbits around the moon and beamed back to earth live images of the moon's surface. On Christmas Eve, astronauts William Anders, Jim Lovell, and Frank Borman read the biblical story of creation to a live television audience as the earth rose like the sun over surface of the moon.[274]

"It was such a huge event in our country's history, and I grew up in New York. This was bigger than the Mets winning the World Series in '69. I remember, as a little boy, looking up to them and thinking, 'these guys are even cooler than the Beatles.' These guys are the epitome of cool."

Mike Massimino, astronaut

It was a strangely comforting moment in a rather *discomforting* year. America was coming apart at the seams in 1968…and with good reason. We experienced the Vietnam Tet Offensive, and the murders of Martin Luther King, Jr. and Bobby Kennedy. We witnessed, race riots, student protests and the disastrous police brutality at the Democratic National Convention. We watched President Johnson decline a second term and Richard Nixon win a razor-thin (.7 percent margin) contentious election.[275]

America needed a "feel good" moment.

Seven months later, as the decade of Kennedy's challenge for America to put a man on the moon ebbed away, Apollo 11 rocketed into history. On July 20, 1969, live television broadcasted the lunar landing to a global audience. *The eagle had landed.* America was on the moon. Eventually, astronaut Neil Armstrong appeared on the outside steps of the space capsule and gingerly stepped to the moon's surface and famously announced, "It's one small step for man and one giant leap for mankind." Later, Buzz Aldrin joined Armstrong to plant an American flag. The whole world stopped in its tracks. It was a glorious moment of wonder and disbelief. Walter Cronkite commented, "After seeing it happen, knowing it happened, it still seems like a dream."[276]

It was no dream. America was *first* to the moon.

Houston, We Have A Problem

Between 1969 and 1972, six more American lunar missions explored that glorious rock we view in the nighttime sky. The Soviets never did make it. Neither did any other country. Only the Americans. It's our story alone.

"All of human experience will be divided into two eras. Before man walked on the moon and after man walked on the moon."
Tom Hanks

The Space generation—save the late-birth (post-1965) members—cannot forget July 20, 1969. Every member of this generation grew up with Americans either headed to space or doing something significant in space. We watched Alan Shepard play golf on the moon.[277] We sent spacecraft to Venus, Mars, Uranus, Neptune, and Saturn. We constructed the International Space Station. But for all these successes there were also momentous failures. We built SkyLabs that plunged back to earth and Space Shuttles that mysteriously exploded. And then there was Apollo 13. This "Houston, we have a problem" aborted moon mission and "successful failure" was a legendary story of human ingenuity and resolve.[278] It's no wonder that Space generation astronaut Mike Massimino professed: "The space program of the 1960s set the standard of what we could do…'Go to Mars, yeah, we can go to Mars. We went to the moon in 1969. We can do anything.'"

America would send the first African-American into space (Guion Bluford, Jr.) on August 30, 1983. We'd also re-send an eager, but elderly, John Glenn back into orbit in October 1998. This mission was the back-end "coming of age" event for the Space generation.

"My generation is the generation that changed the moon from an object to a place and that can never happen again. There can only be one first time."
Jim Slade

But the most memorable event—other than landing on the moon—for the Space generation happened on a fateful day in late January 1986.[279] On that day, the Space Shuttle Challenger was set to launch into space the first civilian school teacher. Her name was Christa McAuliffe and she was one of 11,000 applicants for NASA's coveted "Teacher in Space" project.[280] McAuliffe, a social studies teacher from Concord (NH) High School, was a media darling. She appeared on several television shows—including *Good Morning America* and *The Tonight Show*—to tutor America on her mission, which included educational lectures in outer space.

The Challenger had already experienced delays, from mechanical issues to poor weather, but on the morning of January 28, all systems were finally a go. The blast off, viewed by millions via television, was as glorious as ever. People cheered from the bleachers, including Christa McAuliffe's parents. As the Challenger space shuttle lifted into the blue skies off Cape Canaveral, people snapped photos. Some followed the craft with binoculars. Challenger made a slight roll to the right, then climbed deeper into the heavens, leaving a majestic white cloud billowing behind it. Mission control announcements occasionally broke the peaceful silence. Television cameras followed the shuttle for seventy-three seconds.

And then it happened.

"We will never forget them, nor the last time we saw them, this morning, as they prepared for their journey and waved goodbye and 'slipped the surly bonds of Earth to touch the face of God.'"
Ronald Reagan (January 28, 1986)

An explosion blew the craft into a huge fireball and incinerated the spacecraft into multiple pieces, each with its own trail of smoke. The flight deck fell silent, as did Mission Control in Houston. In the bleachers, McAuliffe's stunned parents looked heavenward in disbelief. As each minute passed, the reality of the situation set in. Men wept. Women fainted. Children questioned. People prayed. The nation watched in shock as the spacecraft—now in dozens of pieces—showered across the Florida sky. Debris fell into the Atlantic Ocean. There were no survivors. An entire seven-man crew was lost.[281] It was the greatest tragedy in American space exploration since Apollo 1, but it wouldn't be the last. Seventeen years later, another shuttle (this time named Columbia) exploded upon re-entry, killing still another crew of seven. In both cases, mechanical failures were to blame.

The launch of the Hubble Space Telescope on April 25, 1990 proved a significant one for NASA. Hubble reimagined everything we knew about space, including how we think of ourselves. The images it returned to earth were brilliant, legendary, and astonishing. Three years later, DirecTV launched its first satellite and "satellite television" was born. Meanwhile, other spacecraft like Galileo and the Mars Pathfinder, explored Jupiter and the red planet.

In 2011, NASA officially retired its space shuttle program with the landing of the craft Atlantis (July 21). The Space generation was now firmly planted in mid-life, between forty and sixty years of age.

―――――――

"Throughout all human history we've always had people look up and think, 'The blue sky, what is it up there? I wonder what it would it be like to go up there? In our time—in our lifetime— we've gone up there.… What a great time to be alive!"
John Glenn

―――――――

It should be no surprise that a Space generation baby—Sir Richard Branson (b. 1950)—is now working on spaceships to shuttle the common man into outer space. Since 2004, the billionaire entrepreneur has promoted his Virgin Galactic spacecrafts.[282] Of course, with ticket prices around $200,000, it's still a rich man's seat. Meanwhile, in March 2019, Elon Musk—an honorary member of the Space generation (born in 1971) and the mastermind behind SpaceX—launched his own unmanned craft into orbit. It's the first step to putting the common man into space.

I Believe I Can Fly

The Space generation (born 1950–1970) uniquely experienced this exploration of outer space. In their youth, they watched the elder Transportation generation pioneer the science to launch spacecrafts into orbit. In middle adulthood, they witnessed tragedy (Challenger shuttle explosion) and triumph (construction of an International Space Station) wrapped in Reagan's "star wars" missile defense strategies. Now, as they enter elderhood, the Space generation sees promising and productive journeys into outer space to establish future civilizations on the moon and Mars.

"You need to live in a dome initially, but over time you could terraform Mars to look like Earth and eventually walk around outside without anything on…So it's a fixer-upper of a planet."
Elon Musk

This generation's first members observed Russians launch a satellite (Sputnik) and cosmonaut into the heavens. They lived through "duck and cover" Cold War rhetoric, when an itchy finger on some button could blow the entire world to smithereens. The last members of this cohort were born just as Americans landed on the moon. They may have missed the original lunar landing, but twelve years later—on August 1, 1981—these kids witnessed a different launch and landing (using a rocket blastoff and astronaut as its opening theme): music television, or MTV.[283]

For the Space generation, life itself has been a rocket ride…especially in the pocketbook. In fact, many in this generation have suffered the *most* economically. As children, teens, and young adults, they faced 1970s Carter administration recession, inflation, unemployment, and economic malaise. As young parents, in the 1980s and 1990s, they endured rising costs for education, home ownership, or entrepreneurialism. As forty- and fifty-somethings, they experienced the stock bubble busts, housing market collapses, layoffs, and unemployment due to a collapsing middle class in the Great Recession (2007–2009). Space generation men in particular struggled to secure full-time employment. Many were forced to retire. Others downsized their homes, used reserve funds, went bankrupt, watched their wives get work, and opted for part-time jobs or self-employment. Space generation parents further drained their savings to send their kids to college only to re-house them when a post-Recession economy struggled to produce jobs. Consequently, this cohort now faces a rapidly arriving retirement with little to no reserves and suspicions that previous safety nets like Social Security and Medicare could be unavailable. Less than one in three Space generation members feel they'll meet their financial goals.[284]

In many ways, their lives have resembled the brief journey of that fateful Challenger rocket. The Space generation was gloriously launched into the clear blue skies of the American Dream, but never fully achieved orbit (culturally, professionally, or financially). The Great Recession exploded their savings, income potential, and career paths. In the end, it was just a long tail of smoky "what ifs."

The Space generation grew up with its eyes on outer space. For this generation, NASA has always existed. They watched *The Jetsons* and imagined a day of flying cars, instant meals, and robots. They experienced original runs of *Star Trek* in the 1960s and the *Star Wars* trilogy in the late '70s and early '80s. In fact, the *Star Trek* and *Star Wars* television and motion pictures franchise grooved the Space generation to believe *anything* was possible. As Yoda famously quipped, "Do or do not, there is no try."

The Space generation is also the most unique of all generations because it's the only American cohort to straddle the great post-modern cultural divide. Half of its generation was born a decade shy of 1960 and the other half a decade after 1960. It spans this post-modern crevice with a unique understanding and experience in two different cultural worlds. Metaphorically speaking, the Space generation has one foot on "modern" planet earth and the other somewhere in "post-modern" outer space. Maybe that's why, as a generation, it's always felt a bit *different*, even jaded. In traditional terms, the Space generation is a blend of late-birth "boomers" mixed with early-birth "Gen Xers," who experienced the maturation of technologies in transportation, motion pictures, radio, vinyl recordings, and television. The Space generation came of age during:

- The emergence of affordable, commercial airline travel and "vacation" travel by sea or plane.
- The promotion of fifty-five and up amenities/retirement communities, "family vacation travel," and "spring break" college retreats.
- The arrival of engine, dashboard, digital/audio/video technology that rapidly evolved cars and motorcycles (1970s–2000s).

- The motion picture as color, mega-screen, IMAX, and digital.
- The end of radio disc jockeys and AM dominance.
- The peak of vinyl records...and its demise, thanks to compact disc and digital music technology.
- The rise of modern television: color, via satellite, time-shifting recording devices (VCR, DVR), and gaming/computing consoles.

While it's true that generations in their shadow would equally experience these grand evolutionary changes in technology and culture, only the Space generation would do it *first*.

They've truly gone where no generation had gone before.

A TIMELINE OF TECHNOLOGICAL EVENTS (1951–1960):

- 1951: Electric power produced from atomic energy. J. Andre-Thomas invents a heart-lung machine for heart operations. Uranium converted to plutonium. Color television first introduced in U.S. First oral contraceptive invented. Direct dial coast-to-coast telephone service begins in U.S.
- 1952: Hydrogen bomb is exploded by U.S. World's first passenger jet produced. Mechanical heart successfully used. First patent for a bar code issued. Polio vaccine and roll-on deodorant introduced.
- 1953: Cosmic ray observatory erected on Mount Wrangell, Alaska. A rocket-powered U.S. plane is flown at more than 1,600 mph. First color TV set goes on sale. Notable inventions: transistor radio.
- 1954: Concern in Europe and America regarding disposal of radioactive waste. U.S. submarine "Nautilus" converted to nuclear power. U.S. flies first Boeing 747 jet. Twenty-nine million U.S. homes have televisions. Rose Bowl parade broadcast in color. Swanson introduces frozen TV dinners. GM produces fifty-millionth car. First organ transplants. Notable inventions: solar cell, robot.
- 1955: Ultra-high frequency waves produced at Massachusetts Institute of Technology. Atomically generated power first used in America. Commercial television begins broadcasting in Britain. Notable inventions: atomic clock, hovercraft, Velcro.

- 1956: Neutrino, an atomic particle with no electric charge, produced. F.W. Muller develops the ion microscope. Bell Telephone begins to develop "visual" telephone. Transatlantic cable telephone service inaugurated. Oral polio vaccine developed. Notable inventions: hard disk, nuclear power, video tape.
- 1957: U.S.S.R. launches Sputnik I and II, first earth satellites. Mackinac Straits Bridge (MI) opens the world's longest suspension bridge. John Glenn sets speed record in a jet, traveling from California to New York in three hours and twenty-three seconds. Ultrasound screening pioneered in Scotland. First nuclear reactor plant opens (PA).
- 1958: U.S. launches Explorer I (first earth satellite). Stereophonic recordings come into use. National Aeronautics and Space Administration (NASA) established. U.S. launches first moon rocket (travels 79,000 miles but fails to reach moon). Notable inventions: microchip, computer modem, remote control.
- 1959: U.S.S.R. Lunik reaches moon. Lunik III photographs moon. First U.S. nuclear-powered merchant vessel (Savannah) is launched. IBM ships transistor-based 1401 mainframe computer. Xerox releases first commercial copier.
- 1960: U.S. launches a radio-reflector satellite. Optical microwave laser constructed. *Triton* (a U.S. nuclear submarine) completes circumnavigation of the globe underwater. Laser device invented. Experimental rocket-powered airplane travels at 2200 mph. First weather satellite launched that allows television images of global cloud cover. U.S. has 85 million television sets. U.S. experimental rocket-powered plane travels 2,200 mph. Notable inventions: telephone answering machine, heart pacemaker.

INFLUENTIAL BIRTHS IN THE SPACE GENERATION:
Presidents:
- Barack Obama (1961)

Business, Education, Athletes and Other Leaders:
- Steve Wozniak (1950), entrepreneur
- Sally Ride (1951–2012), astronaut

- Howard Schultz (1953), entrepreneur
- Bill Gates (1955), entrepreneur
- Steve Jobs (1955–2011), entrepreneur
- Mike Pence (1959), politician
- Mike Tyson (1966), boxer
- Tonya Harding (1970), skater

Entertainers:

- Rush Limbaugh (1951), radio host
- Tom Hanks (1956), actor/director
- Prince (1958–2016), pop singer
- Madonna (1958), pop singer
- George Clooney (1961), actor
- Tom Cruise (1962), actor
- Garth Brooks (1962), country singer
- Whitney Houston (1963–2012), R&B singer
- Jimmy Kimmel (1967), television host
- Maria Carey (1970), pop singer

Authors/Artists:

- Kate Spade (1962–2018), fashion designer
- Gordon Ramsay (1966), chef
- Richie Rich (1970), fashion designer

"In a sense it's in our DNA as a country to try and jump on whatever new form of communications technology is there because it was so essential for our ancestors in building this large a nation."
Steven Johnson

POST-MODERN GENERATIONS

1960 - 2020

2020

Sri Lanka Easter bombings (2019)
End of ISIS in Syria (2019)

Parkland, FL school shooting (2018)
Las Vegas country music festival shooting kills 58 (2017)
Donald Trump elected president (2016)
Same sex marriage legalized (2015)
Boston Marathon bombings (2013)

Barack Obama elected president (2008)
The Great Recession (2007-2010)

 2010 **ROBOTICS**
2010-2030

Hurricane Katrina (2005)
Iraq War (2003)

iTECH **2000**
2000-2020

Terrorist attacks on NYC/DC (2001)
George W. Bush elected president (2000)

Bill Clinton-Monica Lewinsky impeachment (1999)
Columbine School shooting (1999)
Oklahoma City bombing (1995)
OJ Simpson trial (1995)

Los Angeles riots (1992)
Bill Clinton elected president (1992)
Desert Storm in Iraq/Kuwait (1991)

Fall of the Berlin Wall (1989)
George H.W. Bush elected president (1988)
Challenger space shuttle explosion (1986)

1990 **INTERNET**
1990-2010

Sally Ride is first American woman in space (1983)
Charles and Diana wed (1981)
Ronald Reagan elected president (1980)
John Lennon murdered (1980)
Mt. St. Helens erupts in Washington state (1980)
Iran Hostage Crisis (1979-1981)
Camp David Peace Accords (1978)
Jimmy Carter elected president (1976)

COMPUTER and CELLPHONE **1980**
1980-2000

Vietnam War ends (1975)
Richard Nixon resigns after Watergate scandal (1974)
Abortion legalized (1973)
Watergate scandal (1972)

Woodstock music festival (1969)
Man lands on the moon (1969)
Robert Kennedy and Martin Luther King assassinated (1968)

1970 **CABLE TELEVISION**
1970-1990

Civil Rights Act (1964)
John F. Kennedy assassinated (1963)
Cuban Missile Crisis (1962)
Berlin Wall constructed (1961)
Yuri Gagarin is first man in space (1961)
John F. Kennedy elected president (1960)

GAMER **1960**
1960-1980

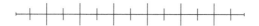

Chapter Ten

Gamer

"People [who] grew up playing this stuff are now paying attention to it and we don't think twice about it. We don't think these games are just for kids. We don't think these video games are destroying the fabric of youth. For us, it's just like music, it's just like TV, it's just like film. It's a part of life."
David Kushner, author of *Masters of Doom*

BIRTH YEARS: 1960–1980
"Coming of Age" Years: 1970–2005
Primary Tech Event: Challenger Explosion
Strauss-Howe Archetype: Nomad
Generation Personality: Recessive/Pessimistic
Iconic Generation Representatives: Princess Diana and Michael Jordan

Historical Influencing Events in Youth and Young Adulthood:
Vietnam, Man on the moon, Kent State, Watergate, Iran hostages, Ronald Reagan, Challenger explosion, End of Cold War, O.J. Simpson, Columbine, 9-11 terrorist attacks, Hurricane Katrina

---

No generation in history has received more bad press than the batch of children born between 1960 and 1980.

Originally labeled "baby busters," this cadre of kids was also framed as a "boomerang" or "new lost" generation. Sociologists Neil Howe and William Strauss originally pushed for the cursed and quirky "13th Generation."[285] Thankfully, that one didn't last. The name that finally stuck like napalm was borrowed from the title of a 1991 Douglas Coupland novel.[286]

But his term was just as ambiguous.

Generation X.

Depending on the source, the "X" means illiterate or promiscuous or "crossed off" (illegitimate) or "knocked out" (incoherent). The "X" is also an "unknown variable...or a desire not to be defined."[287] It's true that *some* in this generation reflected *some* of these characteristics at *certain* points, but is it a compelling, complete label for an entire cohort...or just reflective of one novelist's perspective in 1991?

The truth is out there...claimed the ironically named *X-Files*...so let's explore it using the cultural metaphors that defined them.

Bad To The Bone

As children, Generation X were often described as *bad news bears*. As teens, they were viewed as *breakfast club* delinquents bent on *risky business*. In young adulthood, they were tattooed grunge *freaks and geeks* seeking nirvana. They were the first generation to be legally aborted.[288] Many were left alone in day cares. Still more arrived home after school to empty houses (latchkey kids). For many Xers, their parents ignored, abused, and even abandoned them...and then divorced at record rates.[289] Generally, Gen X was promoted as the "dumb" generation or a youth "nation at risk" (thanks to a 1983 Reagan commission education report).[290] Of course, that wasn't really news. Ever since sociologists, educators, community leaders, and demographers started tracking this class of kids, there had been alarming reports, cultural condemnations, and futile fearmongering.

---

*"Let's face it, we're afraid of our children these days.
We're scared to death of them."*
Alex Williams, district attorney[291]

*"They don't even seem to know how to dress, and they're
almost unschooled in how to look in different settings."*
Paul Hirsch, sociologist[292]

"Students had great difficulty expressing even one substantive thought."
1988 National Assessment of Educational Progress report[293]

"It's incredible how little they know. There's almost a total lack of knowledge."
David Warren, professor[294]

The media didn't help Gen X's tarnished image.

They were also portrayed as *Rosemary* babies, children of the corn, *Exorcist* kids, and *Goonies*. They were *dazed and confused* "singles" with jaded *reality bites* attitudes. The nicer ones were clerks, top guns, geeks, freaks, and nerds looking for revenge. All they wanted was a day off like *Ferris Bueller*, to hang at *Empire Records*, watch *Wayne's World*, and play video games. More clear-minded folk saw these films as *pulp fiction*, but most still wondered *what was eating Gilbert Grape*?

The kids were *not* all right. The proof was in the piercings and tattoos.

"I see the whole concept of Generation X implies that everyone has lost hope."
Alanis Morissette

Gen X boys pushed all sorts of fashion buttons. They wore their baseball caps backwards, sported skinheads, mullets, and mohawks. They untucked their shirts. They wore ripped, baggy, bleached jeans that hung low. They donned heavy metal leathers. The girls dressed like Madonna and Cyndi Lauper. Bright colors. Perms. Fishnet stockings and fingerless gloves.

Gen X epitomized a bluesy George Thorogood tune: *bad to the bone*. Crack cocaine addiction, suicides, and alcoholism skyrocketed.[295] AIDS was the new fear.[296] Gen Xers took raunchy spring break getaways, ditched school, and skipped church.[297] They were grounded, sent to detention, and incarcerated (causing one cultural analyst to label them the "Jail generation").[298] Gen Xers embraced cohabitation, open marriages, homosexuality and other alternative lifestyles. They listened to heavy metal, grunge, and gangsta rap. And a lot of Xers got tattoos and piercings…including the *good* kids. Even Nancy Reagan couldn't get them to "just say no."

Naturally, parents, teachers, and pastors despised this cultural unraveling. The societal consequences were a clear and present danger, most notably in self-esteem. Social historians Neil Howe and William Strauss observed how Gen X was "cursed with the lowest collective self-esteem of any youth generation in living memory."[299]

Maybe they were "bad to the bone."

Or maybe *not*.

The problem? These dumb, confused, and rebellious kids didn't stay that way. In fact, most grew up to be hard-working, street smart, straight-shooting tax payers with college educations, mortgages, and 2.5 kids. Most of them weren't bad apples. Many Gen Xers changed the world.

Maybe they weren't as dumb or as lazy as critics suggested. Maybe they possessed mad skills for a unique time in American history. This cohort of kids would be the last to dial a telephone and the first to log on, download, and uplink. They would engineer the digital revolution and pioneer mobile, wireless, visual, and Internet technologies that most of us now take for granted. It's a generation that produced or first adopted:

- Google, Amazon, eBay, Wikipedia, MySpace, Friendster, Twitter, Wikileaks, and the Netscape browser
- Blogging, bulletin boards, chat rooms, and texting

- VCRs, video game consoles, camcorders, compact discs, DVDs, and DVRs
- Personal computers for uses other than word processing
- GPS, USB, MP3, MOV, JPEG, and PDF
- Email, e-commerce, e-banking, and online education

So maybe they aren't what we dubbed them. Maybe they're not really a Generation X.

Instead this generation has *game*.

They are the *Gamer* generation.

Now there's a label that sticks and says *something*. It also reflects a video game technology that wired this group of kids for life. Nearly every person in the Gamer generation played video games at some point. From *Pong* and *Pac-Man* to *Myst* and *Candy Crush*. You could call them true *Guitar Heroes*.

"Video games are actually the training wheels for computer literacy. I know of no programmers—zero—that are not game players."
Nolan Bushnell

In reality, the Gamer label reflects a more positive, powerful, and productive side to this generation. It's a name that definitely fits their formative "coming of age" years: 1970 to 2005. During this thirty-five-year period—from the "bloop, bloop, bloop" of *Pong* (1972) to the experiential tennis play of the Wii entertainment systems (2006)—the Gamers matured into a fairly respectable, albeit still cynical and jaded, generation. Gamers are the middle children generation. They're that "Jan Brady" generation: stuck in the middle between the gorgeous "Marcia" Television generation (1940–1960) and the precocious "Cindy" Personal Computer generation (1980–2000).

"In the next twenty years, the person who is in the White House will have played 'Super Mario Brothers' and what

will that mean for the way that they think about policy or
resource distribution or think about problem-solving."
Justin Hall, Managing Editor, GameGirlAdvance.com

———————

As with the late Space generation members, the Gamers have faced the worst of America's economic troubles—and usually at a moment when it was least convenient. The Great Recession in the late 2000s proved particularly harsh. The Gamers lost more jobs than any other generation in that period, and many of those jobs never returned. As a result, they also lost their homes, savings, careers, and retirements. It's why the Gamer generation carries a cultural chip on their shoulder. They played by the rules, made the expected moves, took appropriate risks, and then suddenly… "game over."

The Gamers voted heavily for "change" in fellow Gamer Barack Obama. Unfortunately, the politics in D.C. were driven by the same older generation that stiffed them in the Great Recession. President Obama couldn't completely fix the mess. Its why Gamers then voted, more than any other generation, for an outsider named Donald Trump.[300] They've always had an "Alex P. Keaton" conservative streak.[301] Reagan was their first president. Donald Trump promised to *drain the swamp* and *make America great again*—an "extended play" message that resonated with many Gamers.

They've been counting on somebody to make things right since they were computing math problems on pocket calculators. For the Gamer generation, calculators were the first handheld gaming machines. Besides math, there were word games on those calculators too. If you typed "07734" and turned it upside-down, it read "hello." You could even create off-color words ("8008"). It's how Gamer nerds got their revenge.

———————

"The point was to play around and mess with it, keep trying
until you figure out how to find the key to the castle, so to
speak. That's the way we approach technology."
Peter Rojas, co-founder, Gizmodo and Engadget

———————

The Gamers had *game* back then…and they still do today.

THE HISTORY OF VIDEO GAMES

1980

1958: Higinbothan/Dvorak invent "Tennis for Two"
1961: Steve Russell creates "Space War"
1967: Ralph Baer releases first "pong" game
1972: "Pong" video game debuts
1977: Atari begins selling a home gaming console
1980: Namco debuts "Pac-Man"
1981: Nintendo releases "Donkey Kong"

1990

1982: Commodore 64 home computer debuts
1985: Nintendo releases NES with "Super Mario Bros."
1989: Nintendo releases Game Boy with "Tetris"
1989: The Sega Genesis gaming system debuts
1992: First-person shooter game: "Wolfenstein 3D"
1993: "Doom," "NBA Jam" and "Myst" debut

2000

1994: Sony PlayStation is released
1997: "Grand Theft Auto" debuts
2000: "The Sims" debuts
2001: Microsoft releases XBox
2001: Nintendo premieres the GameCube system
2003: Activision debuts "Call of Duty"

2010

2005: "Guitar Hero" debuts
2006: Nintendo releases Wii interactive game
2007: Apple iPhone unleashes new mobile gaming era
2009: "Angry Birds" & "Words With Friends" released
2012: "Candy Crush" is released
2017: "Fortnight" debuts

Play The Game

The genesis of gaming originated in a man who helped create the atom bomb.

The first electronic digital computers were built following World War II and many of these early computers incorporated games for training, research, or demonstration. Consequently, it didn't take long for bored technicians to innovate the first computerized game of checkers[302] and tic-tac-toe.[303] Boys just want to have fun, too.

And that's where William Higinbotham and Robert Dvorak come in. They got the ball rolling (literally) for gaming technology. Their 1958 *Tennis for Two* was the first game to employ a moving image. However, Higinbotham, one of the scientists who developed the atom bomb, saw no long-term use for his game and eventually dismantled it. Three years later, an MIT student named Steve "Slug" Russell invented the first interactive video game: *Space War*.[304] Originally priced at $120,000, its sales were predictably scant. Still, the invention put "Slug" Smith on a computer scientist career path. His work eventually moved him to Washington state. That's where he met and mentored a young Bill Gates and Paul Allen.

For most of the 1960s, primitive video games were consigned to computer programming elites in America's best universities. But by 1970, the price of a "mini-computer" was now under $10,000 and the promise of an arcade game was within reach. Coin-operated pinball games were introduced in the 1930s and proved cheap entertainment in bars and drugstores. By the late 1960s, arcade games like *Periscope* and *Speedway* were moneymakers.

A young engineer named Nolan Bushnell had played Russell's *Space War* game back in college and now wanted to create an electronic video game for arcade use. However, his first attempt—*Computer Space*—failed miserably due to its complex gameplay. Bushnell needed something that regular folk would play. Something fun and "blooping" *easy*.

Meanwhile, another engineer named Ralph Baer feverishly worked to develop a home video game system. The images and gameplay were simple, but the technology for home use was also proving complex. In 1967, Baer added a third moving spot and a "ping pong" game was created. Five years later, the Odyssey system was finally marketed to U.S. homes. It included the first ever gun game. Ultimately, the Odyssey showed promise, although its sales never caught fire.

That same year, Bushnell and computer engineer Ted Dabney partnered to form Atari. Bushnell had seen the Odyssey, particularly the table tennis game. He felt it was a viable contender for a full-size arcade video game. Atari rolled out *Pong* in the fall of 1972, and it was an immediate cultural smash. Everybody wanted to play *Pong*. The arcade game did two things the Odyssey game did not: faster ball play and score-keeping. Oh, and it was "blooping" *fun* to play!

"You just can't fathom that this innocuous black and white ball bouncing back and forth is going to change the world, but sometimes you get some happy surprises."
Nolan Bushnell

The gaming era had begun.

Early Gamer kids couldn't get enough of *Pong*. From bowling alleys to shopping malls to taverns, *Pong* video screens and "bloop, bloop, bloop" sounds lit up adolescent imaginations. The two-player nature of the game created something else fresh: interactive gaming. We forget how the Gamer generation matured within communal game play contexts. Video games were best played with friends.

The Gamer generation is also the first generation to interact with digital technology for *pleasure*. It's why they're called "gamers."

Of course, Odyssey wasn't happy with *Pong's* success. Ralph Baer sued Nolan Bushnell and Atari for copyright violations. Atari settled the case and two years later launched its own home television version of *Pong*, helped by a sweetheart partnership with Sears. However, the Odyssey still couldn't compete. Atari was developing new games with better computer techs and engineers. One of those early Atari hires was Steve Jobs (who let his friend Steve Wozniak tag along). They created the popular *Breakout* game. Eventually, the Atari 2600 home console system was released, featuring gaming cartridges to easily switch games. Initially, the 2600 system failed miserably. So much so that it cost Nolan Bushnell his job. Warner Communications had purchased Atari with hopes of big financial returns. Expectations were high, and Bushnell failed to deliver. His firing from Atari didn't bother him though. He just served up a different American institution: Chuck E. Cheese pizzerias.

Pac-Man Fever

By 1977, arcade gamers were growing bored. Pool and pinball were still royalty in barrooms and bowling alleys. The movie of the year was *Star Wars*. Tennis was okay, but Gamers now itched to battle aliens in space. Meanwhile, a Japanese gaming company known as Taito was looking to invade the American market.

Enter *Space Invaders*.

Like *Pong*, the game was an instant arcade hit. It was the first video game to feature multiple targets, background music, and the ability to record a high score. Its addictive gameplay launched *Space Invaders* into the stratosphere. Not to be outdone, the empire of Atari struck back with *Asteroids* (1979).[305] Soon, other space-themed video games emerged: *Galaxian*,[306] *Missile Command*,[307] *Defender*,[308] and *Galaga*.[309] However, it was the double invasion of the joystick snatchers named *Space Invaders* and *Asteroids* that forever ended the pinball star.

The golden age of video games was here.

In 1980 the first true gaming celebrity emerged: a Japanese sensation known as *Pac-Man* (Namco).[310] *Pac-Man* literally devoured the competition. Originally titled "Puck Man" in Japan, the moniker was changed for American audiences for fear that vandals might have too much fun with that first letter. The attraction to *Pac-Man* was its simple gameplay that proved equally hard to master. It was the first time a character in a video game became a cultural superstar. Pac-Man's name was licensed. He had his own Top 40 song,[311] animated television series, and even made the cover of *Time* magazine. Of course, no Mr. *Pac-Man* is complete without a *Ms. Pac-Man*.[312] She rolled out two years later to the delight of fans and remains one of history's highest-grossing video games.

1980: Pac-Man (Namco)
1980: Centipede (Atari)
1980: Missile Command (Atari)
1981: Donkey Kong (Nintendo)
1982: Q*Bert (Atari)

1982: Dig Dug (Namco)
1982: Pole Position (Namco)
1982: Ms. Pac-Man (Midway Manufacturing)
1982: Robotron 2984 (Vid Kidz)
1982: Pitfall! (Activision)
1983: Star Wars (Atari)
1983: Bomberman (Hudson Soft)
1984: Tetris (Aleksei Pazhitnov)

A King Named Kong

Originally founded in 1889 to market handmade Japanese playing cards, Nintendo (which means "leave luck to heaven") eventually became an electronics juggernaut headquartered in Kyoto, Japan.[313] In 1981, Nintendo unleashed *Donkey Kong* upon the American market—a game that quickly climbed the ladder as an arcade favorite. The game featured a man named "Mario" who tries to rescue a distressed damsel from a giant ape (who loves to roll and toss barrels to keep Mario off balance). This video game was the first to create a "story" in its action, with sequels (*Donkey Kong Jr.* and *Donkey Kong 3*) and knockoffs (*Crazy Kong, Killer Gorilla*).

In the 1980s, the Gamer generation was fully immersed in video gaming. Arcade machines gobbled quarters like a rabid *Pac-Man*. By 1982, Gamers had spent 75,000 hours and 20 billion dollars on video games.[314] For years Atari had sold a home gaming console that featured many Nintendo favorites like *Space Invaders*. The Atari 2600—which debuted in 1977—made the company a fortune, but not all was well. Disgruntled, underpaid Atari game engineers started an exodus. One group of engineers formed Activision and did nothing but create games. Meanwhile, Mattel joined the crowded console market with Intellivision while Magnavox still shopped its Odyssey 2. Coleco focused on handheld devices like the popular "Electronic Quarterback" and miniature versions of arcade games.

But the brain drain of engineers leaving Atari eventually proved fatal. In 1982, the company needed a new star and that particular year everyone was hooked on a certain cute alien. Atari banked its last dollar on Steven Spielberg and bought the rights to produce an *E.T.* video game. Unfortunately, the venture proved a massive failure. Poorly engineered and terrible to play, most of the *E.T.* games were returned. Atari eventually trucked boxes of unsold and returned cartridges into the New Mexico desert, dumped them into a hole, and topped it with concrete. Atari was done.

The whole home market was officially in the dumps.[315]

It was the perfect time for a revolution.

A King's Quest And An Apple

One of the early defectors from Atari was Steve Jobs. He left in the late 1970s to launch his own company with a vision to make the computer *personal*. The success of his Apple II and a rival company's Commodore PET paved the way for home computers in the 1980s. The Commodore 64 was particularly popular with gamers, who could use their Atari joysticks with the machine.[316] In 1984, Apple released the highly-anticipated MacIntosh.[317] Between the Mac and Commodore 64, computer video gameplay evolved quickly with passionate game developers.

Trip Hawkins was one such creator. He left Apple in 1982 to launch Electronic Arts, a sports-driven video gaming company that's now become the second-largest in America.[318] Ken and Roberta Williams helped develop the first "mystery" video games. Early "mystery" games were text-based but Roberta envisioned a "visual" platform and commissioned her husband to make her dream a reality. The result was *Mystery House*—an Apple II game. Eventually, the Robertsons founded Sierra Entertainment and produced the classic adventure game *King's Quest*.[319] This latter game was unique in that it allowed the gamer to manipulate the character inside the game and personalize the story.

1984: Duck Hunt (Nintendo)

1985: Super Mario Bros. (Nintendo EAD)

1985: Oregon Trail (Minnesota Ed Computing Consortium)

1986: The Legend of Zelda (Nintendo)

1986: Outrun (Sega)

1987: Street Fighter (Capcom)

1987: Final Fantasy (Squaresoft)

1987: Tecmo Bowl (Tecmo)

1987: Punch-Out (Nintendo)

1988: John Madden Football (EA Sports)
1988: Galaxy Force (Sega)
1989: Simcity (Maxis)
1989: Teenage Mutant Ninja Turtles (Konami)
1989: Final Fight (Capcom)
1991: Sonic the Hedgehog (Sonic Team)
1991: The Legend of Zelda: A Link to the Past (Nintendo)
1991: Civilization (Microprose)
1992: Mortal Kombat (Midway)
1992: Super Mario Kart (Nintendo)

Beyond computers, it was the Japanese who truly revolutionized video gaming.

Despite a terrible market for home video games, Nintendo fearlessly dived into the home console market in 1985. And they employed the help of an old friend name Mario. Finished with dodging barrels by apes, Mario got a plumbing job with his brother Luigi and the *Super Mario Brothers* game was born. This exciting new game was part of the Nintendo Entertainment System (NES) console that featured yet another old friend: a gun game called *Duck Hunt*. The Nintendo gaming suite, with redesigned console and controls, quickly became a bestseller.[320]

With the home market revived, Sega also jumped in. The company originally serviced arcades and sold pinball machines, but in 1983 released its Sega SG-1000,[321] a machine loaded with well-worn versions of old arcade games.

Nintendo's success with *Super Mario Brothers* sent them searching for a new gaming star and they soon found it...*in Russia*. A Soviet mathematician named Alexey Pajitnov noodled a new video game while at work and shared it with friend. Unfortunately, his communist bosses also enjoyed his new game. So much so that they bought ten years' worth of rights. Then they shopped the game around the world much to Pajitnov's dislike. That's how Nintendo found this addicting game of falling boxes called *Tetris*.[322] Nintendo eventually used *Tetris* to anchor its new Game Boy handheld gaming system in 1989. The Gamer generation, now between nine and twenty-nine, made these portable devices an instant hit. *Tetris* was popular, easy, and fun to play.

In 1989, Sega also released the Genesis gaming system with a warning that "Genesis does what Nintendon't." Like all great games, Sega used "Sonic the Hedgehog" as its mascot and ended every commercial with the one-word punch: "Sega!"

Blood And Doom

In the 1990s, the home market was now fueled by personal computing games that operated using disks. These disks held much more technical information and opened new frontiers in game design. One game that proved particularly popular was the immersive, interactive game called *Myst*. In *Myst*, people could literally get lost in surroundings that looked *real*.[323] Other computing games like *Dune* and *Sim City*[324] were equally popular. Many of these computer games, like the historical *Oregon Trail*, were also educational and that's a fact we shouldn't overlook. The Gamer generation, after all, was the first to grow up playing video games *to learn*.

1993: Doom (ID Software)

1993: NBA Jam (Midway)

1993: Myst (Cyan)

1994: Tekken (Namco)

1994: The Need for Speed (Electronic Arts)

1995: Wipeout (Psygnosis)

1996: Tomb Raider (Core Design)

1996: Crash Bandicoot (Naughty Dog)

1997: Goldeneye 007 (Rare)

1997: Final Fantasy VII (Square)

1997: Gran Turismo (Polys Entertainment)

1997: Age of Empires (Ensemble Studios)

1997: Grand Theft Auto (DMA Design)

1998: Half-Life (Valve)

1999: Medal of Honor (Dreamworks Interactive)

1999: Silent Hill (Konami)

1999: Tony Hawk's Pro Skater (Neversoft)

But in the 1990s video games also took a dark turn.

The gameplay became more bloody, violent, and intense…and it seemed the Gamer generation was its target audience. From *Street Fighter* to *Mortal Kombat*, video games received a black eye in the national press. The rise of first-person shooter games like *Wolfenstein 3D* (1992) and *Doom* (1993) were notably violent and bloody.[325] These first-person shooter games allowed players to completely immerse themselves in the game, looking down the barrel of their own gun to kill the enemy, which was often another human player. The multi-player capabilities of *Doom* were tagged "death-matching." The bloody gameplay and overall violence caught the attention of lawmakers and instigated a 1993 congressional hearing led by Senator Joseph Lieberman.[326] The result was a ratings system for video games, but even that didn't stop the violence. Games like *Grand Theft Auto*, *Silent Hill*, *Soldier of Fortune*, *Call of Duty*, and *Manhunt* routinely used R-rated violence for their storyboards.

Throughout the 1990s, the home console wars were duked out between Sega, Sony, Nintendo, and a newcomer named Microsoft. Sega was the first to introduce a CD-ROM drive. Sony PlayStations remained the most affordable, and could handle 3-D graphics. They also featured popular games like *Tomb Raider* and *Tekken*. Its PlayStation 2 model even played CD music and DVD movies. Microsoft entered the fray with Xbox and an exclusive new first-person shooter game called *Halo*. Nintendo released the GameCube, which was web-connected.

By 2004, more than half of all Americans (145 million strong) played video games. And most of Gamer generation still does. But they don't just play games on their televisions and computers. Today's Gamers play on smart phones and tablets too. From *Candy Crush* to *Angry Birds* to *Words With Friends*, game apps are hot. The video game industry rakes in more money than any other entertainment business, including Hollywood.

———

"There's a perception in the game industry that games are in their infancy. We've achieved a lot but it's far from where it's going to be."
Jane Pinkard (Editor-in-Chief, GameGirlAdvance.com)

———

The Gamer generation was grooved by video games, which became increasingly interactive, immersive, and image-soaked over the years. Consequently, that's how Gamers now process information and experience truth. If you want to communicate, teach, lecture or preach, it's critical to talk their gamer language. Other institutions are certainly doing it. The U.S. military has long used video games to train soldiers for combat.[327] Gamers love to *get in the game*. In a first-person shooter video game called *Quake*, up to sixteen people can play together via the Internet.[328] But that's nothing compared to *Everquest*, an online fantasy video game that's created a 24/7/365 virtual world where tens of thousands participate.[329]

The back end of the Gamer generation's "coming of age" years happened in the mid-2000s. Two significant new games appeared at that time that further evolved the gaming community, who were now mostly parents: *Guitar Hero* and the Nintendo Wii. *Guitar Hero* allowed players to don a plastic guitar and play along with classic rock tunes.[330] The Nintendo Wii was even more immersive. Using a wireless controller, players could hit a golf ball, baseball, or tennis ball. These games opened a new frontier for video gaming.[331]

2000: The Sims (Maxis/Edge of Reality)
2001: Devil May Cry (Capcom)
2001: Halo: Combat Evolved (Bungie)
2002: Mafia (Illusion Softworks)
2003: Call of Duty (Activision)
2003: Manhunt (Rockstar North)
2003: Prince of Persia: The Sands of Time (Ubisoft)
2004: World of Warcraft (Blizzard Entertainment)
2005: Star Wars: Battlefront II (Pandemic Studios)
2005: God of War (SCE Santa Monica Studio)
2005: Guitar Hero (Harmonix)
2006: Wii Sports (Nintendo)

Don't tell these Gamers they don't have game. They do. As they now face mid-life wrinkles and gray hair, this generation continues to play to its last quarter. Like Tommy in The Who's "Pinball Wizard," they are fiercely focused on finishing well, even if the odds are firmly stacked against them.

The truth is, for the Gamer generation, life has always played out like a fast-paced killer video game. And whether it's a *Final Fantasy* or just a *Fortnite*, this generation ain't going down without a fight. It's not "game over" yet.

A TIMELINE OF TECHNOLOGICAL EVENTS (1961–1970):

- 1961: Russian Yuri Gagarin orbits the earth. Alan Shepard makes first U.S. space flight. Atlas computer installed at Harwell. First in-flight movie shown on TWA airlines. Electric toothbrush introduced. Niagra Falls starts to produce hydroelectric power. First quasar is discovered. IBM introduces Selectric typewriter "Golfball."

- 1962: U.S. spacemen (Glenn, Carpenter, and Schirra) orbit separately. Telstar satellite launched from Cape Canaveral. Mariner 2 launched to probe Venus. Fossil algae "revived" by Russian scientist. Telstar relays first live transatlantic television signal. Television sets in 90 percent of U.S. households. First use of silicone breast implants. Notable invention: LED.

- 1963: Anti-xi-zeno discovered. Russian Valentina Tereshkova becomes first woman astronaut. Gordon Cooper completes twenty-two orbits in Atlas rocket. Friction welding invented. Artificial heart used to take over patient's blood circulation during heart surgery. AT&T introduces touch tone phones. U.S. introduces zip codes. Notable inventions: cassette tape, pull tab can.

- 1964: Fundamental particle omega-minus discovered. New theory of gravitation postulated (Hoyle and Marlikar). Ranger VII produces first photographic close-ups of the moon. BASIC computer code created. World's first high-speed rail network opens in Japan. Sony introduces home video recorder. First driverless train runs in London. Notable inventions: computer mouse, bubble wrap.

- 1965: Soviet astronaut Leonov exits spacecraft and floats for ten minutes. U.S. astronaut Ed White repeats the feat for twenty-one minutes. First

French satellite launched. Rare earth complexes first separated by gas chromatography. First flight around the world over both poles. Notable inventions: optical disc, hypertext, respirator.

- 1966: Plastic arteries implanted leading to an artificial heart inside thirty-seven-year-old woman. Soviet spacecraft Luna 9 makes soft landing on moon. U.S. spacecraft Surveyor I does the same and transmits over 11,000 television images of the moon. Color television becomes popular. First disposable diaper introduced. U.S. has 78 million registered cars. Notable inventions: Kevlar, fiber optics.

- 1967: Biochemists produce synthetic version of DNA. China explodes its first hydrogen bomb. World's first human heart transplant performed. Cryosurgery developed to help Parkinson's disease. 100 million U.S. telephones in service. U.S. has 74 nuclear-powered submarines in operation. First ATM goes into service. Pulsars are discovered. Boeing 737 makes maiden flight. Notable invention: pocket calculator.

- 1968: U.S. Surveyor 7 spacecraft successfully lands on the moon. First manned Apollo (7) mission launched. Intelsat 3A, first of new series of communication satellites, launched. U.S. has 78 million television sets. Emergency 9-1-1 telephone service begins. U.S. explodes hydrogen bomb. Notable invention: airbags.

- 1969: The Concorde supersonic aircraft makes first test flight. Apollo 11 lands on the moon and Neil Armstrong becomes first man to walk on the moon. Two Mariner space probes return photos of Mars. Creation of ARPANET. UNIX developed at Bell Labs. Boeing 747 jet debuts. 225 million telephones in service worldwide (114 million in U.S.). First transplant of human eye. Seiko sells first quartz watch. Notable invention: battery-powered smoke detector.

- 1970: First complete synthesis of a gene. Soviet Venera 7 lands on Venus. Nuclear-powered heart pacemakers implanted to correct a condition called "heart block." 150-inch reflecting telescope at Kitt Peak (AZ) Observatory completed. An estimated 231 million television sets in use around the world. First jumbo jet goes into service. Concorde makes first supersonic flight. First remote-controlled robot introduced.

INFLUENTIAL BIRTHS IN THE GAMER GENERATION:

Politicians:

- Sarah Palin (1964)
- Ted Cruz (1970)

Business, Education, Athletes and Other Leaders:

- Michael Jordan (1963), basketball player
- Joel Osteen (1963), religious leader
- Jeff Bezos (1964), entrepreneur
- Brett Favre (1969), football player
- Tony Hawk (1968), skateboarder
- Elon Musk (1971), entrepreneur
- Peyton Manning (1976), football player
- Kobe Bryant (1978), basketball player

Entertainers:

- Bono (1960), rock singer
- George Clooney (1961), actor
- Eddie Murphey (1961), actor
- Jeff Probst (1962), game show host
- Russell Crowe (1964), actor
- Kurt Cobain (1967–1994), rock singer
- Jimmy Kimmel (1967), television host
- Tim McGraw (1967), country singer
- Jennifer Lopez (1969), R&B singer
- Jay-Z (1969), rapper
- River Phoenix (1970–1993), actor
- Tupac Shakur (1971–1996), rapper
- Eminem (1972), rapper
- Leonardo DiCaprio (1974), actor
- Kanye West (1977), rapper
- Heath Ledger (1979–2009), actor
- Macaulay Culkin (1980), actor

Authors/Artists:
- J.K. Rowling (1965), author
- Guy Fieri (1968), chef

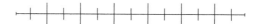

Chapter Eleven
Cable Television

"I think that cable TV is a great venue to do something interesting."
Bob Odenkirk

BIRTH YEARS: 1970–1990
"Coming of Age" Years: 1980–2015
Primary Tech Event: VCR/DVR
Strauss-Howe Archetype: Nomad-Hero
Generation Personality: Recessive/Pessimistic
Iconic Generation Representatives: Tom Brady and Joanna Gaines

Historical Influencing Events in Youth and Young Adulthood:
Iran hostages, Ronald Reagan, Challenger explosion, End of Cold War,
O.J. Simpson, Columbine, Monica Lewinsky-Bill Clinton, 9-11 terrorist attacks,
Hurricane Katrina, Great Recession, Barack Obama

Television changed the world.

As a medium, it completely rearranged how we communicated, learned, socialized, and were entertained. Television moved us from a word-centered modern world to a visually centered post-modern culture. It changed how we received and processed current events. It altered how we experienced live sports. It re-imagined the direction and place of visual entertainment. Until television arrived, a person had to *go* to a movie house, grange hall, church building, school room, or community center to watch a film, see a play, view a speaker, or experience a concert. Television brought visual entertainment *home*. News was now delivered visually through breaking bulletins, nightly newscasts, and magazine-style shows. Religion now arrived in televised Billy Graham crusades and Pat Robertson prayer circles. Pop music was now distributed via Dick Clark dance floors, Ed Sullivan variety shows, *Saturday Night Live*, and MTV.

---

*"Television is like the American toaster, you push
the button and the same thing pops up every time."*
Alfred Hitchcock

Television proved a post-modern, mega-technology that evolved a new cultural language communicated through images. It was so "mega" that three generations—Television, Gamer, and Cable—were influenced by its technological imprint. As we've already observed, the emergence of television and video gaming were important technologies for the Boom and Gen X generations. However, what gets lost in this conversation is the significant influence of *cable* television, particularly upon the kids of the 1980s and 1990s.

After all, if we overlook cable television, technological history would tell a different story.

That's because until cable arrived television had its *limits*.

"The perfect date for me would be staying at home, making a big picnic in bed, eating Wotsits and cookies while watching cable television."
Kim Kardashian

Yes, the technology was improving. The innovations of remote controls, color, better sound, and reception were wonderful enhancements. Television programming also greatly evolved, some for the better and others for the worse. There's a world of difference between *Father Knows Best* in the 1950s and *All in the Family* in the 1970s—not just in how the family is portrayed but also in how these shows were produced. In 1970, American television was confined to three big network channels (four, if you count PBS) that controlled the programming pot. Consumers only saw what network brass and their sponsors wanted viewed. Movies were heavily edited and censored for broadcast. News was clipped to protect the powerful. Some quiz shows were rigged for ratings. Controversial (and popular) television shows—particularly politically smart ones like *The Smothers Brothers*—were unexpectantly canceled. In general, the big networks targeted the "middles" of America culture: a white, male-dominated, married-with-kids, middle-class audience. Most of the shows reflected this template until the late 1960s.

The Day Television Lost Control

Live sports were equally subjected to strict programming rules. This was certainly true when the famous *Heidi* game was played between the New York Jets and Oakland Raiders (November 17, 1968).[332] Broadcasted by NBC, the game was viewed as a delightful revenge match from the previous year, a contest considered "one of the most vicious in Jet history."[333] The bitter rivalry featured two elite quarterbacks: the flamboyant playboy Joe Namath and the cool field general Daryle Lamonica. To say these two teams hated each other would be an understatement, and NBC salivated at the knowledge that sports fans would enthusiastically tune in. To sweeten the programming schedule that particular Sunday, NBC slated the popular children's film *Heidi* to immediately follow the game as a nightcap treat. On paper, it seemed a perfect idea. In reality, it proved a nightmare.

"When the Jets played the Raiders, it wasn't a rivalry. It was war."
Frank Ramos, Director of Public Relations, New York Jets

Between penalties and thrilling gameplay, the contest soon pushed the limits of its two-and-a-half-hour televised time allotment. It was the game that NFL fans wanted, and NBC executives needed. At halftime, the Raiders were winning 14-12. The game went back and forth until the final minute. With sixty seconds remaining, the Jets precariously clung to a narrow three-point lead, but the Raiders now had the ball. It was going to be a fantastic finish. However, it was also nearly 7 p.m. in the eastern time zone and that generated a problem for NBC executives. The *Heidi* movie was scheduled to start at 7 p.m. For most of the second half, NBC brass debated (and eventually decided) to delay *Heidi* to let the game finish. The only problem was that word never got to the supervisor of Broadcast Operations Control (who desperately tried to reach executives by phone). Consequently, as the 7 p.m. hour neared, NBC phone lines were jammed with inquiries from nervous football fans and impatient preteen girls waiting for *Heidi*.

The supervisor couldn't get through.

At 7 p.m., just as the Raiders received the kickoff for a desperate final march to victory, NBC Broadcast Operations Control cued the closing football theme music and switched to the start of *Heidi*. The NBC brass went nuts. They thought word had been relayed to let the game finish. Football fans also exploded in outrage. In reality, the decision only impacted those in the eastern half of the country, as viewers in the western U.S. stayed with the game. But all hell broke loose in huge eastern market cities, particularly those blindsided Jet fans in New York. In retrospect, it's probably better they never saw the ending. Amazingly, the Raiders scored not one, but two touchdowns in that final minute of play. Bob Valli, a reporter for the *Oakland Tribune*, penned, "Television missed one of football's most exciting and exhausting minutes of emotion. In that minute, Oakland fans saw despair turn to delirium."[334]

Unfortunately, NBC then made matters even worse.

As a public courtesy to jilted football fans, NBC posted a scrolling bulletin to report the Raiders had indeed won the game (since no one knew the outcome except those in the western U.S.). Unfortunately, NBC also chose to make *that* announcement during one of the most pivotal, emotional points in the entire movie. And now *Heidi* fans were ticked. The phones at NBC (and even local police departments) rang off the hook. It got so bad that NBC installed special "Heidi" phones to handle all the calls. There was even a very public apology.

In 1968, America was clearly coming apart at the seams.

The *Heidi* game was indicative of a wider cultural change that was happening. And to be fair, it also capped a hard, desperate year for the nation. Arguably, 1968 was a year to forget, if that was even possible. *Martin Luther King, Jr. and Bobby Kennedy were assassinated. Riots broke out at university campuses as well as the Democratic National Convention in Chicago. Forty-six Americans per day were dying in Vietnam, now considered a lost battle according to Walter Cronkite. Race wars tore apart urban neighborhoods while "black power" athletes sparked controversy at the Summer Olympics in Mexico City. Richard Nixon was narrowly elected in a heated contest.* Americans were on edge, weary, and desperate for some relaxation. All they wanted was a great football game. They just wanted to unwind.[335]

What they received was more agitation and fury.

Can You See Me Now?

But it wasn't just the current events that created problems for the medium. Television also had an image problem: *reception*. It was a serious limitation. After all, if you can't *watch* television, what use is it?

"Life doesn't imitate art, it imitates bad television."
Woody Allen

In the late 1960s, television was predominantly transmitted "over the air" and that meant television sets required antennae. Whether it was telescoping rods or rooftop spires, every television needed to be "tuned" for optimal reception. It helped if the skies were clear or nothing obstructed the signal. However, interference was a common problem. Rain and snow. Hills and trees. Buildings and landmarks. Some channels, particularly those of distance or low transmission outputs, created their own "weather" and were said to be "snowy." Neither the image nor the sound was clear. No matter how high the antenna or how much tinfoil a frustrated television junkie wrapped around the tips, nothing improved the clarity.

You can't watch what you can't see.

That's why cable television was so revolutionary.

This technological innovation created crystal-clear viewing that had no interference issues. Furthermore, it opened new specialized channels for movies, sports, news, music, and religion. Initial cable lineups had only a dozen channels, but even that paltry number was *four times* what most people had received with over-the-air transmissions. By 1990, the average cable company boasted a premium service featuring hundreds of channels.

And, surprisingly for some couch potato cynics, there *still* wasn't anything to watch.

For others there was *too much* to view.

Consequently, cable television helped to launch parallel television technology, like the remote control and video cassette recorder.[336] With so many channels from which to choose, a new American sport emerged: *channel surfing*. In the hands of certain individuals, most of them male, the television channeled a nonstop stream of visual entertainment. Of course, with all those options came the need to "time-shift" programming. No one could watch every channel at once. Consequently, the video cassette recorder allowed couch potatoes to cook their own television menu, watching what they wanted, *when* they wanted. Later, DVR technology permitted viewers to pause live television and then catch up when ready.

"I was a member of the VHS generation. I used to study movies as a kid because I had a VCR and could record a movie on HBO and just watch it repeatedly."
Derek Cianfrance

It was a whole new ball game in television.

Perhaps no American generation experienced the rise of this new medium more than the Cable Television generation (born 1970–1990). Cable television wasn't just a novelty or fad to these kids. It was a window to the world. It was a game changer in how all Americans viewed television. In fact, it's safe to say that without cable television, we might still be stuck with preempted *Heidi* games, manipulating tin-foiled antennas, and griping that there was "nothing good" to watch on our three network channels.

Cable television was a monumental leap forward in visual entertainment.

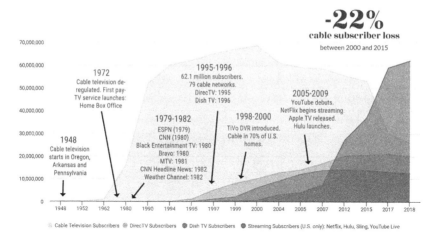

CABLE TELEVISION
The history, growth and decline of cable and satellite television

The Cable Television generation's "coming of age" years (1980 to 2015) mirror the meteoric rise, and now decline, of this media giant. The front end is framed by the emergence of cable news, sports, and music television—all revolutionary changes in how Americans watched television. Meanwhile, the back end marks the dominance of new streaming media that renders cable television obsolete. Many Americans started "cutting the cable" in 2015 and the writing is on the wall for both cable and home satellite television.[337] By 2030, some futurists predict, cable television will be extinct.[338]

Nevertheless, for thirty-five years, "must-see" television was driven by cable. What was produced on cable pushed the big networks (ABC, CBS, NBC, and, later, FOX) to produce edgier, better-written, entertaining content. MTV's *The Real World* carved relationship reality shows. Cable news dragged networks into a 24/7/365 news cycle. Documentaries on HBO, History, and A&E forced better storytelling and smarter dramas. Black Entertainment Television (BET), Telemundo, and Univision encouraged networks to launch more ethnic-centric programming. ESPN sparked better coverage of sports—from curling to soccer to basketball.

"Cable TV has become where the best actors, writers and directors have gone to work because they are allowed to do character-driven stories."
Kevin Spacey

The social history of the Cable Television generation is told by the channels it produced. From a Watergate scandal to Reagan's Iran-Contra hearings to Bill Clinton's impeachment, the Cable generation viewed politics through network lens that eventually camped left or right. The states were either blue or red. The players either a leftist deep state or a "vast right-wing conspiracy." The 24/7/365 nature of post-1980 news created a perfect cauldron for reality television. *Reagan's assassination attempt. The Challenger explosion. The fall of the Berlin wall. Operation Desert Storm. L.A. riots. O.J. Simpson. Waco and Ruby Ridge. Oklahoma City and Columbine. The tragic death of Princess Diana. The Monica Lewinsky-Bill Clinton affair. The terrorist attacks on 9-11. Katrina. The elections of Barack Obama and Donald Trump.* A simple survey of these unique events framed the psyche and soul of the Cable Television generation.

It's no wonder they're cynical, although decidedly less so than their Gamer peers.

That's because the 1980s and 1990s were better times for kids in America. The nation was in a better mood. Ronald Reagan had vowed to "make America great again" long before Donald Trump trademarked the phrase.[339] So, as "morning in America"[340] dawned in the mid 1980s, Americans were generally feeling happier and more hopeful. The Carter recession years were history. The economy improved for most families. Interest rates and unemployment fell.[341] Home prices rose.[342] Churches focused on specialized ministries to children and teens. Social and community organizations—from the YMCA to scouting programs—enjoyed a renaissance. Kids were more favorably viewed in film, music, and commentary. Cable television, video games, and computers gave children more entertainment options.

That doesn't mean every American enjoyed the prosperity of the Reagan/ Bush/Clinton years. Many were still being left behind or out. The welfare state widened, and homelessness expanded.[343] College tuition costs climbed, as did student loan debt.[344] With the escalation of home prices, renting (and rents) also skyrocketed.[345] Many Cable Television young adults found it difficult to buy a home until their 30s.

Nevertheless, more discretionary money was available for Cable generation kids to enjoy, and they spent it on everything from video games and skateboards to high-priced jeans and low-rider cars.

Plugging In The Cable

The cable television story begins in 1948 when Community Antenna Television (CATV) was developed for people who lived in the hills of Pennsylvania, Arkansas, and Oregon. Over-the-air signals were getting lost in the trees and coaxial cable provided a clear-cut path to better viewing. One enthusiastic appliance store owner in Tuckerman, AR advertised seventeen channels, from as far away as Memphis, and offered the service for only three bucks a month.[346] By the early 1950s, there were over 14,000 CATV subscribers.[347] Throughout the 1950s, cable television was a novelty. As translator towers were better positioned, the coverage of over-the-air transmissions improved. So much so that only those in rural locales couldn't access the signals. Cable television filled that gap, but since it provided channels that others already enjoyed for free "over the air," it was viewed as unnecessary.

NICKNAMES FOR TELEVISION:

Boob tube, idiot box, one-eyed monster, chatter box, electric babysitter, flicker box, home wrecker, magic screen, man's home companion, moron magnet, picture machine, squawk box, vidiot

---

But that would soon change.

In 1958, cable operators began to carry FM radio stations and "weather scans" for customers. By 1963, over 1,200 cable systems served more than one million American homes.[348] The rapid rise of cable television prompted the Federal Communications Commission to monitor, regulate, and even freeze development in various markets. Nevertheless, by the end of the 1960s, nearly four million homes were now wired for television (thanks to over 22,000 cable systems).[349]

The 1972 deregulation of cable is what freed the industry to revolutionize the world. Finally, cable systems could expand and grow. That same year, Charles Dolan and Gerald Levin of Sterling Manhattan Cable brought a new idea to the television world called *Home Box Office*. HBO was the first-ever pay television network. This innovation was assisted by NASA launching communication satellites in the 1960s. The ability to beam a transmission across the United States (not to mention the world) opened all sorts of possibilities.

Home Box Office initially enjoyed little attention for most of the 1970s. In fact, one early survey of potential subscribers found that 99 percent were opposed to paid television...*any kind* of paid television. Nevertheless, Dolan pushed his vision and finally found a cable television system in Allentown willing to carry his new movie channel. The first feature film on November 8, 1972 was *Sometimes a Great Notion* starring Paul Newman. There's irony in that title. "Sometimes a great notion" also sparks a cultural and technological revolution. Home Box Office would eventually prove everyone wrong and become the flagship channel of premium cable services across the United States. Currently, there are over a dozen specialized HBO "multi-plex" channels (comedy, family, Latino, and signature) and over 130 million subscribers around the world. Millions of people also subscribe to its streaming service, HBO Now.

Not bad for a man with a "great notion."

Windows To The World

Another man with vision was Ted Turner.

Turner lived in Atlanta and enjoyed baseball, particularly his hometown Braves. He also owned a local station that he decided to convert to a satellite station in 1975. The call letters for his station were WTCG which Turner promoted as "Watch This Channel Grow." And grow it did. WTCG carried Atlanta Braves and Hawks games, professional wrestling, syndicated television shows, and classic movies. WTCG would eventually be included in cable systems from coast to coast and emerge as the first national "superstation."[350] Turner launched another local Atlanta station called WTBS that mirrored the WTCG national feed. In 1979, these feeds blended formally as WTBS and a decade later became TBS.

But Turner's TBS was just the beginning.

On June 1, 1980, Ted launched the Cable News Network.[351] It was the first twenty-four-hour news channel and it revolutionized how Americans consumed current events. A second channel (CNN2) launched two years later but was eventually renamed CNN Headline News. Headline News (HLN) featured twenty-four hours of repeating half-hour broadcasts. Throughout the 1980s, CNN found increased traction among Americans hungry to get their news as it happened. In many ways, CNN did more to end the reign of the newspaper than the Internet. Web news was less filtered, but it wasn't more breaking in nature.

"Television news before this was stuff that had already happened. For the first time CNN brought the world to people in real time."
H.W. Brands

CNN's coverage of the 1991 Gulf War forever separated it from the networks. During "Operation Desert Storm," CNN had boots on the ground in Baghdad.

Americans received exclusive live coverage from the al-Rashid Hotel through the crack reporting of Bernard Shaw, John Holliman, and Peter Arnett. The "big three" news networks of NBC, CBS, and ABC couldn't compete as millions of Americans switched to CNN to watch live coverage. When the U.S. began bombing Baghdad (January 16, 1991), CNN was there with cameras rolling. Americans watched the bombs fall and explode only on CNN. It was the first time the nation experienced a war *live* from their *living* rooms.

"We began to realize that the best way to get a message to a foreign leader was to have the President go in the Rose Garden and make a statement because everybody was watching CNN."
James A. Baker III, former Reagan chief of staff

It was "must-see" television.

CNN (and cable television) made the world smaller in 1991. You couldn't get this news coverage "over the air" with an antenna. You needed to be hooked up and cable subscriptions continued to mushroom, particularly among early Cable Television generation young adults, now in their 20s.

CNN's coverage of the O.J. Simpson trial was also unprecedented. Even though another cable channel, Court TV, offered a gavel-to-gavel live feed of the trial, it was CNN that led the coverage. Millions of Americans tuned in to watch live courtroom drama of a football hero charged with murdering his wife. The suspense was further helped by Simpson's legal "dream team" defense.[352] CNN and Court TV also made California's district attorneys (Marsha Clark and Christopher Darden) and bit players like Mark Fuhrman, Judge Lance Alito, and Kato Kaelin into celebrities. Once again, the big networks couldn't compete.

CNN featured money advice from Lou Dobbs and introspective interviews by Larry King. But it was a hard-hitting political and social commentary show called *Crossfire* that revealed how America was dividing left and right. *Crossfire* featured opposing viewpoints on a variety of issues and had similarities to the long-running, high-brow *The McLaughlin Group* (PBS). Ironically, *Crossfire* almost didn't air.

Ted Turner vehemently opposed the idea, but eventually relented due to signed contractual agreements. *Crossfire* proved political commentary at its best and worst, revealing a growing rift between the left and right in the 1990s.[353] Eventually, *Crossfire* lost its appeal as similar shows like *Hannity and Colmes* (Fox News) and *Hardball* (MSNBC) peeled off audiences.

"I didn't do Cable News Network because someone told me it couldn't be done, I figured it was a very viable concept and I went ahead and did it… CNN was a breakthrough. It changed the whole world."
Ted Turner

CNN's commentary—originating in the liberal views of its founder Ted Turner—clearly positioned the channel to the political left. Meanwhile, the national network news also increasingly leaned to the left in the 1990s. With MSNBC's debut in 1996, the rift between the American left and right was growing clear and evident. The right-wing conservatives need their own voice.

Enter Fox News.

Fox did what CNN and MSNBC did, except from a conservative perspective. Founded in 1996 by media mogul Rupert Murdoch and masterminded by CEO Roger Ailes, a former GOP strategist, Fox News quickly gained traction among America's conservatives during the Clinton administration. Fox News featured headline and breaking news stories plus hour-long commentary shows. Early Fox News influencers were Bill O'Reilly's *The Factor* (1996–2017)[354] and *Your World with Neil Cavuto* (1996–present). The 2000 presidential race between George W. Bush and Al Gore put Fox News on the map and atop the cable news ratings. With tens of millions of households within its reach, the channel witnessed an explosive 440 percent uptick in viewership.

"We have seen the news and it is us."
Peter Jennings

In 2018, Fox News was the number one cable news network. In fact, seven of the top ten news commentary shows were on Fox News, including the number one show *Hannity*, featuring Sean Hannity.[355] CNN, the originator of cable news, surprisingly failed to place a single show in the top twenty. It's currently a two-horse, conservative-liberal race between Fox News and MSNBC.

Cable Comes Of Age

Cable television experienced its renaissance in the early 1980s.

In fact, between 1977 and 1985, the heart of cable television programming formed. The *Christian Broadcasting Network* (1977). *Nickelodeon* (1977). *The PTL Network* (1978). *ESPN* (1979). *C-SPAN* (1979). *The Movie Channel* (1979). *Black Entertainment Television* (1980). *Cinemax* (1980). *Bravo* (1980). *Music Television* (1981). *The Weather Channel* (1982). *Home Shopping Network* (1982). *The Disney Channel* (1983). *American Movie Classics* (1984). *Arts & Entertainment* (1984). *Lifetime* (1984). *The Discovery Channel* (1985). *Video Hits One* (1985).

Cable company offerings differed from city to city. Originally, most local companies boasted a dozen channels (of the twenty-eight available in 1980). At the decade's end, there were three times that number. In 1996, the average cable consumer feasted upon as many as fifty-seven different channels. Six years later, lineups exploded to 280 channels. Today, there are over 800 specialty channels, including dozens of regional sports networks. From news to outdoors to music to shopping to movies, there's a channel just for *you,* particularly if you're religiously inclined. If you're Catholic, there's EWTN. If you're an evangelical, there's TBN and INSP. If you're a Mormon, there's BYUtv. There's even a Scientology channel.[356]

Cable television's lack of restrictions allowed it to carry content that wasn't available on network television. Furthermore, the changing attitudes and morality of Americans created an explosion of new shows on NBC, CBS, and ABC that cable television clearly influenced.

From the 1980s nightly soap operas (*Dallas, Knot's Landing,* and *Dynasty*) to the 1990s adult cartoons (*The Simpsons, American Dad, King of the Hill,* and *South Park*), the television landscape drastically shifted during the Cable Television generation. A lot of it focused on the family—which fractured into a variety of sitcom contexts. Affluent black Huxtables (*The Cosby Show*). Lower white middle-class Connors (*Roseanne*). Upper middle-class Taylors (*Home*

Improvement). Family shows also focused on adult-child relationships (*Everybody Loves Raymond*) and portrayed unconventional families that showed a *Full House* with *Charles in Charge*.

Network television got grittier and more authentic in the 1980s and 1990s, no doubt reflecting new realities on cable television. From "shaky camera" *Hill Street Blues* to the profanity-laced *NYPD Blue*, from *St. Elsewhere* to *ER* and *LA Law* to *The West Wing*, television shows embraced more authentic storytelling that focused on the personal lives of characters. Americans watched television passively until the 1980s. But fresh storylines about deeply flawed characters—fathers, mothers, cops, preachers, lawyers, businessmen, doctors—created new realities.

Enter *reality* television.

The "reality" genre had been around for decades but until the late 1980s had never been fully explored. The emergence of video camcorders allowed regular Joes and Janes to film stuff that cameras never previously captured. It was a home video recording of a Rodney King beating that sparked violent riots and destruction in south-central Los Angeles (1992). The Cable generation was the first to consume reality television, starting with *Real People* (1979), *That's Incredible!* (1980), and *The People's Court* (1981). With the raw video of *Cops* to homegrown family fare like *America's Funniest Home Videos*, both of which first aired in 1989, the groundwork for reality television was laid. Everything that followed in the competition reality category—from *Survivor* to *The Bachelor* to *American Idol*—featured mostly, if not all, Cable Television kids. The explosion of reality shows on cable television after 2000 further cemented the format into the American psyche, although not without criticism for its tendency toward "scripted" fare. Nevertheless, reality television introduced us to *The Osbournes* and the Robertsons (*Duck Dynasty*), the Teutuls (*American Chopper*), the Gaines (*Fixer Upper*), the Roloffs (*Little People, Big World*) the Harrisons (*Pawn Stars*), and the Kardashians. Hopefully, we're "keeping up."

We're The One Worth Watching!

Televised sports forever changed on September 21, 1970—the first birth year of the Cable Television generation. That's when ABC unleashed *Monday Night Football* upon America. Prior to that date, professional football was a Sunday sport. Monday Night Football turned it into a national, must-see, three-ring circus hosted by the straight man Frank Gifford, the goofball clown "Dandy" Don Meredith, and the blustery egotist Howard Cosell.

The combination was magical even if the games weren't.

Cosell's halftime highlights of Sunday's games were popular fare and Meredith's crooning to "turn out the lights, the party's over" signaled yet another game was in the bag.

The success of ABC's *Monday Night Football*, and sister program *Wide World of Sports*, no doubt influenced a father and son named Bill and Scott Rasmussen, and fellow sports enthusiast Ed Eagan, to create a new cable television channel known as the Entertainment and Sports Programming Network (ESPN). The channel featured all sports around the clock. On December 7, 1979, ESPN launched with some 30,000 viewers. Thanks to its flagship program, *Sportscenter*, and its catchy "we're the one worth watching" theme music, ESPN quickly became a fan favorite, picked up by cable systems all over America.

At first, ESPN struggled financially. They had no contracts with major sporting leagues (the networks owned all rights) but somehow slowly built their sports empire. In 1982, ESPN snagged a contract with the NBA and then a new professional football league known as the USFL. By 1987, ESPN had partial rights with the NFL and *ESPN Sunday Night Football* was born. In 1990, baseball was added. ESPN eventually launched ESPN Radio, ESPN 2, ESPN 3, ESPNews, and ESPN Classic, among other specialty sport networks.[357]

ESPN is the most successful national sports network—and no doubt contributed to the regional sports networks so popular today. In the 1980s, sports became character-driven. John McEnroe vs. Bjorn Borg. Chrissy Evert vs. Martina Navratilova. Magic Johnson vs. Larry Bird. Mike Tyson vs. Leon Spinks. And don't forget the emergence of Michael Jordan, the first iconic sports brand. It's why ESPN is the undisputed sports channel for the Cable Television generation.

I Want My MTV!

Of all the cable channels, there is none that was more transformative than MTV. Music television didn't just introduce a new television genre (music videos), it changed how we thought about music and the role music played in our entertainment.

"Music videos may seem old hat now, but let me tell you, in the summer of 1981, MTV was…the coolest thing ever invented."
Julia Quinn

On August 1, 1981, a transmission of a rocket on the launchpad greeted viewers. With a countdown, the spacecraft launched and landed on the moon. Out stepped an astronaut who firmly planted an MTV flag into the lunar landscape. The message was clear: Music television wasn't just another technological innovation like television or radio. Music television was *as big as walking on the moon*. It was as revolutionary as space travel.

At the time such an idea seemed far-fetched, but in the decades since the landing of MTV in American culture that prophetic notion has proven incredibly true. MTV, it turns out, was everything (and more) that it promised. So much so that I initially debated naming this particular generation the "MTV generation." MTV was *that* critical and influential. The problem is that MTV isn't a technological innovation as much as a cultural revolution. MTV is a cable channel. You can't control it like a car or radio or television.

Furthermore, while MTV could single-handedly represent this cohort of children born between 1970 and 1990, it's not the only influencer. CNN and ESPN are also co-parents, so to speak. That's why I eventually landed on the Cable Television generation tag. It's the only moniker that covered all these influencers. Without cable, and later satellite television, there would be no MTV or CNN or ESPN. There would be no superstations like TBS or WGN. Cable television is the technology that makes those revolutionary channels possible.

MTV claimed to be "the best of television combined with the best of radio." Like ESPN and CNN, it was round-the-clock videos. Mark Goodman, one MTV's first veejays, stated, "We're going to do for TV what FM did for radio." The first video played on MTV was "Video Killed the Radio Star" by a British band named The Buggles.[358] In reality, the Brits had long produced clever music videos for their music, while American artists relied upon concert footage and Dick Clark "Bandstand" lip-synching to promote their music. MTV needed a video vault and quickly turned to artists across the pond to furnish the goods. The "new wave," or second British invasion, hit America in the early 1980s like a tidal wave and MTV was the reason. *The Human League. Psychedelic Furs. Thompson Twins. Eurythmics. Culture Club. Duran Duran. A Flock of Seagulls. Spandau Ballet. The Police. The Cure. Depeche Mode. The Smiths. New Order. Peter Gabriel. Gary Numan. The Pretenders.*

Another problem MTV faced was the first American artists to create music videos weren't white rockers but black musicians who sang rhythm and blues, funk and disco. MTV initially positioned itself as a "rock" channel and that created a "blackball" for many African-American music artists. But that door didn't stay shut long. Michael Jackson's electrifying "moon walk" performance at a Motown music tribute (May 16, 1983) showed MTV what they were missing.[359] Within a week, the Prince of Pop's new album "Thriller" sold a million copies. MTV rightly saw the light, conceded its purely rock mantle and happily embraced Michael Jackson. Suddenly, the channel blew open for black artists from Lionel Richie to Stevie Wonder to Kool and the Gang.

"MTV had a giant impact: visually and musically on every part of the TV culture that came next."
David Bianculli

During the 1980s, MTV was the place that young America hung out.

From Bruce Springsteen and Prince to Madonna and Whitney Houston, music videos were a new and rising art form that influenced everything from commercials to television shows like *Miami Vice*. Music videos and MTV created new genres. *Heavy metal. Hip hop. Alternative rock. Grunge.*

"MTV was the first network really focused on the youth market, and it becomes hugely influential because they understand each other, the audience and the network."
Chris Connelly, ESPN reporter

MTV also helped spread cultural messages about AIDS, voting, and world crises. On July 13, 1985, the Cable generation communed around MTV to watch a "global jukebox" known as Live Aid. The brainchild of musicians Bob Geldoff and Midge Ure, "Live Aid" was a simultaneous concert held in two locations: London's Wembley stadium and Philadelphia's John F. Kennedy's stadium. All proceeds from the concert were targeted for the Ethiopian famine. It was one of music's best days, and only MTV aired it in the U.S. from start to finish. Nearly 173,000 concert-goers packed the two stadiums while satellite link-ups allowed a televised audience of 1.9 billion people to also tune in. On this one day in world history, nearly half (40 percent) of the planet's entire population grooved to musical artists from the obscure (Status Quo, Style Council, Ultravox) to the legendary (Queen, The Who, Elton John, and Paul McCartney).[360]

MTV launched many new artists, but few more dynamic than U2. They were the 1980s version of the Fab Four. Led by the charismatic Bono, the band preached a message that mixed rock and roll with spiritual themes of peace, love, and joy. U2 music was beautiful, artful, and sensual. And they were the perfect band for video. Their music and lyrics were already wrapped in visual hooks. *New Year's Day. Sunday Bloody Sunday. Where the Streets Have No Name. The Fly. Numb.* The four lads from Ireland even replicated the famous Beatle rooftop concert stunt.

It could be argued that U2 is the Cable Television generation's band.

Irish, yet American. Spiritual, yet agnostic. Optimistic, yet cynical. A little rock and roll. A little blues. A little pop. A little country.

As a generation, the Cable Television cohort has always been leaning into the future.

It's like they still haven't found what they're looking for.

But that's okay with them.

A TIMELINE OF TECHNOLOGICAL EVENTS (1971–1980):

- 1971: U.S.S.R. soft lands on Mars. Human growth hormone is synthesized. Two new galaxies discovered. Intel releases world's first microprocessor. First Internet chat rooms and email created. Notable inventions: CAT scanner, floppy disk, and LCD. Soft contact lens, pocket calculator, and Kevlar polymer first sold.

- 1972: Apollo 17 astronauts spend record seventy-five hours on moon surface. Soviet spacecraft soft lands on Venus. HBO launched. Space shuttle program starts. Digital watches and Atari "Pong" video game introduced. Notable inventions: artificial heart and optical fiber.

- 1973: First U.S. space station SkyLab launched. Pioneer 10 space probe transmits televised pictures from within 81,000 miles of Jupiter. Sears Tower opens. Notable inventions: barcodes and Jet Skis.

- 1974: Skylab III astronauts spend eighty-four days in space. Mariner 10 satellite transmits detailed pictures of both Venus and Mercury. India becomes sixth nation to explode a nuclear device. U.S. Air Force jet flies from New York to London in under two hours with speeds reaching 2,000 mph. MRI Scanner invented. Primitive word processor released.

- 1975: The unmanned Viking is launched to Mars to seek signs of life. U.S. and U.S.S.R. astronauts complete a link-up in space: the first international space flight. First commercially-developed supercomputer (Cray-1). Bill Gates and Paul Allen develop BASIC program. Microsoft registered as a trademark. Motorola patents mobile phone. Sony introduces Betamax videotapes while Matsushita/JVC introduce VHS. Notable inventions: laser printer and digital camera.

- 1976: First detailed radar observation of the surface of Venus. Viking I and II land on Mars and transmit first photos of the surface. Concorde jets cuts transatlantic flying time to 3.5 hours. Apple Computer Company formed by Steve Jobs and Steve Wozniak. Olympics broadcasted globally to one billion viewers. Notable invention: ink jet printer.

- 1977: British scientists report they've identified the complete genetic structure of a living organism. Voyager I and II launched to explore outer reaches of solar system. First Apple II computer released. NAVSTAR Global Positioning System (GPS) is inaugurated by U.S. Department of Defense.

- 1978: Soviet cosmonauts live in space a record 139 days. "Test Tube Baby" born in England on July 25. Illinois Bell Company introduces first cellular mobile phone system. Space Invaders video game released. Television is in 98 percent of all U.S. homes.

- 1979: VisiCalc is first spreadsheet program. Sony Walkman introduced. Voyager I photo reveals the rings around Jupiter. Notable invention: snowboards.
- 1980: Japan releases first domestic camcorders and fax machines. Voyager I returns hi-res images of Saturn. Pac-Man arcade game released. Cable News Network (CNN) launches. 3M sells a new paper product: Post-It Notes.

INFLUENTIAL BIRTHS IN THE CABLE TELEVISION GENERATION:
Politicians:
- Ted Cruz (1970)

Business, Education, Athletes and Other Leaders:
- Shaquille O'Neal (1972), basketball player
- Monica Lewinsky (1973), White House intern
- Tiger Woods (1975), golfer
- Tom Brady (1977), football player
- Ivanka Trump (1981), business executive
- Michael Phelps (1985), swimmer
- Stephen Curry (1988), basketball player

Entertainers:
- Leah Remini (1970), actress
- Mariah Carey (1970), R&B singer
- Tina Fey (1970), actress
- Willy Robertson (1972), reality star
- Jim Parsons (1973), actor
- Jimmy Fallon (1974), television host
- Chip Gaines (1974), reality star
- Ryan Seacrest (1974), television host
- Blake Shelton (1976), country singer
- Kim Kardashian (1980), reality star
- Nicki Minaj (1982), rapper
- Drake (1986), rapper
- The Weeknd (1990), R&B singer

Authors/Artists/Social Media Stars:
- Daniel Handler (1970), novelist
- Kat Von D (1982), tattoo artist

Chapter Twelve

Personal Computer-Cell Phone

"Technology has forever changed the world we live in. We're online, in one way or another, all day long. Our phones and computers have become reflections of our personalities, our interests and our identities."
James Comey

BIRTH YEARS: 1980–2000
"Coming of Age" Years: 1990–2025
Primary Tech Event: Cell phone
Strauss-Howe Archetype: Hero
Generation Personality: Dominant/Optimistic
Iconic Generation Representatives: Mark Zuckerberg and Megan Markle

Historical Influencing Events in Youth and Young Adulthood:
End of Cold War, O.J. Simpson, Columbine, Death of Princess Diana, Clinton-Lewinsky scandal, 9-11 terrorist attacks, Hurricane Katrina, Great Recession, Barack Obama, Las Vegas shooting, Donald Trump/2016 election, Kavanaugh SCOTUS hearings

---

Baby on board.

It was a simple yellow sign suction-cupped to rear car windows.

But in the early 1980s those three words on plastic signaled a major generational lane shift. The times were changing again. A new crop of kids was being born to more enlightened, attached, and attentive parents. This wasn't your father's family anymore. These kids were born with a mission, money, and moxie.

It's doubtful any American generation has created a bigger cultural splash than those born between 1980 and 2000. Social historians Neil Howe and William Strauss labeled them a "hero" generation in the same vein as the kids born at the turn of the twentieth century. And don't forget that *those* kids—whom we've recast as the Transportation and Telephone generation—grew up to become the "greatest" in America. They were Rosie the Riveters and Lucky Lindys. They built suburbs, dams, interstates, and moon rockets. They won wars and survived economic depression. Consequently, when a batch of babies born in the early 1980s matched that optimistic heroic frame, it commanded attention.

The first problem was finding these tykes a suitable name.

Generation Y. Too simple.

Baby Boomlets. Too cheesy.

Echo Boom. Too abstract.

The one thing all these tots had in common was the millennial year 2000. The children uniquely born in 1982 were scheduled to graduate in 2000 and dubbed "millennium" babies. The rest of the brood crossed over into the new millennium during their youth. Consequently, they were "Millennial" kids. And they were *different* because we christened them as *different*. Attitude is everything, and the Millennial babies matured beneath a new national outlook. They mirrored their Transportation and Telephone (TNT) generation President: Ronald Reagan. In 1980, the TNT cohort (with their Gipper in the White House) was comprised of optimistic, positive, and influential senior adults settling into retirement. These "millennial babies" were a new American hope. They were still *in diapers* when Anna Quindlen of *Newsweek* gushed: "Meet the Millennials and rejoice."[361]

Rejoice, indeed.

It was "morning in America," Ronald Reagan style.

The Big Bang Theory

For the Millennials, the 1980s and 1990s proved to be a brave new world where families grew closer, conspicuous consumption reigned supreme, social institutions evolved, and new technologies changed the world. The Millennials witnessed a renaissance in family television. *Cosby. Family Ties. Growing Pains. Full House. Family Matters. Home Improvement.* Hollywood produced movies that made babies cool (*Three Men and a Baby, Baby Boom, Look Who's Talking?*) and cast kids as creative, intelligent heroes (*Spy Kids, The Rookie, Home Alone*). Even Disney got in on the act. From animated feature films to mall stores to a revival of the Mickey Mouse Club (headlined by soon-to-be Millennial icons like Britney Spears, Christina Aguilera, Justin Timberlake, and Ryan Gosling), Disney was an entertainment tour de force.

The Millennials savored a cultural anointing from every social institution. Churches launched children's and youth ministries with professional staff, specialized facilities, and targeted programming. Public education reinvented pedagogy and promoted outcomes-based learning. Montessori teaching methods re-emerged. *Hooked on Phonics*, abstinence, *True Love Waits*, and character education were popular. Homeschooling, private Christian schools, daycares, and charter schools blossomed. SAT scores jumped. Child "Doogie Howser" prodigies were everywhere. Girl and boy scout troop membership experienced revival. Kids were particularly targeted by retailers. McDonalds built Playlands. Restaurants offered child menus and opened experiential eateries like *Chuck E. Cheese* and *Rainforest Café*. Hotels offered breakfast bars. Toys R Us launched Babies R Us.

Everything became "family-friendly" and "family-focused." Maternity wards were reimagined into birthing centers with fathers welcomed. Fetal phones, crib cameras, and baby monitors sold like hotcakes. Breastfeeding and parental leave was cool. There were family days at ballparks, zoos, fairs, and theme parks. Family size products were trendy, as were family-friendly workplaces and "bring your kid to work" days.

Children were more protected after 1980. Neighborhood watches, adult safety patrols, and curfews. Child protection services, Medicaid for children, and Amber alerts. We put safety covers on sockets and medicine bottles, v-chips in televisions, airbags and safety seats in cars, helmets on heads, and changing tables in restrooms.

Kids were cool. Kids were smart. Kids were wanted.

And kids were *different*, as Mary Ann Johanson noted (circa 1997):

The first tough, cranky, pragmatic, independent Generation Xers are gonna start hitting [forty] in the next couple of years, and rearing up behind them are the Millennials, the first batch of which are the high school class of 2000. These kids are, as a group, pleasant, cheerful, helpful, ambitious, and community-oriented.[362]

Of course, such glowing terms were generalized in application, but there was little doubt the Millennials—eventually defined as children born between 1982 and 1998—were a sanctified generation. Gen X "helicopter" parents in particular wanted their kids to enjoy a better childhood than they had experienced. In many ways, the Millennials were parented by *reaction*. Mothers stayed home. Divorces were fewer and friendlier. Fathers spent more time with their kids. Parents showered their children with praise, trophies, money for grades, backyard play equipment, toddler beauty pageants, sports leagues, birthday party extravaganzas, preschool graduation exercises, and countless other "blessings" to make them *feel good*. Thirty-something Boomers, with the biological clock winding down, also joined this emerging positive parenting "focus on the family" frame.

As a generation born between 1980 and 2000, there were two clear phases: The Reagan/Bush Millennials (b. 1980–1989) and the Clinton/Bush Millennials (b. 1990–1999). The differences between these phases caused many social historians and demographers to demarcate this cohort into the more ambiguous "Y" and "Z," but these labels contribute little productive insight. In their youth, Reagan/Bush Millennials experienced the fall of the Berlin Wall, the L.A. riots, "Operation Desert Storm," the O.J. Simpson trial, and the Oklahoma City bombing. In contrast, the Clinton/Bush Millennials witnessed Princess Diana's death, Clinton's impeachment, Columbine school shooting, Persian Gulf War, Katrina hurricane, and the Great Recession.

The binding moment for all Millennial children was September 11, 2001: a dark day in our nation's history when three hijacked planes plowed into the twin towers in downtown Manhattan and the Pentagon in Washington D.C. This day of "terror" culturally glued a generation of children and teenagers together. From this day forward, the "war on terror" marked their story.

It was also on September 11, 2001 that two technologies merged to better define Millennials as an American generation: the personal computer and cell phone. The computer (aided by the Internet) became a continuing source of raw information. Meanwhile, the cell phone demonstrated how American communication was evolving. On that fateful day, Americans listened to last cell phone conversations from desperate people inside the twin towers and aboard United Airlines Flight 93.[363] They also used a new emerging communication tool: texting. It's how a shell-shocked nation stayed in touch.

It's why the "Millennial" tag isn't the best description for those born during this time. The fact that this generation of kids came of age with the turning of the millennium is significant and helpful, but that event in itself isn't what defined "who" they truly were as a cohort. The television show *The Big Bang Theory* perfectly represents this group of American kids and portrays them as uber-smart, hip, empowered, multicultural, communal nerds. From Sheldon Cooper to Penny, these twenty-something Millennials are a "connected" generation. The two technologies that guide nearly every episode in this top-rated television show: computers and cell phones.

It's why there's no better tag than "PC generation."

After all, the Personal Computer generation uniquely experienced a digital and cyber revolution that completely reimagined American life. The PC generation was the first cohort of Americans to fully learn on computers at home, to surf the Internet using Google, and to embrace a world of clouds and streams. They are the "e" generation, growing up as digital natives. They used emails, e-banking, and e-learning. They are comfortable navigating a cyber culture. Indeed, many early wave entrepreneurs in social media were "PC" kids, most notably Mark Zuckerberg, the founder of Facebook.

But there's more to "P.C." than first meets the eye. Like any good "flip phone," these kids are also "C.P." for "cell phone."

Post-1980 children entered adolescence just as their parents discovered mobile phone technology. Many families purchased their first "family" cell phone in the 1990s. Back then, a mobile phone was transitory, moving from parent to parent and sibling to sibling (depending on who needed it most). Those born later in the cohort embraced a new type of phone that was "smart." They also enjoyed affordable "family plans" that permitted each family member a private line. That's when landlines were put on notice.

Indeed, cell phones significantly shifted and changed American communication. Literally, cellular phones flattened how we lived and transformed us into a world without borders, margins, or limits. Isn't it interesting the most permanent thing in our new world is our cell phone number? We can change addresses, switch spouses, upgrade phones, and travel to new locations, but our number *goes with us*. It's one of the most permanent things we possess.

Since its emergence in American homes in the early 1900s, the telephone was wired to the wall. These "landlines" linked conversations to a particular time and space. Our phones were locational devices. You had a phone in the living room. Another one in the kitchen. Maybe a third line in the bedroom. If you wanted to talk to someone, you had to go to a *particular* phone at a *certain* time.

Answering machines eventually helped save missed connections, but they still demanded a "space and time" return conversation. It wasn't until the cell phone emerged that communication completely flattened into *any time* and *any place*. Its why landlines are now nearly dead in the American home and phone booths are a cultural artifact. It's an antiquated form of conversation. Indeed, by the time the last "PC/CP" generation kid turns twenty-five in 2025, the landline will likely be extinct (with the desktop computer not far behind).

James Meigs, editor of *Popular Mechanics*, noted the cultural importance of the personal computer and cell phone:

> Your first pocket knife. Your first bicycle. Your first car. Today, your first cellphone. Your first laptop. All these are badges of gaining control of your world. I mean, to live life better because you have a better tool and the skill to use it. That's something deeply appealing to the American psyche.[364]

It's no wonder the personal computer and cell phone defined the PC generation. For one group of American kids, similar to those two terrorized towers in lower Manhattan, the cell phone and personal computer serve as twin apex technologies. It's why we must investigate their history and understand their influence.

Big Blue Beginnings

Ever since Alan Turing first imagined a computing machine in 1937, there has been a code rush to discover what computers can actually do. From eggheads

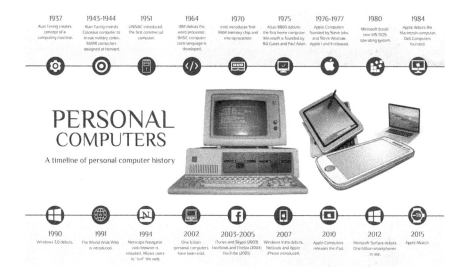

PERSONAL COMPUTERS

A timeline of personal computer history

1937	1943-1944	1951	1964	1970	1975	1976-1977	1980	1984
Alan Turing creates concept of a computing machine.	Alan Turing invents Colossus computer to break military codes. MARK computers designed at Harvard.	UNIVAC introduced. The first commercial computer.	IBM debuts the word processor. BASIC computer code language is developed.	Intel introduces first RAM memory chip and microprocessor.	Altair 8800 debuts: the first home computer. Microsoft is founded by Bill Gates and Paul Allen.	Apple Computers founded by Steve Jobs and Steve Wozniak. Apple I and II released.	Microsoft builds new MS-DOS operating system.	Apple debuts the Macintosh computer. Dell Computers founded.

1990	1991	1994	2002	2003-2005	2007	2010	2012	2015
Windows 3.0 debuts.	The World Wide Web is introduced.	Netscape Navigator web browser is released. Allows users to 'surf' the web.	One billion personal computers have been sold.	iTunes and Skype (2003) Facebook and Firefox (2004) YouTube (2005)	Windows Vista debuts: Netbook and Apple iPhone introduced.	Apple Computers releases the iPad.	Microsoft Surface debuts. One billion smartphones in use.	Apple Watch

in educational institutions (like Harvard and Stanford) to engineers in business companies (like IBM and Hewlett-Packard), everyone sought to computerize the business world. IBM (International Business Machines) had been around since 1911 and enjoyed a stellar reputation for business products. They produced the office machines—from typewriters to calculators to punch cards—that companies demanded for everyday transactions.

IBM not only created the business culture of a post-war America; it *was* the business culture. The word "business" was IBM's middle name. If you were doing business, IBM was your supplier. They developed the mainframe computer that drove banks, office centers, and retail stores. Only the finest and smartest worked for IBM—in research, management, or sales. If you were an IBM "suit," you were something *special*. It was this institutional confidence, some might say arrogance, that would eventually prove their Achille's heel.

"If the automobile had followed the same development cycle as the computer, a Rolls-Royce would today cost $100, get a million miles per gallon, and explode once a year, killing everyone inside."
Robert X. Cringley

IBM was mostly focused on producing mainframe computers. Consequently, our journey towards "personal" computing starts with a company named Intel.

Intel—a blending of "Integrated Electronics"—was founded in 1968 by chemist Gordon Moore and physicist Robert Noyce.[365] Moore is famously noted for his "Moore's Law" that postulates every two years the transistors in an integrated circuit will *double*.[366] His law was later attached to other digital matters, such as computer memory, processing speed, microprocessor, and pixels. When Intel invented the microprocessor in 1971, it fueled the evolution of personal computing. In fact, Intel processors still power every Apple, Hewlett-Packard, Lenovo, and Dell computer.

Enter Ed Roberts and his minicomputer the Altair 8800.

In 1974, Roberts worked for Micro Instrumentation and Technology Systems (MITS) when he invented a computer he named the Altair 8800. Except to computer nerds with calculators and pocket pen holders, the machine wasn't much to look at. The Altair 8800 was a box kit with blinking lights and flip switches. It contained no keyboard, monitor, or printer. And yet it got major press. *Popular Mechanics* was so impressed they featured the Altair on their January 1975 cover.

The Altair 8800 proved to be breakthrough home-computing technology, wildly popular with programming hobbyists.[367] One computer enthusiast who purchased the Altair 8800 was none other than Paul Allen. At the time, Allen was working for Honeywell in Boston. He immediately shared the "personal computer" kit with his good friend Bill Gates (a student at Harvard University). Gates was instantly hooked and soon programmed a simple operating system for the Altair 8800 that he called BASIC.

The Altair 8800 was ripe with potential uses, but without a working operating system, none of those applications mattered. It's like a beautiful car without an engine. Gates and Allen visualized the computer's potential and contacted Ed Roberts with a query. Was he interested in their BASIC program chip for the Altair 8800? It was just a couple college kids chasing an idea.

But that's the day Microsoft was born.

"I think it's fair to say that personal computers have become the most empowering tool we've ever created. They're tools of communication, they're tools of creativity, and they can be shaped by their user."

Bill Gates

Bill Gates and Paul Allen were now on their way to becoming zillionaires. Of course, you wouldn't have known it in 1976. They were just programming fools who coded all night, ate stale pizza, listened to hard rock, and drank cases of Coca-Cola. Eventually, the dynamic duo returned to their hometown of Seattle to seed their programming business.

Meanwhile in the San Francisco bay area, a motley bunch of hippie nerds, tech geeks, and computer programmers were also gathering regularly. Known as the Homebrew Computer Company, they convened to discuss various applications for the Altair 8800.[368] One of those nerds was Steve Wozniak. "Woz" had another computer geek friend who occasionally tagged along with him by the name of Steve Jobs. Steve soon became consumed with a grand vision to make the computer "personal." He only needed a programming wizard like Wozniak to engineer the reality…plus a little money and his parents' garage.

That's when Apple Computers was born.[369]

In 1977, a "trinity" of personal computing machines were unveiled to the American public. Beside the Apple II, there was the Commodore PET, and Radio Shack TRS-80. Computer nerds were hip to be square, but the general public wasn't yet hooked. The personal computer needed a bigger fish in the pond, and IBM was now hungry for opportunity.

Insanely Great

In 1980, Microsoft caught the attention of Big Blue. The business goliath IBM saw money in personal computers but needed a partner to create an operating system.

The suits of IBM tapped Bill Gates for the job.

Microsoft was still a small, struggling company. However, Big Blue wanted something pronto and so Gates procured an operating system from another Seattle company, shined it up, and exclusively leased "PC DOS" to Big Blue for $50,000.

A year later, IBM released the 5150. The computer had no hard drive and a paltry 640K of random-access memory (RAM), but it was a glorious machine. IBM positioned itself to become the computer titan of the world.[370] Big Blue literally put the personal computer on the map. *Time* magazine even named the personal computer as its "Man of the Year" in 1982.

Therefore, it's no coincidence the first babies of the PC generation were born just as the age of personal computing dawned.

The only thing IBM didn't fully consider was the moxie of that little computer company in Seattle. Bill Gates wasn't interested in exclusively feeding Big Blue with operating systems. His vision was to ensure every computer on the planet ran only the *Microsoft* operating system. It didn't have to be an IBM machine at all. Gates counted on clone companies to make his money. After all, IBM only *leased* DOS from Microsoft. They didn't own all rights. Consequently, because the hardware was simple to replicate, Microsoft began to sell MS-DOS to competitors hell-bent on busting Big Blue's dominance. IBM and clone companies constructed the car, but Microsoft delivered the engine.

Consequently, clone computers—from Amstrad to Hewlett-Packard and Compaq to Dell—emerged in the 1980s. These machines used "IBM-compatible" software, such as Lotus 1-2-3 and WordPerfect. And almost every computer, save notably the Apple II, ran MS-DOS. Microsoft got rich in the process. Bill Gates and Paul Allen were overnight millionaires.

Back in California, Steve Jobs and the Woz weren't so fortunate. The Apple II was revolutionary and sold well, but Jobs knew its days were limited. That's because Steve had seen the future of computing back in 1979, during a highly-privileged tour of Xerox's Palo Alto Research Center (PARC).[371] On that day, Steve Jobs was introduced to "graphic user interface" (GUI or "gooey") technology. Essentially, it was a brand of computing that was focused *visually* through icons, graphics, and windows. MS-DOS featured text-based computing. It required users to manually type in commands to start programs, copy documents, or explore directories. "Gooey" computers employed a mouse that could "drag and drop" or "click and save" or "cut and paste." Steve Jobs was enamored by the intuitive graphic-user interface. He was convinced that's where Apple needed to go.

"Computer themselves, and software yet to be developed, will revolutionize the way we learn."
Steve Jobs

What's more fascinating is that Xerox didn't seem to mind. They fully cooperated with Apple. Even when PARC researchers angrily protested and lobbied for Xerox to adopt "gooey" computer technology itself, the suits in New York never bought the vision. Now these same executives were offering the Apple development team an open-door, free-range, intimate tour of their highly-protected, graphic-interface computer. Essentially, Xerox handed Apple the recip to the secret sauce. Steve Jobs later reflected, "Basically [Xerox executives] were copier-heads that had no clue about a computer and what it could do…Xerox could've owned the entire computer industry today…it could've been the Microsoft of the 90's."[372]

Steve Jobs now controlled, literally, the "X-Factor" and feverishly led his Apple troops in developing his own "gooey" computer. The only problem was Jobs' leadership style. He quickly proved a corporate contradiction. Charismatic, yet obnoxious. Visionary, yet impatient. Moving, yet menacing. Jobs was as inspiring as he was perspiring.

He was a benevolent dictator on a mission to rule the world.

Jobs immediately hired a hundred engineers who worked to create something "insanely great." In January 1984, Apple finally unveiled the "gooey" MacIntosh[373]—a computer introduced to America in a famous Super Bowl advertisement.[374] The Mac sold for $2500 (over $6000 in today's dollars) and featured only two programs: Mac Paint and Mac Write. Initially, its sales were modestly good, but it wasn't long before the Mac started to slide. People wanted more productivity. Maybe the IBM-compatible computers weren't as flashy, but they possessed powerful business software.

Apple needed serious help.

That's when a little-known company named Adobe came calling.

John Warnock and Charles Geschke launched Adobe in 1982. They were former Xerox employees at PARC who developed creative software. Photoshop was one of their first success stories, but it was the portable document format (.PDF) that truly put Adobe on the map. Apple and Adobe formed a partnership and delivered to the creative class—particularly photographers and videographers—a computer with robust, intuitive graphic design capabilities. With the introduction of laser printing, a desktop publishing revolution exploded.

But even that infused success didn't salvage Apple. Their computer sales remained sluggish. The MacIntosh was simply too expensive for the average user. IBM-compatible machines and software were what most people could afford. Steve Jobs recognized Apple needed higher-level vision and fresh perspectives. Jobs found his visionary in Pepsi's CEO John Sculley.[375] On paper, Apple's hire of Sculley seemed a perfect fit for the failing company. Apple and Pepsi were clearly focused on "new generation" targets and both companies' featured marketing that was youthful and edgy. Sculley was himself a decisive, determined leader and wasted no time casting a fresh vision for Apple computers. In the end, Sculley's influence went too far. He eventually persuaded the Apple board to prefer his "sugar water" visions to Steve's "insanely great" dreams. Steve Jobs suddenly found himself losing influence.

As a result, Jobs left the company he founded.

The soul of Apple was *gone*.

Ironically, the absence of Steve Jobs initially helped Apple computer sales to better compete. In 1987, Apple matched IBM, computer for computer, and sold a million MacIntosh machines. Beating "Big Blue" was the battle cry. Unfortunately, IBM wasn't Apple's true rival. Their real nemesis was in Seattle. Microsoft hungered for a slice of Apple's pie. And, believe it or not, Apple did *exactly* what Xerox had done in 1979. In need of some minor software, Apple reached out to Bill Gates and Microsoft in 1983. And then Apple gleefully, some might even say arrogantly, revealed their coveted Lisa computer to Bill Gates. Lisa was a "gooey" prototype for the MacIntosh. Gates was equally fascinated. Steve got the idea from Xerox and now Gates "creatively borrowed" the concept for his Microsoft empire. Apple learned quickly that Bill Gates was no fool. He recognized that visual computing was also the future. Armed with a new "gooey" vision, Gates commissioned his Microsoft minions to create its own graphic-user interface.

Windows To The World

The result of that Apple-Microsoft meeting was a program called *Windows*.

And it looked remarkably like the MacIntosh operating system.

At first, Apple didn't care. They were selling computers and making money. But with every revision of Windows, new features popped up that attracted more buyers. During the 1990s, Microsoft Windows soon became the de facto operating system platform to replace MS-DOS in every computer. It was that reality that caught Apple's attention. They sued for copyright infringement but lost. Steve Jobs used to preach Big Blue was the Darth Vader of the computer empire, but now the company from Cupertino fingered Bill Gates and Microsoft. Apple refused to play with Windows and that further isolated the company, costing even more sales.

By 1996, Apple computers was near death, controlling less than 4 percent of the computer market and teetering on bankruptcy. The clock was ticking.

Meanwhile, Bill Gates and Microsoft built a glorious computer kingdom. They constructed their own web navigator named "Explorer." They released a series of powerful "windows" operating system upgrades. They got into video gaming (Xbox) and cable news (MSNBC). They released the popular Microsoft Office suite that featured Word, PowerPoint, Excel, and Outlook. They launched a tablet computer named Microsoft Surface. They bought LinkedIn and Skype. In 2018, Microsoft became the most valuable publicly-traded company on the planet.

Paul Allen and Bill Gates were billionaires.

As for Apple?

They'll make their own comeback in the 2000s, thanks to the "i's": iMac, iPod, iTunes, iPad, iPhone, and iWatch. Steve Jobs' 1997 return to Apple as its interim CEO sparked a "think different" revolution. Three years later, Jobs replaced and rebranded the interim "i" in "iCEO" with "Internet."[376]

It was the year 2000. Steve Jobs wasn't going to lose his company again. Instead, he was going to create one of the world's most iconic brands for the emerging PC generation, now starting to enter young adulthood. The millennium year was the final birth year for the Personal Computer generation. In 1980, their first birth year, only 300,000 personal computers existed in America. By the year 2000, that number had exploded to over 168 million. Nearly six in ten U.S. households now owned a personal computer.[377] The tipping point for a technology had happened.

Can You Hear Me Now?

The 1980s was the decade of conspicuous consumption.

The Boomers were out of college and ready to spend money. Known as young urban professionals or "yuppies," the Boom generation morphed into the "splurge generation," according to journalist Tom Wolfe. During the 80s and 90s, credit cards, easy payments, and debt were big business.[378] "Shop 'til you drop" was the cultural mantra. Materialistic Americans bought stuff like crazy, especially in technology. *Microwaves. Video-cassette recorders. Walkmans. Video game consoles. Boom Boxes. Camcorders. Personal computers. Compact disc players. PalmPilots. DVD players.*

And the cell phone.

It was the fastest technology to reach total mass consumption in American history. In 1980, hardly anyone had a cell phone. By 2020, hardly anyone doesn't own one. The first truly mobile phone hit the market in 1983 carrying a hefty price tag of nearly $4000: The Motorola DynaTAC 8000x. With a battery life of sixty minutes, its most advanced feature was a redial button.

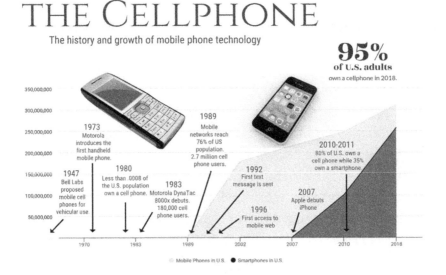

THE CELLPHONE
The history and growth of mobile phone technology

95%
of U.S. adults
own a cellphone in 2018.

1947 Bell Labs proposed mobile cell phones for vehicular use

1973 Motorola introduces the first handheld mobile phone.

1980 Less than .0008 of the U.S. population own a cell phone.

1983 Motorola DynaTac 8000x debuts. 180,000 cell phone users.

1989 Mobile networks reach 76% of US population. 2.7 million cell phone users.

1992 First text message is sent

1996 First access to mobile web

2007 Apple debuts iPhone

2010-2011 80% of U.S. own a cell phone while 35% own a smartphone

Mobile Phones in U.S. ● Smartphones in U.S.

That's probably why only 180,000 Americans owned a cell phone in 1983.[379] Or maybe it's the weight (the Nokia Senator weighed in at a whopping twenty-two pounds). Or perhaps its coverage. Even if you owned one of these "bricks," there wasn't much connection. Cell towers were limited in the early 1980s. The largest network was Bell Telephone in New York City and the best it handled was twelve calls at one time. Can you hear me now? I didn't think so.

In 1986, the Federal Communications Commission stepped to the plate. They held a lottery for the rights to construct fifteen new cellular networks in U.S. cities like Pensacola, Santa Barbara, and Atlantic City. A year later, Americans caught their first look at cell phones thanks to a rich, corporate raider named Gordon Gekko (portrayed by Michael Douglas) in the movie *Wall Street*.[380] His "greed is good" lifestyle made the mobile phone a status symbol for the upper crust.[381]

For the rest of America, there was little interest. Who cared if you could phone a friend from a car or a beach? Why would you *want* to?

———————

"You have to take into account it was the cell phone that became what the modern-day concept of a phone call is, and this is a device that's attached to your hip 24/7. Before that there was 'leave a message' and before that there was 'hopefully you're home.'"
Giovanni Ribisi

———————

The idea of mobile phone technology had been floating around since 1947. That's when Bell Labs engineers first proposed "cells" to transfer phone calls. In the 1960s, the idea was expanded to the use of cell towers. In theory, as long as a phone was in proximity of a tower, a call could connect. That's why multiple towers were needed for true mobility. Cars moved quickly beyond a tower's coverage. On April 3, 1973, a Motorola engineer named Martin Cooper made the first mobile telephone call, but it would be another decade before cell phones got much more than a hello. Even when the 1980s closed—with over three-quarters of America under cell coverage—only a meager 2.7 million people owned the mobile technology (less than 1 percent of the total population).

Call Me…*Anytime, Anyplace, Anywhere!*
In 1980, the new wave punk group Blondie released a prophetic hit song titled "Call Me." At the time, the idea of "anytime, anyplace, and anywhere" phone

calls were relegated to science fiction. The phone was wired to the wall or inside a box (pay phones). Even "cordless" landline phones weren't introduced until the mid-1990s.

Most Americans were comfortable with landline technology.

It would take something truly big to change their phone behaviors.

And that game changer was the emergence of 2G networks in the early 1990s.

"The cell phone has become the adult's transitional object, replacing the toddler's teddy bear for comfort and a sense of belonging."
Margaret Hefferman

Digital technology in phone circuitry unleashed the cell phone revolution that improved connections and increased coverage. It made companies like Sprint, Verizon, and T-Mobile household names (even AT&T joined the fray). Furthermore, these dueling mobile phone businesses made cell phones more affordable to average Americans. In 1994, IBM introduced *Simon*, a device considered by many to be the first true smartphone. Designed for the business crowd, Simon was a phone, fax machine, pager, and personal digital assistant (PDA) all in one.

And then 2G gave way to 3G broadband. This innovation allowed cell phones to connect to the Internet. Suddenly there were new possibilities, most notably the ability to send text messages via the phone. The PC generation quickly discovered that texting provided distinct advantages over verbal conversations, especially with intrusive parents, teachers, and other authority figures nearby. Adolescents everywhere started "thumbing" their messages. Unfortunately, their texting also got behind the steering wheel.

The PC generation literally texted itself to death.[382]

The real question was where was this technology headed? What was on the horizon? In the mid 2000s, most Americans owned cell phones. They were comfortable with basic features to call and text. That's what phones did, after all. They were for *communicating* with people.

Or so we thought.

In a riveting 1996 PBS documentary on personal computer history, the final minutes of the last episode turned toward the future. Larry Ellison, then CEO of Oracle, crafted an insightful, bold vision for how the personal computer would eventually be replaced by an "information appliance" that was a "glorified television" able to "access information...by connecting to giant computers via the Internet."[383]

An information appliance? A television? A computer?

What Ellison essentially described was the *smartphone*.[384]

And the PC generation was ready—perhaps *born* ready—to blend its personal computer and flip phones into one seamless, wireless, and diskless technology. The smartphone was a personal computer, a television, and a phone packed into one convenient, touchscreen "information appliance."

"Millennials regular draw ire for their cell phone usage. They're mobile natives, having come of age when landlines were well on their way out and payphones had gone the way of dinosaurs. Because of their native fluency, Millennials recognize mobile phones can do a whole lot more than make calls, enable texting between friends or tweeting."
Chelsea Clinton

When Apple released the iPhone in 2007 and androids hit the market a year later, everything changed again—especially in applications or "apps." We have an app for everything. We use our smartphones to shop, find love, map a destination, watch YouTube or Netflix, play fantasy sports, Facetime a friend, read or watch news, take photos and video, plan vacations, change flights, monitor health, play games, find a restaurant, social network, and countless other activities.

Smartphones are the PC generation's tool of choice.[385]

From a socio-historical view, those born between 1980 and 2000 can be summarized as a "www" generation. Essentially, they were *wanted* ("baby on board"), *watched* ("helicopter" parenting and family-focused institutions), and christened *worthy* (culturally anointed by the media, politicians, and cultural leaders).

It's no wonder Millennials are making a ruckus.

From Alexandria Ocasio-Cortez, the lightning rod junior Congresswoman from New York City pushing her progressive socialism to Mark Zuckerberg, the Facebook founder considering a presidential run, to entertainers Lady GaGa, Bruno Mars, Kelly Clarkson and Mandy Moore, the PC generation is a wrecking-ball force to be reckoned with.

They may have started as babies on board.

But now they're chairing those boards, baby.

In the early 1980s, these tykes demanded attention. In reality, nothing has changed. The PC generation is generally ambitious, enthusiastic, positive, and focused. Maybe even a bit heroic.

Can you hear me now?

Good.

A TIMELINE OF TECHNOLOGICAL EVENTS (1981–1990):

- 1981: The AIDS virus is identified. First flight of the Space Shuttle Columbia. IBM launches its first personal computer with MS-DOS (Microsoft). The term "Internet" is first mentioned. Artificially-produced insulin introduced.
- 1982: Japan sells first compact disc player. The Weather Channel debuts. Genetic engineering develops insulin produced by bacteria.
- 1983: ARPANET officially changes to use the Internet Protocol. Lotus 1-2-3 and Microsoft Word are released. IBM debuts the PC XT computer. First artificial heart implanted. The Swatch watch is introduced.
- 1984: AT&T breaks up into "baby Bells." First Apple Macintosh is sold. Sony and Philips introduce CD players. Sony makes first 3.5" computer disk. DNA profiling developed for forensic investigations.
- 1985: Blood test for AIDS approved by FDA. First ".com" domain name is registered. Microsoft releases Windows 1.0. Compact discs are sold in America. Space shuttle Atlantis is launched. Scientists discover a hole in the earth's ozone layer.
- 1986: United Kingdom and France announce plans to build the Channel Tunnel. Space Shuttle Challenger explodes after takeoff. Soviets launch Mir space station. First laptop computer introduced by IBM. First triple transplant (heart, lung, and liver) performed by British surgeons. Email

is invented. Intel releases 386 microprocessor. Human Genome Project launched. Notable inventions: high temperature superconductor, nicotine patch.

- 1987: The FDA approves anti-AIDS drug AZT. First criminal convicted with DNA evidence. Z88 portable computer (under 2 lbs) is released. Disposable contact lens sold to public. Notable invention: kitty litter.
- 1988: Transatlantic fiber-optic cable allows 40,000 phone calls simultaneously. First major computer virus. The Stealth bomber rolls out of production. Laser eye surgery and Prozac are introduced.
- 1989: First of twenty-four satellites for the Global Positioning System are launched. Nintendo releases GameBoy. Voyager II passes Neptune and transmits pictures back to earth. Intel introduces 486 micro-processor. Microsoft Office is released.
- 1990: Space Shuttle Discovery launches Hubble space telescope. The World Wide Web is formed. First web page created. Microsoft releases Windows 3.0. A 16-megabit computer chip is introduced. First in-car satellite navigation system is sold.

INFLUENTIAL BIRTHS IN THE
PERSONAL COMPUTER GENERATION:

Politicians:
- Ilhan Omar (1981)
- Pete Buttigieg (1982)
- Alexandria Ocasio-Cortez (1989)

Business, Education, Athletes and Other Leaders:
- Meghan Markle (1981), duchess
- LeBron James (1984), basketball player
- Mark Zuckerberg (1984), entrepreneur
- James Harden (1989), basketball player
- Aaron Judge (1992), baseball player
- Simone Biles (1997), gymnast

Entertainers:
- Brittany Spears (1981), pop singer
- Kelly Clarkson (1982), pop singer

Katy Perry (1984), pop singer

Mandy Moore (1984), actress/singer

Bruno Mars (1985), pop singer

Lady Gaga (1986), pop singer

Adele (1988), pop singer

Ed Sheeran (1991), pop singer

Miley Cyrus (1992), pop singer

Justin Bieber (1994), pop singer

Kylie Jenner (1997), reality star

Authors/Artists/Social Media Stars:

Laura Lee (1988), YouTube star

Erika Costel (1992), model

Pete Davidson (1993), comedian

Kendall Jenner (1995), model

Kristen Hancher (1998), Instagram star

Chapter Thirteen

Internet

"It's like the Wild West, the Internet. There are no rules."
Steven Wright

BIRTH YEARS: 1990–2010
"Coming of Age" Years: 2000–2035
Primary Tech Event: Wi-Fi
Strauss-Howe Archetype: Hero/Artist
Generation Personality: Dominant/Optimistic
Iconic Generation Representatives: Justin Bieber and Miley Cyrus

Historical Influencing Events in Youth and Young Adulthood:
George Bush presidency, 9-11 terrorist attacks, War on Terror, Hurricane Katrina, Great Recession, Sandy Hook shooting, Barack Obama, Las Vegas shooting, Donald Trump/2016 Election, Kavanaugh SCOTUS hearings, Parkland school shooting, Christchurch massacre, end of ISIS in Syria, immigration and border crisis

---

I n 1968 the Fab Four declared a "revolution."[386] They wanted to change the world. This Beatle's clarion call would prove powerfully prophetic.

At the time they released this classic song from their White album, America was mired in a mess. *The Vietnam War. Racial unrest. Political assassinations. College campus riots.* The Summer of Love was history. Nearly every cultural corner of the American fabric was worn thin by angst, agitation, and anger. In 1969, things did seem rosier. A man walked the moon. The Mets relished in a baseball miracle. And nearly half a million hippies flocked to a farm in upstate New York to rock and roll.

In 1969 a group of dedicated computer scientists also forged the foundations for what we now know as the Internet. It's possible these highly-educated lab rats didn't know or care who the Beatles were, let alone any desire for "revolution." Nevertheless, these geniuses still managed to lay the fundamental building blocks to the greatest technological and cultural transformation since the printing press. In fact, perhaps only fire-making was a greater human innovation.

The Internet changed everything.

Since its introduction in the early 1990s, the Internet has transformed every corner of culture that it's touched. It's anointed every person a journalist, artist, singer, dancer, film producer, politician, lawyer, pastor, teacher, entrepreneur, community organizer, counselor, doctor, and any other profession on the planet. The Internet made handwritten postal mail obsolete. The Internet revolutionized how people would buy and sell, worship, learn, and interact. It introduced a new constellation of virtual real estate, from .com to .edu to .org.

"The Internet has made us richer, freer, connected and informed in ways its founders could not have dreamt of. It has also become a vector of attack, espionage, crime and harm."
George Osborne

However, the Internet also possesses a sinister underbelly that carries a creepy name known as "the dark web." From hacking to pornography, identity theft to cyber bullying, the Internet often reflects the worst in humanity. A good, innocent person can be smeared and destroyed overnight. Secrets can be revealed to end marriages, careers, and reputations in a mouse click. The Internet is a breeding ground for fake news, unverified reports, deceptive memes, and destructive tweets.

It's also become a gruesome live window to the world.

On March 15, 2019, a lone gunman entered a Christchurch mosque hell-bent on chaos and carnage. Prior to his violent killing spree, the self-professed white nationalist instantaneously emailed a seventy-three-page manifesto to media outlets and other influential persons, including the New Zealand prime minister. He then livestreamed on Facebook the massacre that left fifty people dead and dozens more wounded. It's not the first time a crime was livestreamed but unlike previous isolated incidents, this particular video was reproduced and disseminated on social media platforms faster than web masters could remove them. It was the first viral livestream of mass murder.[387]

Historical benchmarks are nothing new for this medium. The Internet has been pushing societal evolution for thirty years. Just when you think you've seen it all, there's a new innovative play on this transformative technology.

And one particular American generation suckled on this cyber culture from its emergence. The Net generation (born 1990 to 2010) is a cohort of children, teens, and young adults who've never lived without web access. The oldest came of age just as Google, Napster, and Pandora found cultural traction. They experienced the entire social media revolution—Facebook, YouTube, Twitter, Instagram, Pinterest, Snapchat—and watched hard drives evolve into clouds and cables morph into streams. They witnessed flip phones transform into Internet devices. From the moment they wake until they close their eyes in sleep, the Net gen is welded to their smart phones.

The information superhighway is their gateway to a "selfie-style" stardom on Instagram or YouTube. This generation measures success in followers, likes, and shares (and some have millions to their name). Many Net gen kids are pathologically obsessed with their social media status. They live for the "like" and even die for it too. The quest for dangerous "selfies" has resulted in hundreds of deaths since 2011.[388] A 2017 research study on rising suicide rates among adolescents identified a direct link to social media. The "perfect life" portrayals combined with cyberbullying has proven deadly for some adolescents. As one teen confessed: "After hours of scrolling through Instagram feeds, I just feel worse about myself because I feel left out."[389]

> *"Millennials, and the generations that follow, are shaping technology. This generation has grown up with computing in the palm of their hands. They are more socially and globally connected through mobile Internet device than any prior generation."*
> **Brad D. Smith**

It's a cyber culture consequence that Internet pioneers never imagined in 1969. Have you noticed the Internet is the only technology that gets capitalized when we write it? We don't give that type of reverence to anything but proper names and God. We don't capitalize cars, planes, telephones, films, radio, vinyl records, televisions, rockets, satellites, or computers. There's something different about *the* Internet. We recognize it's bigger than us. It's beyond us. It's uncontrollable and often beyond censor. It holds the answer to every question. You can't even spell "googled" without G-O-D in it.

So what historical "big bang" produced the Internet? What cosmic event sparked this cyber revolution? Would you guess a Russian rocket? It's true.

THE INTERNET
The history and growth of cyber communication since 1960

89%
of U.S. adults
use the Internet (2018)

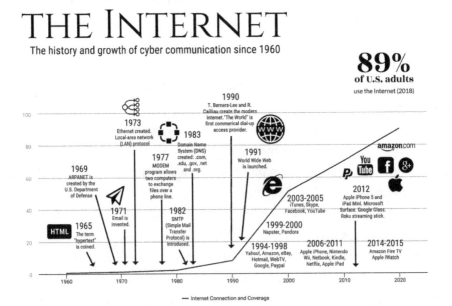

— Internet Connection and Coverage

The real story for the "world wide web" begins in 1957, thanks to the Soviets and their Sputnik spaceship. That's when America woke up to a new reality: we were losing the space race (and most Americans didn't even know there was one). In response, the Eisenhower administration created the Advanced Research Projects Agency (ARPA) as part of the Department of Defense in 1958. Four years later, a visionary named J.C.R. Licklider—who also directed ARPA—released a series of memos describing an "Intergalactic Computer Network." He was a man beyond his time, imagining "graphical computing, user-friendly interfaces, digital libraries, e-commerce, online banking, and cloud computing."[390]

"To join the industrial revolution, you needed to open a factory.
In the Internet revolution, you need to open a laptop."
Alexis Ohanian

In 1966, ARPA tasked Robert Taylor[391] to lead a team to build a computer network. Taylor was frustrated that he had to work from three different computer terminals and wanted them to "talk" to one another and transfer files. He recruited Lawrence Roberts,[392] who had experience in computer networks, to build an ARPA network (eventually known as ARPANET). Roberts created a process he called "packet switching" that allowed data to flow between computers in different locations. By 1968, Roberts had constructed the framework for the network using "interface message processors" (IMPs) to transfer messages and files. In 1969, the first "imp" was delivered to UCLA and four other universities, including the University of Utah and Stanford Research Institute.[393]

On October 29, 1969, Dr. Leonard Kleinrock[394]—who also helped innovate "packet switching"—attempted the first networked communication. In order to log into the system, Kleinrock had to simply type "l-o-g." To ensure success, he had scientists from the other terminal on the phone, listening in. First, he typed "L":

"Do you see the L?"

"Yes, we see the L," came the response.

We typed the O, and we asked, "Do you see the O."

"Yes, we see the O."

Then we typed the G, and the system crashed…

Yet, a revolution had begun.[395]

Kleinrock was right. A revolution had begun. And isn't it ironic the ARPANET was born with what amounts to the single *angelic* word: "Lo?"

As in "lo, you say you want a revolution?"

Unfortunately, an Internet revolution wasn't on anyone's mind in 1969, other than a few mad scientists. Computers were for data entry, computations, and word processing. They weren't intended for communication. That's why we called them "computers."[396] The other concern involved phone lines. These cables were wired for talking, not file transfer. It's why the ARPANET remained primarily a Department of Defense and research university tool for two decades. It was just a place for the academic community and military to share information. Even still, by 1970, there were eighteen mainframe computers hooked to the ARPANET.

The problem now was a common language.

Enter Robert Kahn and Vint Cerf.

Kahn and Cerf created a protocol language called TCP/IP that eventually became the "gateway" to the Internet. In fact, that's where we get the word "Internet." Kahn and Cerf originally called their project "Internetworking" (but later shortened it to "Internet").[397] The credit for email goes to Raymond Tomlinson, the mastermind who created the code and language for electronic mail (including that little "@" symbol).[398] The first email was sent in 1969. Fifty years later, over 281 billion emails a day are received, and two-thirds of those emails are read on mobile devices.[399]

That's what makes the Internet different from other communication inventions. In most cases, a single person was responsible for the technology. Alexander Graham Bell innovated the telephone. Thomas Edison invented the motion picture camera. Philo T. Farnsworth developed television. Steve Jobs and Steve Wozniak made the computer personal. With the Internet, it was a team of unknowns who pioneered it. And, yes, a certain Tennessee senator named Al Gore did play a significant role.[400]

For the next two decades, the ARPANET remained confined to an elite user. It wasn't for the average Joe or Jane. But, then again, neither were computers until they got *personal* in the early 1980s. As homes became more plugged into computer terminals—thanks to the silicon chip, mouse, and modem—the idea of opening up the Internet made more sense. Licklider's original vision for an "intergalactic computer network" was suddenly within reach. By 1990, the ARPANET had connected around 300,000 computers.

It was time to go big *and* go home.

The Information Superhighway

In 1989, Tim Berners-Lee had a burning desire to craft a new democratic, global place to expand Licklider's vision into what he called the "world wide web" or "www" for short. Berners-Lee poured the foundations for the Internet as we know it today.[401] He created the first web server, browser, and page. The Internet begins with him. It's why we still type, even if it's no longer necessary, "www" to travel anywhere online.

"Getting information off the Internet is like taking a drink from a fire hydrant."
Mitch Kapor

But then Berners-Lee did something even more remarkable.

After creating this new cyber world, he turned around and, on August 6, 1991, gave it away…for *free*. The Net generation was just a year old, but they would grow up to love Berner-Lee's gift baby. The following June, the United States Congress passed a bill that took the Internet out of government's hands and fully gave it to the people. It was a landmark declaration of independence as radical as what our founding fathers penned in 1776.

Suddenly it was "we the people" who drove the content of the world wide web. "We the people" would build this new world, not a government. The idea was grand, but it didn't take long for "we the people" to recognize that it meant little if it took a degree in computer science to access it. Maybe it didn't matter much anyway. In 1992, there were only fifty web pages on the Internet to access.

In 1993, that changed, thanks to Marc Andreesson.[402]

Andreesson was fascinated with Berner-Lee's "open-source" Internet concept and invented a user-friendly, free web browser called "Mosaic." He later founded a company called "Netscape" and recast his Mosaic browser as "Navigator." The

Netscape Navigator browser opened the door for the common man to surf the web and became the predominant browser during the 1990s.[403] Thanks to Andreeson's free tool, web traffic exploded. The Navigator had unlocked the Internet, and nothing would be the same again. Internet usage skyrocketed into the stratosphere, growing at unbelievable rates (2300 percent per year). It created an entirely new culture and region known as Silicon Valley. It was a period when people took high risks for high rewards. In the 1990s, 30,000 new tech companies were launched with a million new jobs. *Yahoo!*

Most technologies take a decade to influence a particular generation's psyche, but not the Internet. Once it was open and available in the early 1990s, its rate of influence and cultural impact was immediate. In one famous and rather comical 1994 television moment, three NBC *Today Show* hosts—including Bryant Gumbel and Katie Couric—tried to wrap their frustrated minds around this new technology:[404]

Gumbel:	"That little mark with the 'a' and the ring around it?"
Third host:	"At."
Gumbel:	"You see, that's what I said. Katie said she thought it was 'about.'"
Couric:	"Yeah."
Third host:	"Oh."
Gumbel:	"But I've never it heard said. I've only seen the mark. And then it sounded stupid when I said it: 'violence@nbc.' [NBC displays email address] You see, there it is: 'violence at nbc.ge.com."
Couric:	"Well Allison should know."
Gumbel:	"What is the Internet anyway?"
Couric:	"Internet is that massive computer network. The one that's becoming really big now."
Gumbel:	"What do you mean? Do you write to it like mail?"
Couric:	"No, a lot of people use it to communicate. I guess they can communicate with NBC writers and producers. Allison, can you explain what 'Internet' is?"
Gumbel:	"No, she can't say anything in ten seconds or less." (hosts laugh, recognizing Allison isn't even in the studio)
Off-Stage:	"It's a giant computer network…(Gumbel cuts him off)"

Gumbel:	"Oh, I thought you were going to tell us what 'this' (makes @ symbol) was?"
Third host:	"It's like a computer billboard."
Off-Stage:	"Right, it's a computer billboard and it's nationwide, and its several universities all joined together."
Gumbel:	"And others can access it?"
Third host:	"Right."
Off-Stage:	"And it's getting bigger and bigger all the time."
Gumbel:	"Just great."
Third host:	"It came in real handy during the quake. A lot of people that's how they were communicating to tell family and loved ones they were okay because the phone lines were down."
Couric:	"You don't need a phone line to operate the Internet?
Third host:	"No, no."

Of course, that last punchline was particularly hilarious. In 1994, wireless (Wi-Fi) networks for computers wouldn't be available for another three years. The only way to go online *was* via a phone line.

The World Is Fat

In 2000, half of American adults—by choice or circumstance—could not access the Internet. Two decades later, according to a 2018 Pew Research study, around 10 percent of the U.S. population remained disconnected. The greatest percentage of adults who remain off the Internet grid is not surprising: it's the over-65 crowd (34 percent).[405] They are the last vestiges of a modern (pre-1960) culture…and it's a culture that's fading fast.

———

"We are all now connected by the Internet, like neurons in giant brain."
Stephen Hawking

———

In 2005, *New York Times* columnist Thomas Friedman penned an international bestseller book titled *The World is Flat: A Brief History of the Twenty-first Century* that argued for a globalized view of commerce. Friedman was right. Thanks to the Internet, everything had changed for business in a global marketplace. But it wasn't just commerce. The Internet has also reimagined education (e-learning), entertainment (streamed content), and even religion. A church's web page is the new cultural steeple. It's how people locate a place of worship.

In reality, the emerging cyber culture isn't just "flat" but also F-A-T. It's a "fast and fluid" multiverse in which a person can surf and stream. It's also "accessible." Suddenly, the world (and all the information in it) is at our fingertips. Finally, it's a "temporary and transparent" culture. From social media secret revelations to Snapchat disappearing posts to "cloud-based" computing, the Internet reimagines how we store and distribute information. Is there anything more transparent and temporary than a "cloud?" And yet, that's where we now preserve our most precious digital content.

Since the mid 1990s, a second wave of founding fathers made the Internet work for the rest of us. It's how we now navigate this new f-a-t world.

On July 5, 1994, Jeff Bezos wrote his own personal declaration of independence and launched an online store he called "Amazon" (because the Amazon is the world's largest waterway and its "A" moniker made it appear high in search and alphabetical listings). Initially, Amazon sold books but eventually added videos, electronics, clothing, toys, and furniture. Today, it sells everything under the sun (including groceries, after it's 2017 acquisition of Whole Foods). It's the undisputed champion in the Internet marketplace. In fact, Amazon is the second largest employer in the United States and the most valuable retailer. In January 2019, over 260 billion people visited the website.[406]

In 1999, *Time* magazine named Jeff Bezos its "man of the year."

And that was before he introduced the Kindle, Amazon Prime, Fire television, and the Echo (featuring a know-it-all voice named "Alexa"). Bezos and Amazon pioneered the modern Internet experience.

But there were other players too.

Pierre Omidyar founded eBay auctions in 1995 as the first person-to-person online trading place. It found immediate appeal for collectors on the hunt for a unique, long-lost item. Email companies like Juno and Hotmail emerged, as well as wholesale, one-stop web services like America Online, Compuserve, Prodigy, and

Yahoo! For those looking to build a website there was Angelfire (1996) that was, at one time, the fourth most popular website (behind AOL, Microsoft, and Yahoo!).[407]

The massive explosion of Internet traffic and websites created a new problem: getting noticed. If there are 100,000 websites on dog training, which one is best or most relevant? In the 1990s, search engines like WebCrawler (1994), Lycos (1994), Excite (1995), Altavista (1995), and Ask Jeeves (1996) had varying algorithms to score websites.

And then came Google Search, created by Larry Page and Sergey Brin.

Launched September 15, 1997, Google quickly became the search engine of choice among inquisitive minds. Google better positioned websites (using a "PageRank" algorithm) and allowed for new custom searches. In October of 2018, nearly 93 percent of all web searches were done through Google (or more than 3.5 billion searches daily). Google has expanded searches for everything from images to flights to weather. Google is currently creating the world's largest library with card catalog entries and "snippets" to every book known to man.[408] For the Net generation, the first place they go for information is Google. They have known no other search engine.

In January 2001, another significant website emerged: Wikipedia.

Founded as a nonprofit venture by Jimmy Wales, Wikipedia bills itself as the "people's encyclopedia." It's an open-source, shared website that allows anyone to input, correct, or flag entries. For those born after 1990, they've never known a printed encyclopedia (like *World Book* or *Encyclopedia Britannica*). Before students enjoyed wholesale access to the Internet, these printed book sets were the starting point for research. Digital versions like Microsoft's *Encarta* were transitional encyclopedias, but few in the Net generation used them. Wikipedia quickly became the online encyclopedia, thanks in part to high page rankings in Google searches. Ask any question to Google and Wikipedia is right there to answer.

"This spirit of liberty, of freedom, of openness has been a core part of the Internet…a sort of basic idea that everyone should be able to participate equally in this new medium. It's a very American spirit of an idea; this idea that everyone should have access to knowledge."

Jimmy Wales

The English version of Wikipedia has over 5.8 million article entries. For the *Encyclopedia Britannica* to produce the same information, it would require 2500 volumes. Despite its disparaging reputation among academics, Wikipedia has proven a productive place to research any and all topics. And it's "flagging" of topics ensures the reader is duly warned that there might be problems in the description. But that's the point. It's the "people's encyclopedia," and people make mistakes. They can also correct them. Unlike other printed encyclopedias that were highly editorialized, even slanted on certain topics, Wikipedia lets "we the people" do the corrections, modifications, improvements, explanations, and definitions (and include links to original research).

Not surprisingly, Wikipedia is a top-five website for overall web traffic.[409]

On September 11, 2001, the oldest Net generation members were mere children and preteens. But the terrorist attacks in New York and D.C. brought a fresh reality: live television and fast information. For the Net generation, it meant their world was instantly changed. They'd grow up in an age of terror. From natural catastrophes like Katrina to a Vegas country music festival mass murder to Parkland school shootings, the Net generation relied more and more upon cyber communication and information. They grew up with metal detectors, TSA inspections, zero tolerance rules, and heightened parental protection. Most of the generation would have little to no actual recollection of September 11, 2001, but all lived with its consequences.

Friends Like And Share

The open-source nature of the Internet is what sparked another revolution in the mid-2000s. By this time, the oldest members of the Net generation were teenagers and ready for their own social media movement. The Internet was already brimming with conversation. Chat rooms.[410] Message boards.[411] Instant messages.[412] Online diaries (eventually known as "blogs").[413] But these conversations were text-driven and hyperlinked. The Net gen is more visual, interactive and experiential in their psyche. They were primed for something we now call *social* media.

In 2002, a social gaming site known as *Friendster* was launched. It was the first social media website. Confined to the Philippines, Malaysia, and Singapore, *Friendster* allowed members to share photos, videos, and messages (and even dating information).[414] It proved a precursor for everything to come.

Back in the United States, a business-oriented social media site known as *LinkedIn* also emerged in 2002. Primarily used for the professional class to network, *LinkedIn* featured profiles, skill sets, and employment opportunities for over 610 million people from 200 different countries.[415] A year later, *MySpace* was introduced. It was the American version of *Friendster* and instantly proved a popular place to share news, photos, videos, and blogs. It was a particularly trendy site for those who enjoyed music, movies, and pop culture. Between 2005 and 2009, it was a social media juggernaut.[416]

However, in 2004, a bigger social media giant was born.

"Right now, with social networks and other tools on the Internet, all of these 500 million people have a way to say what they're thinking and have their voice be heard."
Mark Zuckerberg

With current headquarters in Menlo Park, CA, *Facebook* quickly became the darling of social media. Founded by Mark Zuckerberg and a few of his Harvard buddies, *Facebook* was originally limited to Harvard students. Eventually, membership slowly opened to other colleges and universities, but for two years it remained a collegiate site. In 2006, *Facebook* finally allowed anyone thirteen years and older to join, which included the majority of Net generation kids hankering for a place to hang out. By July 2010, there were half a million users and by 2012, a billion people used the site to post status updates, photos, videos, and memes.

For the Net generation, *Facebook* was their cultural "mall" of the world.[417] With the advent of the smartphone, *Facebook* single-handedly introduced the "selfie" to the cultural lexicon. *FaceTime* video chats and livestream video allowed users to become self-styled promoters, producers, and propagandists. Most of it was good and innocuous, but *Facebook* (like the Internet) also had its darker side. In the 2016

Presidential election, the heated and bitter rhetoric between Donald Trump and Hillary Clinton sparked angry and acrimonious interactions between right- and left-wingers, Republicans and Democrats. Fake news was everywhere. Derogatory, dishonest, and divisive posts flooded *Facebook*, even long after Trump was elected. *Facebook* was just like any other public venue: full of opinionated, loud, and passionate voices. It also turns out that *Facebook* contributed to the contentious environment by allowing foreign operatives to post and propagate information that many felt helped Donald Trump win the election.

"Journalism has changed tremendously because of the democratization of information. Anybody can put something up on the Internet. It's harder and harder to find what the truth is."
Robert Redford

Caught in the fray were the members of the Net generation.

They were a large voting block for Hillary Clinton and deeply struggled with her loss. Media footage of the tear-streamed faces of Net generation voters didn't help, nor did parallel events where Net generation kids proved "less resilient and more prone to take offense." Many placed the blame on overprotective (helicopter) parenting that shadowed these Net gen children from the day they were born. These parents showered their kids with undue praise, completed their homework, cleaned their rooms, handed them money, gave them anything they wanted (materially), and, in some cases, even helped to cheat the system for college admission.[418] As a result, the Net generation is generally viewed as entitled, fragile, lazy, uninformed, and hyper-sensitive. They can cry foul if they lose, fail, or mess up. They might shut down (or shout down) anyone with whom they disagree. Some even require "safe places" to protect them from "hate speech" (usually of the conservative and right-wing type).

That's given rise to another derogatory moniker: Generation Snowflake.[419]

Of course, like real snow, it remains to be seen if that label will stick for long. After all, similar tags were hung over the Gen X parents who produced this brood. What goes around, comes around.

In the wake of *Facebook* came other social media giants: *Reddit* and *YouTube* (2005). *Twitter* (2006). *Tumblr* (2007). *Pinterest* and *Instagram* (2010). *Snapchat* (2011). *Marco Polo* (2014). And, once again, the Net generation welcomed each one with open arms. The emergence of micro-communication that's brief like *Twitter* (280 characters) or temporary like *Snapchat* (post disappears shortly) has redefined social media. *YouTube* has actually impacted attention spans, since the average *YouTube* video is a little over four minutes.[420] That changes drastically how we communicate to younger generations. The Net generation, in fact, prefers *YouTube* to traditional television two to one.[421]

YouTube isn't the only thing the Net gen is watching on their screens.

They're also leading a revolution to cut the cord.

The Net generation is turning to Netflix, Hulu, Sling, Roku, Fire, Apple Television, and other streaming options rather than traditional cable and satellite packages. Unlike their older PC generation siblings, who grew up in a "silver disc" (CD/DVD) world, the Net generation is happy to float the "streams" and ride the "clouds."

"Access to computers and the Internet has become a basic need for education in our society."
Kent Conrad

For the Net generation, access to the Internet is a human right and owning a smartphone is a civic duty. The Internet is another utility like water and electricity. And it's not just a connection to the wider world. The Internet *is* the wider world. It's how they gain employment, discover eateries, map destinations, broadcast news, buy stuff, get a date, research a topic, relax and recreate, share, and communicate. The worst thing that can happen is to be out of touch, offline, or off the grid. Many even suffer from nomophobia, or the fear of losing their cell phone.[422]

The youngest Net generation members won't turn twenty-five and complete the coming of age window until 2035. It's anybody's guess what Internet innovations lie ahead, but it's safe to say the "Internet of Things" will fully be in bloom. Essentially, any and everything will be connected. All information (including entertainment) will be streamed. We'll live in *smart* homes with *smart* appliances that cook *smart* food. We'll watch *smart* screens through *smart* devices on *smart* furniture. We'll wear *smart* clothes that will log every heartbeat, body temperature, blood pressure, and calorie. These fashions will communicate to us—probably via self-styled advertising—that we need to eat, sleep, or drink…or even buy something.

The Net generation is the first fully digital, wireless, and mobile cyber generation.

And they may be, as some contend, a "snowflake" generation. But beware: we all know the big things that can happen when snowflakes stick together.

A TIMELINE OF TECHNOLOGICAL EVENTS (1991–2000):

- 1991: Internet is available for unrestricted commercial use. Number of personal computers reaches one million. Linux operating system released. Galileo spacecraft probes an asteroid. Genetic engineering produces blue roses. The first web browser is introduced. Airbag debuts in American cars.
- 1992: Microsoft releases Windows 3.1 and Microsoft Works. AT&T debuts video telephone. Space shuttle Endeavor is launched.
- 1993: Intel introduces the Pentium microprocessor. A bagless vacuum cleaner introduced. Human embryo is cloned. U.S. drops the Strategic Defense Initiative ("star wars" missile interception).
- 1994: Satellite digital television is launched. Netscape Navigator web browser released.
- 1995: Windows 95 released by Microsoft. JavaScript introduced. The online auction company *eBay* debuts. Soviet cosmonaut Valeri Polyakov spends record 438 days in space. Galileo spacecraft arrives at Jupiter. DVD media format is announced.
- 1996: Number of Internet host computers explodes from one to ten million. Internet Explorer 3 web browser released. Duke Nukem 3-D

shareware made available to public. First cloning of a mammal (Dolly the sheep). "Ask Jeeves" debuts. IBM's Deep Blue defeats human for first time in chess. MSNBC launches.

- 1997: Microsoft is the world's most valuable company ($261 billion). ThrustSSC sets supersonic land speed record (763 mph). Mars Pathfinder lands on Mars. Steve Jobs returns as interim CEO of Apple computers.
- 1998: Windows 98 released by Microsoft. E-commerce rises in popularity as more businesses and shops have online presence. *Google* search engine founded. FDA approves Viagra as a treatment for male impotence. Apple computers releases the iMac. India and Pakistan test nuclear weapons.
- 1999: "Melissa" email virus infects over one million computers globally. America successfully tests new intercontinental missile defense system. The "Y2K" problem and millennium bug creates fear. *MySpace* and *Napster* debut. Bluetooth technology is announced.
- 2000: Microsoft releases Windows 2000. AOL and Time Warner merge. The "dot com" bubble bursts and thousands of tech companies close. World's largest passenger plane (Airbus A3xx) is built (able to hold 656 passengers). Destructive ILOVEYOU virus shuts down computers globally. First draft of the Human Genome distributed. Fifty-one million viewers watch the first season finale of *Survivor*.

INFLUENTIAL BIRTHS IN THE NET GENERATION:

Business, Education, Athletes and Other Leaders:
- Mike Trout (1991), baseball player
- Gabby Douglas (1995), gymnast

Entertainers:
- Selena Gomez (1992), pop singer
- Chance the Rapper (1993), rapper
- Harry Styles (1994), pop singer
- Olivia Holt (1997), actress
- Skai Jackson (2002), actress
- Cash Baker (2003), pop singer
- Coco Quinn (2008) dancer

Authors/Artists/Social Media Stars:

- Zoe Sugg (1990), YouTube star
- Hannah Stocking (1992), Instagram star
- Savannah LaBrant (1993), YouTube star
- Karina Garcia (1994) YouTube star
- Jake Paul (1997), YouTube star
- Olivia Jade (1999), YouTube star
- Saffron Barker (2000), YouTube star
- Haley Orona (2002), Instagram star
- Piper Rockelle (2007), YouTube star

Chapter Fourteen
iTECH

*"Smart phones and social media expand our universe. We can connect
with others or collect information easier and faster than ever."*
Daniel Goleman

BIRTH YEARS: 2000–2020
"Coming of Age" Years: 2010–2045
Primary Tech Event: Smartphone
Strauss-Howe Archetype: Artist
Generation Personality: Dominant/Pessimistic
Iconic Generation Representatives: Barron Trump and Loren Gray

Historical Influencing Events in Youth and Young Adulthood:
*Barack Obama, Las Vegas shooting, Donald Trump/2016 Election, Parkland school
shooting, Kavanaugh SCOTUS hearings, Christchurch massacre, end of ISIS in Syria,
Sri Lanka Easter massacre, border and immigration crisis*

Since 1998, Beloit College has issued its annual "Mindset List"—a collection of cultural declarations to help professors, college admission counselors and university administrators to understand the mentality of incoming freshmen. This popular list revealed what recent high school graduates remember in regard to current events, technology, and lifestyles.

In 2018, the Mindset List captured the first cohort of kids born since the millennium. Here were a few of their more notable revelations (guaranteed to make anyone over forty feel their age):[423]

- Outer space has always had human habitation.
- They've always had Wikipedia as a reference tool.
- They've grown up afraid that a shooting could happen at their school.
- The Prius has always been on the road.
- There's always been a *Survivor* and *Big Brother* reality show.
- A visit to the bank is rare.
- Light bulbs have always been shatterproof.
- Mass market books have also been available as ebooks.
- Films have always been distributed via the Internet.
- The computer mouse is nearly extinct.

It's a bit unbelievable.

An amazing cultural transformation happened.

We moved from analog to digital, from print to electronic, from landline to online, from Gutenberg to Google. We've become a post-modern cyber culture. Instant communication. Visual experiences. Social media. We now live within a fast, fluid world of "clouds" and "streams." In fact, we've seen more change in the past two decades than the previous century combined. Ever since the clock struck 01/01/00, we've witnessed:

- The emergence of Wikipedia, LinkedIn, MySpace, Facebook, Twitter, Pinterest, Instagram, Snapchat, Tinder, eHarmony, Match, Skype, FaceTime, Zoom, Marco Polo, Tik Tok,
- The rise of iTunes, YouTube, Hulu, Netflix, and Sling,

- The advent of flash drives, DVRs, hybrid cars, BlueRay, Bluetooth, 3-D scanners, iPods, touch screen tablets, smart phones, 3-D printers, holograms, smart watches, FitBits, hover boards, self-driving cars, robots, artificial intelligence
- The arrival of Gmail, electronic payments, Google Maps, Kindle
- Computer-generated images, augmented reality, synthetic organ transplants, embryonic stem cell research.

We are a technologically driven culture. We may not be tech savvy, but we are certainly tech *reliant*. We count on technology to serve, salve, and save us. From the womb to the tomb, technology is reinventing every aspect of our lives.

And nobody knows this new world better than one of our youngest generations.

It's a cohort of children and teens born between 2000 and 2020 that I refer to as the iTech generation. It's a moniker that pays rightful homage to the influence of Apple in the 2000s, but also the general technologies that shifted our culture: iPod (MP3/MP4), iTunes (streaming content to electronic devices), iPhone (smart phones with killer apps), iPad (touch-screen tablets), and iWatches (smart devices and appliances). Steve Jobs and Apple certainly led this revolution in "iTechnology," but it was the children born after 2000 who suckled upon it. The little "i" highlights the individualistic, personal, and narcissistic tendencies of this post-2000 group of kids. Their ability to personalize their life is unlike any previous generation. They are a "Selfie" generation that comfortably dwells with web-connected technology.

"The Internet has made us richer, freer, connected and informed in ways its founders could not have dreamt of. It has also become a vector of attack, espionage, crime and harm."
George Osborne

It's why I call them iTechs.

But they have other nicknames too: Posts, Plurals, ReGen, Centennials, Plurals, Linksters,[424] and Homeland Generation.[425] Generational expert and psychology professor Jean Twenge has labeled them iGen for similar reasons as mine:

> A generational label needs to capture something about the generation's experience, and for iGen'ers, the Internet and smartphones have defined many of their experiences thus far—thus the name iGen, like iPhones and iPads. One survey found that 2 out of 3 teens has an iPhone (specifically an iPhone, not just a smartphone).[426]

Perhaps the only weakness in "iGen" is it doesn't go far enough (focusing more on "generation" than "technology"). It's also redundant: "iGen generation." Around 2007, I started to employ the term "iTech" to define those born after 2000. My audiences found the designation helpful, particularly in the wake of the iPhone. Smartphone technology radically shifted the uses of a cell phone from an audio and text communication device to photography, videography, social media, video gaming, GPS, and countless other applications. When I surveyed the technology that emerged since 2001—particularly those produced by Apple—I noticed an "iTrend" emerging. The generation coming of age under the influence of iPods, iTunes, iPads, and iPhones were more appropriately viewed as *iTechers*. It's a name that made sense.

Surprisingly, and unfortunately, the most common label for these children and teens is Generation Z. To be honest, it's an intellectually lazy moniker that has little meaning other than to follow Generations X and Y (Millennials). This alphabet generational name game has run its course. As one Millennial quipped, "I wonder what they'll do when they run out of letters in the alphabet?"[427] Evidently, it's to go back to "A." The youngest kids are now being labeled as "The Alpha Generation."[428] The good news is that we have twenty-three American generations to go before we hit double "X."

But if naming this crop of kids is difficult, it's even more challenging to identify their birth year frames. On this matter, there is even less agreement. In fact, it's a messy endeavor and all over the map. I think partly because there's confusion over what is a "wave" within a generation and what is a *complete* generation. As

I've already argued, every generation has a first and second wave that's contained within a roughly two-decade time frame. Gen X, for example, had its "Pong/Pacman" wave (1961–1971) and "Mario Brothers" (1972–1981) wave. Millennials are either Reagan/Bush babies (1982–1991) or Clinton/Bush babies (1992–1998). Technically, the former is Gen Y and the latter is Gen Z (for those who prefer alphabetical labels), but both Gen Y and Gen Z are part of the larger "Millennial" generation (1982–1998).

That's why any stretch of Gen Z past the year 2000 creates problems.

"The digital universe is a kind of wild west. Largely unregulated. Parents worry about inappropriate content, children's privacy, safety and all the hours they're spending staring at a screen."
Kate Snow, *NBC News*

So, what are the Gen Z birth years? It depends on who you ask.

Jean Twenge argues that iGen was born between 1995 and 2012.[429] William Strauss and Neil Howe state the Homeland Generation (which followed the Millennials) was first born in 2005.[430] Most proponents of a Gen Z designation argue for a 1996 start to the generation but vary on when the generation ends (from 2010 to present day). The Pew Research Center concluded that 1997 to 2012 is their definition for Generation Z.[431] The Barna Group identifies Gen Z as 1999 to 2015, while the Center for Generational Kinetics contends for a 1996 to "TBD" frame, suggesting Gen Z might still be born yet today.[432]

For this work, the blended frames of the Net generation (born 1990 to 2010) with the iTech Generation (born 2000 to 2020) help to eliminate these contradictions. Nevertheless, there's a huge difference between flip phone Net gens and smartphone iTechs. There's a clear demarcation between those born prior to social media (which fully blossomed in 2007) and those born after social media. That's the problem with Gen Z crossing those technological lines. And don't forget the iTech generation didn't start coming of age until 2010, just as social media and smartphone technology had their cultural tipping points.

"We want to reinvent the phone. What's the killer app? The killer app is making calls! It's amazing how hard it is to make calls on most phones. We want to let you use contacts like never before—sync your iPhone with your PC or Mac."
Steve Jobs

If there's a single event that marks the memory of the Net generation (which includes late wave Millennials), it's September 11, 2001. Every person born prior to 1997 possesses a distinct recollection of this horrific day of terror. But it can also be argued that the younger the person on 9/11/01, the less direct impact it had upon their lives (other than temporary fear). My son was seven years old on that terrible day. He remembers watching the news with his mother and feeling afraid that terrorists might strike our house. But, within days, that fear subsided. He was back to watching Barney and chasing the dog. The oldest Net Gens were eleven on September 11, 2001—old enough to understand and remember, but still young enough that the event carried little lasting impact.

However, let's fast-forward six years to the Great Recession (2007–2010).

Now these *same* kids were seventeen and younger. And it could be argued the Great Recession probably had a larger impact on those born after 1990 than the attacks of September 11, 2001. This economic downturn impacted these children's and teen's general lifestyles, limiting opportunity and changing preferences. In the Great Recession, American families downsized and deserted their homes. Layoffs were common. Job prospects were few. Money was tight. Just like in the Great Depression, when the technology of the radio was a necessity, the smartphone proved indispensable during the Great Recession. Even those on limited incomes found a way to own one.

Americans have always processed transformative historical moments in the technology we own—whether its radio, television, or smartphones. They are our windows to the world. This was particularly true for the iTech Generation, as Jean Twenge validates:

Due to these [technological] influences and many others, iGen is distinct from every previous generation in how its members spend their time, how they behave, and their attitudes toward religion, sexuality, and politics. They socialize in completely new ways, reject once sacred social taboos, and want different things from their lives and careers. They are obsessed with safety and fearful of their economic futures, and they have no patience for inequality based on gender, race, or sexual orientation. They are the forefront of the worst mental health crisis in decades, with rates of teen depression and suicide skyrocketing since 2011.[433]

Dr. Twenge describes the iTech Generation to a "T." And that "T" stands for "technology." And the "i" technologies in particular have been a guiding force for this generation. The smartphone is their preferred information and entertainment device. It's how they listen to music, find an address, search for a friend, read a book, watch television, launch a business, take a photo, capture a video, play a game, stream a movie, monitor their health, look for housing, track a flight, make a bank deposit, and chat with family. The iTech generation has only known a world with smartphones, Kindles, iPads and electronic payments.

But that isn't the only "T" the iTechs have known. Socially, they grew up with another "T": terrorism.

Columbine predates their first birth year only by months (April 20, 1999). And just as these tykes were old enough to process death and tragedy, they faced horrific mass shootings at an Amish schoolhouse (2006), Virginia Tech campus (2007), Aurora, CO movie theater (2012), and Sandy Hook Elementary School (2012). Even places of worship were no longer safe zones, whether in Charleston, SC or Sutherland Springs, TX or Pittsburgh, PA. Holiday parties (San Bernardino), nightclubs (Orlando), and restaurants (Thousand Oaks) were all targets. The most lethal mass shooting was on October 1, 2017 when a lone gunman opened fire from his Mandalay Bay hotel room in Las Vegas, killing fifty-eight people and injuring 489 others. Since the first year of the iTech's birth in 2000, there have been thirty-eight high-profile mass shootings in America (nearly four times the number between 1980 and 1999).[434] Many of these shootings happened in schools.

The iTechs have only always known America at war and a world with tragedy. They've witnessed costly and deadly hurricanes from Katrina (2005) to Harvey

(2017). They've seen deadly tsunamis from Indonesia (2004) and Japan (2011) to earthquakes in Haiti (2010) that killed hundreds of thousands. Scott Stenholm, writing for the *Huffington Post,* astutely recognized how technology impacted awareness of current events:

> [Between 2001 and 2011] we have seen something coincidently accompany these tragedies: a massive media boom. Twenty-four-hour-a-day cable news, the full-fledged explosion of the Internet highlighted by Twitter and Facebook. And the constant use of cell phones, as if they were never not in our lives, has made our world wildly smaller.[435]

The iTechs matured within this technological shift. Consequently, to best understand those born between 2000 and 2020, we must recognize how technology—especially those "i" technologies—served as windows to their worlds. Essentially, they've grown up in a 3-D culture: digital, diverse, and decentralized. Let's unpack each characteristic.

Digital!

The iTechs grew up in a completely digital culture.

By the year 2000, the printed photograph had enjoyed its final sunset. The age of .jpegs, .pdfs, .mp3s, and .mp4s had dawned. In the next two decades, everything became *electronic*: mail, literature, commerce, education, business, banking, advertising, religion, and entertainment. The old "box" and "print" technologies of the modern age faded fast. Boxy analog televisions converted to flat-screen digital HD. The VCR morphed into DVR. Physical map books evolved into GPS. Tactile media (CD/DVD) transformed into streaming formats. Hard drives melted into "cloud" storage. Film cameras, cassettes, fax machines, phone books, and landlines died a slow death. The newspaper's demise became its own headline.

During the 2000s, the "middles" collapsed.

The middle man disappeared as we increasingly did things ourselves. Authors no longer needed a publisher. Filmmakers distributed movies freely through the Internet. Travelers booked their own flights, cars, and hotels. Mainline denominations experienced declining attendances.[436] Mainstream media—particularly the Big Three of NBC, CBS, and ABC—watched their ratings dwindle.[437] Middle management was laid off. Middle-aged men and women were suddenly unemployable. Mid-range (starter) homes were hard to find. Mid-range model car sales slowed as Americans opted for either giant Hummers or tiny smart cars.

For the iTech generation, the most pronounced change was in media formats.

The "silver disc" (CD/DVD) of their older Net generation siblings was so last century. The compact disc reached its summit in sales—943 million—during the first year of the iTech's birth (2000). However, throughout the iTech's lifespans, thanks to MP3 streaming and downloads, CD sales plunged 94 percent to a paltry 52 million in 2018.[438] Physical DVD sales also took a dive, while subscription streaming services like Netflix and Hulu climbed steadily.[439] At the present rate, the CD and DVD will be dead by 2025, joining the VHS, cassette and 8-track.

Physical hard drives, satellite dishes, and cable television are on a death march too. Gen X and Boomers are the only ones keeping these technologies alive.[440]

That's because the Net and iTech generations are comfortable swimming in "streams" and riding "clouds." They store, interact, and process information differently than previous generations. They will gladly store their photos, videos, documents, passwords, and other digital valuables on cloud-based systems. They prefer streamed content to cabled television and home satellite dishes (and will end their dominance around 2030). Wireless technology will be the norm. In their tactile touchscreen world, there is no mouse. There are no "points, clicks, and drags," only "pinches, swipes, and taps." A 2014 study of iTechs discovered that four in ten spend over three hours a day using computers for activities other than schoolwork (nearly double the rate from 2004).[441]

"Everyone has a really short attention span nowadays with our social media, our phones. Even me—I can't go without touching my phone every five minutes."
Alexa Bliss

The irony is those computers are now in iTechs' hands 24/7/365. The smartphone is the new *personal* computer. In fact, desktop computers sales are declining and, as the iTech enters the workplace, these "boxy" machines will likely be replaced by tablet and smartphone technology.[442] A 2018 Pew Research study revealed that 95 percent of iTech adolescents possess a smartphone and nearly half disclose they're "almost constantly" online.[443] Nearly three in ten iTechers confess to smartphone use every night *after midnight* and 67 percent are highly stressed if they lose or break their phone.[444] Their favorite mode of social media is YouTube (85 percent), Instagram (72 percent) and Snapchat (59 percent). Facebook is the big loser (down 20 percent in the past three years).[445]

A digitized world allows the iTechs to transmit and transfer content fast.

For them, life happens in a livestream.

Thanks to social media, YouTube, cable news, FaceTime, and other "live" media, the iTechs experience historic moments through a camera's eye. From school to church to street corners to home, cameras capture every angle, turn and moment. Whenever there's a newsworthy event, the smartphones light up, cameras point, and photographs or video are transmitted instantaneously anywhere and to anyone they choose. The difference between a Net generation "Columbine" tragedy (1999) and an iTech "Parkland" school shooting (2018) cannot be overstated. There were no smartphones to record the carnage in Colorado and any surveillance video was released through controlled channels. But that wasn't the case in Florida. The students at Marjory Stoneman Douglas high school were texting and "tweeting… posting on Snapchat and sending videos to friends and family."[446]

These iTech students were fully engaged in communication to outsiders…in *real* time…while bullets flew. That's a true gamechanger.

What does a digital mindset mean for the iTech as they grow into adulthood?

First, it possibly signals the end of brick and mortar education as we know it. The last bastions of the modern world are the school and church. The iTech generation is comfortable with online learning, digital platforms, electronic transmissions, and social media interactions. Just as streaming subscriptions are supplanting cable and satellite television, boxed radio sets, newspapers and print technologies, so will digital learning find a tipping point sometime between 2018 and 2038 as the iTechs graduate into college. That doesn't mean the transition to a more personalized, digital, and collaborative learning environment will be smooth. In 2018, Gen X parents, iTech students and teachers from Connecticut to Kansas launched outright war against a Mark Zuckerberg-backed online program known as Summit Learning (currently used by nearly 400 schools across America).[447] Nevertheless, online schools continue to grow in number and students. One educational study found that online schools have a 6 percent annual enrollment growth that attracts over 310,000 American students. Another 420,000 students are involved in virtual schools taking over a million online courses.[448]

For the iTech, the world of information is a click away. Between Google and YouTube, most of life's answers are readily available and that spells trouble for colleges and universities that have made education increasingly expensive during the Net generation years. The iTechs grew up in the shadow of the Great Recession. They watched their parents lose their jobs, careers, cars, and homes. They also witnessed how their older Net gen siblings graduated from college as "ninjas" (no income, no job or assets) drowning in the deep waters of educational loan debt. For the iTechs, the Internet is a free education and time will tell if they'll invest good money for information they can easily obtain online. More likely, iTechs will pay for personal coaching and mentoring, leaning toward live-experience retreats, conferencing, and interactions with people they admire. Just as the school used to hire faculty, in the future, students will secure their own professors through online portals.

The hyper-connectivity of the iTechs will also transform how they interact with brands through contextualized marketing. Imagine a day when clothes are "smart" (and connected to your smartphone and the Internet). Now imagine how vendors will interact with you through digital billboards and texts based upon your heart rate, thirst, hunger, and body temperature. Imagine how first responders will be notified the moment a heart attack occurs (even if you're physically unable to call) while GPS tracks your location. Imagine how your clothing will allow churches, clubs, and community gatherings to take attendance, communicate announcements, and create personalized experiences.

One more thing: the iTechs inherently value collaborative environments and solutions. Consequently, they possess a "sharing" perspective that seeks to help and serve others. This collaborative attitude carries a "selfie" transparency that forfeits privacy. They recognize that no one can hide, at least not for long. They also know it's easy to steal in a cyber culture. Consequently, the iTechs will swiftly adopt security clearances that protect and hide their true identities through iris and facial recognition technology.

Diverse!

The iTech generation is America's most diverse generation.

According to a 2018 Pew Research study, 48 percent of Americans born since 1997 are non-white.[449] However, a comprehensive U.S. Census Bureau's report in the same year revealed among children under age nine that there are more non-white than white births. The Brookings Institution referred to this phenomenon as "Generation 'Z-Plus.'"[450] In general, the white population is now a minority (49 percent) to other racial groups, as the Hispanic (26 percent), Black (14 percent), Asian (5 percent), multi-racial (5 percent), and Native American (1 percent), collectively, hold a slight majority edge.[451]

But we've seen this tipping point coming for years. This change in racial cultures is particularly noticeable in restaurant and supermarket fare. *Asian. Italian. Mexican. Indian. Mediterranean. French.* American diets not only include traditional Chinese but Thai, Korean, Japanese, and Vietnamese cuisine. We enjoy Cajun, Tex Mex, Greek, and kosher. Even American barbecue is diverse: Memphis, Kansas City, Texas, Carolinas, Alabama, Chicago, Hawaiian, and St. Louis, each one with different rubs, sauces and sides.

The iTechs have grown up in a culture in which different is normal. Reality television spotlights this diversity. From *Little People, Big World* to *Sister Wives* to *Married at First Sight*, unique families and relationships are celebrated and normalized. Social movements like *Black Lives Matter*, *#MeToo*, and LGBTQ rights highlight inequalities in the American culture. The iTechs have grown up in a socially diverse "rainbow flag" world. They've never known a world without a black U.S. president, women as CEOs, or television without lead gay characters.

Even religion has gotten more diverse for the iTech.

"…the percentage of young adults who believed in God changed little between 1989 and 2000. Then it fell off a cliff. By 2016, one out of three 18-to 24-year-olds said they did not believe in God."

Jean M. Twenge

In a post-9-11 culture, they've interacted with Islam like no other American generation. The influx of Asian and Indian immigrants has brought new awareness to eastern religions like Buddhism, Hinduism, Taoism, and Sikhism. American Christianity has also faced new diversity as conservative and liberal churches have divided over various social issues, most notably abortion and homosexuality. Consequently, since 2000, American churches have experienced an attendance decline among younger post-modern generations. Non-denominational, evangelical congregations attempted to reach these disenfranchised young adults by ditching denominational names for more visual monikers like Oasis, Journey, Bridge, Summit, and Rock. Unfortunately, this did little to stem the tide of an eroding biblical worldview. A 2018 Barna Group study concluded that iTechs essentially possess no "religious identity."[452]

- While nearly six in ten iTechs still profess either a Catholic (17 percent) or non-Catholic (42 percent) faith, there's a growing irreligiousness. iTechs are non-religious (14 percent), atheist (13 percent), or agnostic (8 percent) in their religious preference. The rise in iTech atheism is double other generational cohorts (which runs between 5 and 7 percent)
- 37 percent of iTechs agree it's impossible to absolutely know God exists.
- More than half (58 percent) embrace relativism or the concept that all religions lead to God and there is no one true faith system.
- Of iTechers who attend church, most retain a positive view of the experience, but four in ten view church as intolerant and another 36 percent believes Christians are hypocritical.
- More than half (54 percent) view church participation as unimportant.

Religious diversity for the iTech generation is normal and good. To them, differences are positive and attractive. As one teen confessed to me, "It doesn't matter what you believe as long as you believe something." They are the true "whatever" generation.

This diversity in belief, values, and opinion creates a distinct individuality for the iTech. From hair color to nail polish to music preferences, they pursue uniqueness. Social media has grooved them for interaction with various cultures, ideologies, philosophies, religions, and lifestyles. Even their names are unique or spelled distinctively (like one girl I know named "Uneek"). I have granddaughters named Scottlyn and Aliyah. No American generation has more unique names than the iTechs, and it's likely this value for individuality will influence their self-worth, digital footprint, and personality.

The iTech generation has also grown up in a deeply divided, red and blue America. NBC political analyst Tim Russert coined the terms to represent Republicans (red) and Democrats (blue) during the 2000 presidential election, the first birth year of the iTech generation.[453] The election of George W. Bush over Al Gore proved contentious and controversial, carving a left versus right/ Democrat versus Republican power struggle that's never gone away. With each presidential election cycle, the political rhetoric grows more heated, combative, and dishonest. Gridlock, fake news, and partisan politics rule press conferences, Congressional hearings and mainstream media feeds. Neither the left nor the right is immune or guiltless.

By the 2016 presidential election, just as the oldest iTech generation members reached adolescence, all hell broke loose. The election of Donald Trump, a former reality star and real estate tycoon was shockingly divisive. Trump is cocky, sarcastic, and uncouth, but his promise to drain the swamp and "make America great again" resonates with many conservative Americans. Just like Roosevelt used radio in the 1930s and Reagan employed television in the 1980s, Trump adopted Twitter to directly communicate to the American people. Unfortunately, the Trump presidency only split the country deeper. Social media exploded with politically divisive memes, partisan posts, and contentious opinions. The iTech's mass exodus from Facebook coincidentally paralleled the rising political rhetoric that has soaked the social media website since the 2016 election.

The oldest iTechs will cast their first vote for a U.S. president in 2020.

But which way they lean is anyone's guess.

Some have argued the iTechs are the most conservative generation since 1945.[454] But that might be optimistic. A 2019 Pew study suggests a more moderate to liberal perspective for the iTech generation. In that study, only one in three approved of Donald Trump while seven in ten felt government should do more to fix America's problems. Not surprisingly, 62 percent agreed that racial/ethnic diversity is a good thing for the country. The iTechs also tend to be more moderate on social issues. They generally possess no conflict with gay marriage, legalized marijuana, or transgender rights. Nevertheless, they do lean toward "Make America Great Again" nationalism[455] and fiscally conservative policies (probably due to being raised during the Great Recession).

In general, the diversity of the iTech generation is widespread. It's a part of their generational DNA, thanks largely to social media.

Decentralized!

In 2006, leadership experts Ori Brafman and Rod Beckstrom penned an insightful bestselling leadership book titled *The Starfish and the Spider: The Unstoppable Power of Leaderless Organizations*. The metaphor proves helpful to understand the cyber culture of the iTech generation. Throughout their lives, they've experienced decentralized, web-driven communities and organizations that have flattened hierarchies and created an open-source culture.

From Wikipedia and YouTube, to the Tea Party and #MeToo movements, to al Qaeda and Isis terrorist cells, the iTechs matured within decentralized formats and contexts. Once again, it was technology that leads the way. The iTechs routinely use decentralized social media sites like Snapchat, Tik Tok, and Instagram. Thanks to the Internet, they enjoy multi-player video games like *Minecraft* and *Fortnite*. As students, they self-style their learning through educational websites like the Khan Academy and attend online schools like Northstar Academy, Franklin Virtual High School, and the Keystone School.

YouTube and Instagram have catapulted many iTech generation kids into high-earning superstars followed by millions. Many iTech kids have turned their hobbies into cash. It's no wonder that nearly three in four teens hope to start their own business. In their world, the Internet creates a ripe opportunity where anyone, anywhere, anytime can become rich and famous. You just have to figure out how to do it.

This decentralized attitude will likely influence entrepreneurial careers for the iTech generation. They won't value working "*for* the man" as much as working "*with* the man." This independent yet collaborative entrepreneurship will prove invaluable in the 2030s and 2040s—just as the bulk of their generation reaches young adulthood. With the emergence of robotics and artificial intelligence, the iTech generation will quickly learn that jobs once awarded to lower- and middle-class workers will be outsourced to machines. From transportation to food preparation and product delivery, robots will be pervasive in tomorrow's workplace. Consequently, those who can creatively self-sustain an income will possess the edge.

A decentralized culture means that information is fast, accessible, and temporary. What we need to know today might be completely irrelevant tomorrow. What is useful today might be totally impractical tomorrow. And what is ingenious today might be unreasonable tomorrow. The iTechs will be comfortable in a world spinning at the speed of life. Unlike older generations today who struggle to multi-task with technology—such as texting while driving—the younger generations will become increasingly proficient. But that thought shouldn't bring alarm. Self-driving vehicles will eliminate that possibility. In the future, we'll all text and *ride*.

If there's a dark side to this decentralized culture, it would be the inability to focus. With so much information, visual stimulation, and choices flying around, the iTech generation often struggles to maintain attention. Thanks to micro-media like Twitter and Snapchat, the iTech generation operates within abbreviated thoughts, emoticons, and shortened words. Java, for example, already deletes vowels in its strings.[456] Acronyms like "btw," "idk," and "noyb" are common.[457] Some acronyms also carry multiple messages. The lovable "lol" (laughing out loud) can also stand for flirting, nervousness, and creepy.[458]

"In the next decade we may see more young people who know just the right emoji for a situation—but not the right facial expression."
Jean Twenge

Another consequence of decentralization is the emergence and acceptance of relative truth. This is particularly troubling for those in religious communities who promote a belief in Absolute Truth. If all truth is decentralized (meaning all truth is on equal ground), then no single truth is right or superior. Judaism, Islam, and Christianity are rooted to absolute truth claims. Both the Roman Catholic and Mormon profess to be the only true church. In an increasingly decentralized culture that embraces relative truth, it creates difficulty for exclusive religions. But it's also problematic for science, which operates on objective truths and verifiable facts. From climate change to gender dysphoria to evolutionism, what happens when the facts don't match the presuppositions? Or worse, what happens when new facts disrupt old ideas? How does humanity handle genetic engineering without playing God?

These are the theological and philosophical questions that the iTech generation will debate their entire lives. Despite abbreviated acronyms and emoticons, there are some issues and certain problems that can't be fixed without the truth, the whole truth, and nothing but the truth.

"The blue light emanating from our cell phones, our tablets and our laptops is playing havoc on our brain chemicals: our serotonin, our melatonin. It's screwing up our sleep patterns, our happiness, our appetites...."
Harley Pasternak

The good news is the iTech generation is comfortable with the quick evolution of technology and the sudden changes that certain technologies bring. That will be critical in the coming years as America and the world experiences even bigger and more disruptive change.

I hope you're still buckled in for this ride.

A TIMELINE OF TECHNOLOGICAL EVENTS (2001–2010):

- 2001: Apple releases the iPod and iTunes. Wikipedia is launched. World's first contraceptive patch is marketed.
- 2002: First drone strike. The Odyssey finds water deposits on Mars. LinkedIn debuts. First camera phones are released.
- 2003: The Human Genome Project completes 99 percent of the human genome. Skype and MySpace debut. First cloned horse in Italy. Space Shuttle Columbia disintegrates upon re-entry, killing seven astronauts. Concorde makes last commercial flight. Blu-ray disc and players released.
- 2004: Facebook and Gmail debut. A 1 gig SD card is released.
- 2005: YouTube, Reddit, and Google Maps debut. Xbox 360 is released. Steve Fossett completes first non-stop, non-refueled solo flight around the world.

- 2006: Twitter debuts. Sony PlayStation 3 and Nintendo Wii are released. One billionth song purchased at iTunes. Google purchases YouTube. Pluto downgraded from planet to dwarf planet.
- 2007: Kindle debuts. The Apple iPhone and iTouch (built in wi-fi and touch screen) are released. Honda sells zero-emission, hydrogen-fuel-cell powered vehicle.
- 2008: Hulu debuts. Apple releases new ultra-thin MacBook Air notebook
- 2009: American and Russian satellites collide over Siberia. NASA launches probe to search moon for water near its south pole. Mobile phone 3G networks debut.
- 2010: Square, Instagram, and Pinterest debut. Apple released the iPad. Microsoft's Bing and Yahoo! combine search technology to compete with Google. Android phones outsell Apple iPhones.

INFLUENTIAL BIRTHS IN THE iTECH GENERATION:

Business, Education, Athletes and Other Leaders:
- Sophie Dossi (2001), gymnast
- Barron Trump (2006), political family member

Entertainers:
- Rowan Blanchard (2001), actress
- Loren Gray (2002), pop singer
- Grace VanderWaal (2004), pop singer
- Mason Ramsey (2006), country singer
- Josie Duggar (2009), reality star

Authors/Artists/Social Media Stars:
- Hunter Rowland (2001), YouTube star
- Jade Weber (2005), model
- Ruby Rube (2006), YouTube star
- Zircon (2007), YouTube star
- Tydus Talbott (2014), YouTube star

Chapter Fifteen

Robotics

"We're seeing the arrival of conversational robots that can walk in our world. It's the golden age of invention."
David Hanson

BIRTH YEARS: 2010–2030
"Coming of Age" Years: 2020–2055
Primary Tech Event: TBD
Strauss-Howe Archetype: Artist-Prophet
Generation Personality: Dominant/Pessimistic
Iconic Generation Representatives: TBD

Historical Influencing Events in Youth and Young Adulthood:
Donald Trump/2016 Election, Immigration and Border Crisis

S uper Bowls don't tend to be weird.

But the 2019 Super Bowl in Atlanta wasn't your typical football game.

For starters, it was a low-scoring affair. Neither the New England Patriots nor the Los Angeles Rams—both reputable scoring offenses—could find the end zone. At the conclusion of the third quarter, a combined six points was on the board in a 3-3 tie. The Patriots eventually pulled away to win a 13-3 Super Bowl LIII victory, but it remained the lowest scoring game in NFL championship history.

Not surprising, the commercials were the real winners…some were even memorable.

Particularly, a series of Intuit Turbo Tax commercials featuring an android named "RoboChild."[459] This lifelike bot was part machine and part human. The spooky part was how much Robochild acted like a *real* person. It conversed like a *real* person. It talked back, dreamed, and thought like a *real* person. And that was the point. Intuit's central message its tax preparation company is composed of "real humans, not robots." Robots may look and sound human, but they're not. And we need to understand the difference.

That's good to know.

Because RoboChild was a bit *weird*. Social media buzzed with reactions. Some viewed the mechanical kid as creepy, especially when he (she or it) stood next to snoozing dad and murmured, "Wakey wakey, papa." America is clearly not ready for lifelike android alarm clocks. Some commentators dreadfully imagined RoboChild as the beginning of the end for human civilization, fearing the apocalyptic notion called the *singularity* (the moment when humans and androids merge into one race). However, most viewers found the subtle humor in the commercials. RoboChild as cute, coy, and cool. Nothing to see here; just keep moving.

But perhaps we shouldn't be hasty. Perhaps there is something to see here.

Perhaps RoboChild wasn't just another cute and cuddly Super Bowl commercial.

Perhaps RoboChild is revealing a brave new world reality with a foreboding truth: the robots are *here*. This isn't science fiction anymore. It's science fact-ion. The age of robots and artificial intelligence is in its infancy—just a RoboChild— but it's about to completely transform our lives. Robots will do more than vacuum floors, roam Mars, and mow lawns. These humanoids will converse and interact with our world. The age of "smart" robots is now upon us, and RoboChild is exhibit number one.

"If you look at the field of robotics today, you can say robots have been in the deepest oceans, they've been to Mars, you know? They've been all these places, but they're just now starting to come into your living room. Your living room is the final frontier for robots."
Cynthia Breazeal

Robotics will shape the youngest American generation their entire lives. The current crop of kids, born since 2010, will inherit a world baptized in artificial intelligence. By the end of their birth years in 2030, an Intuit "RoboChild" will likely be the *norm*. And these humanoid mechanical creations won't be the only "artificially intelligent" things. From smart appliances to smart clothes to smart cars, everything will be "intelligent." If you think your "smartphone" made you feel dumb, you ain't seen nothing yet.

In fact, for this new emerging generation, it's no coincidence the "smartphone" found its cultural tipping point in 2010, the first year of their birth. Apple released the iPhone in 2007 and android phones soon followed. Initially, these "smartphones" were a luxury. In fact, between 2007 and 2009, smartphone sales were unremarkably sluggish, although with an annual uptick (moving from 122 to 172 million sales per year). But then, smartphone sales exploded through the roof. In 2010 alone, smartphone sales nearly doubled (to 296 million units sold). In just five years—2010 to 2015—smartphone sales quadrupled. By 2018, 1.5 billion smartphones were sold in a single year.[460] No technology in the history of man has sold so many units, so quickly. The smartphone's rise in dominance is unprecedented.

Wakey, wakey, papa.

The smartphone signaled a sea change in how humans communicate. Smartphones produced their own *singularity*. It's not a smart phone (two words) but a smartphone (one word). It's a phone, MP3 player, gaming device, GPS, television, health monitor, camera, flashlight, social media platform, news feed, photo album, alarm clock, digital book reader, and personal computer—all rolled into a *single* machine. Unlike the flip phone which stored only an address book, memos, texts, and low-quality photos, the smartphone is a technological extension of our identity as a person (which is why its loss, failure, or destruction is akin to death). We carry our life on our smartphones. They are personalized to our specific preferences. Some people even name them. For many Americans, their smartphone are omnipresent. It wakes them up and sends them to bed. Even as I write this sentence, my smartphone buzzes with notifications…and I (robotically) check my phone.

Which begs a question: who's the "robot" here? Do I control my smartphone, or does it control me? Some futurists suggest the smartphone is the first step toward androids that interact with humans (perhaps that's why we call non-Apple smartphones *androids*). A smartphone is just a tiny square robot that can't move. But imagine the day when it looks human, possesses mobility and interactive skills.

Wakey, wakey, papa.

"We humans have a love-hate relationship with our technology. We love each new advance and we hate how fast our world is changing…The robots really embody that love-hate relationship we have with technology."
Daniel H. Wilson

And yet again, one generation will *uniquely* experience this artificially intelligent technology in their "coming of age" years. Robots will be common and normal. But as with the iTechs, the problem is finding this cohort of kids, born between 2010 and 2030, a suitable name. After all, most of this generation will witness the turning of another century in 2100. They'll also experience a coming technological transformation we can't even imagine. The future advances in human engineering, holograms, robotics, and artificial intelligence will revolutionize medicine, education, work, play, housing, transportation, religion, and entertainment. By the end of the emerging generation's "coming of age" year in 2055, America will be a radically different world. Our current cyber culture will look like a horse and buggy world in comparison.

In fact, Intuit's RoboChild will be primitive in contrast to the robots that our youngest American kids will experience by their fortieth birthdays. It's why I call them the Robotics generation. Or, and as I'll affectionately dub them from this point forward: *The Robo generation*. This moniker is certainly more appropriate than the unimaginative "Alpha generation" that's been promoted in some circles.

All Robo generation kids are currently under ten years of age. Consequently, the demographic research is still emerging. Nonetheless, many of their characteristics are similar to the iTechs. Some demographers project this emerging generation will be slightly larger in number (over 2.5 million babies are born weekly).[461] Australian generational expert Mark McCrindle notes they'll be the "most formally educated generation ever, the most technology-supplied generation ever, and globally the wealthiest generation ever."[462]

A few notable trends? The Robo generation is already watching less television—and when they do it's streamed content. They prefer digital interactive devices (from touchscreen tablets to FitBit Ace watches to smart speakers). If this trend continues, network television and mainstream news is history. In the future, people will choose entertainment ala cart by subscribing to channels they prefer. Many Robo generation kids are "influencers" on social media, enjoying millions of followers. Most notable Robo is a Texas kid named Ryan who does toy reviews on his YouTube channel. With over nineteen million subscribers, he's a marketer's dream. And he became a millionaire before losing his first tooth.[463]

For our purposes, we'll daringly lean into the future with the Robo generation. Unlike other generations with a historical technology footprint, we'll need to do more prediction and projection. What will tomorrow look like for these young Americans? What technologies will define the coming decades and imprint their generational persona?

In a word, I think the future for the Robo generation is H.A.I.R.Y.

Holograms. **A**rtificial **I**ntelligence. And **R**obots.

Let's unpack each one.

Wholly Hologram, Batman!

Holograms aren't new. In fact, in some forms, they've become quite common. Holograms are printed into our money, credit cards, and passports to prevent forgery and identity theft. A lot of art is holographic, most notably those crystal blocks sold at county fairs, flea markets, and bazaars with 3-D images inside. When properly lighted, the crystal images come to life.

The origin of holograms emerges in the work of a Hungarian-British physicist named Dennis Gabor. In 1971, he won a Nobel Prize for developing the holographic method. It only took three decades for his work to be recognized, but he proved a critical figure in the field. Gabor penned in his 1963 book *Inventing the Future* that the "best way to predict the future is to invent it."[464] It's a thought he personally applied. His invention of electron microscopy is foundational to today's holography.

However, Gabor wasn't the only contributor. A team of two physicists at the University of Michigan—Emmett Leith and Juris Upatnieks—and a Russian named Yuri Denisyuk significantly moved the holographic bar with their invention of the laser in 1962.[465] This innovation allowed for the projection of 3-D objects. Lasers later appeared in millions of DVD recorders to read and write discs. Essentially, every DVD contains a hologram.

Holograms are popular on video chats. As we try to hold serious conversations with our beloved, we can mask our face with various disguises from goofy animals to roving stars to silly face markings. Consequently, the Robo generation is maturing in a culture that's comfortable with augmented (AR) and virtual (VR) reality. It's now possible to wear a VR mask that transports us to amazing destinations. We can swim in a reef, climb a mountain, visit a monument, walk a forested path, or ride a roller coaster…and never leave our couch. Augmented reality allows us to manipulate objects, change scenes, and alter materials in three dimensions. We can learn a skill without risk or consequence. We can explore a hobby without failure. Soldiers can train for battle without injury.

For the Robo generation, life will continually float between the actual and the augmented, the real and the simulated. In fact, for them there'll be little difference. Augmented and virtual reality holograms will permit Robo generation students to (virtually) visit the entire earth and known universe. History will be taught as if the person is *living* it. Students can learn to play the piano using augmented keyboards. Even physical screens (like televisions and monitors) will eventually be replaced by virtual screens that disappear when not in use. Robo kids will no doubt remind their grandchildren how they remember a day when 2-D physical screens were in every room…and get a strange "you're kidding" look in return.

The final frontier of holographic technology—which the Robo generation will likely experience in their lifetimes—is the transmission of 3-D images from one space to another. The ability to teleport live persons is still in its infancy, although it was roughly demonstrated by a Microsoft technical fellow Alex Kipman in a riveting 2016 TED Talk. Kipman used augmented reality (AR) to introduce a colleague—as a 3-D hologram—to the TED stage. His friend was "live"—but not in person.[466] As holographic teleportation technology improves, it'll be possible to attend meetings "in (virtual) person" anywhere. Speakers, trainers, and consultants will deliver their messages via hologram. Students will go to school (virtually) to learn, gathering in digital space populated by other holograms. People will attend community forums, conferences, symposiums, social gatherings, parties, and even church services as holograms.

Holy hologram, Batman!

Of course, this level of holographic teleportation technology remains decades away, but it's on the horizon. The Robo generation is already being grooved by virtual and augmented reality (holograms) in their youth to embrace this final frontier that'll fully emerge by mid-century. It's not a matter of if, but *when*.

Elementary A.i., My Dear Watson Computer

In 1968, a supercomputer named HAL 9000 proved no joke for those who viewed Arthur C. Clarke's *2001: A Space Odyssey*. The diabolical computer could control the spaceship and interact with humans. This last part wasn't new. On *Star Trek*, the crew regularly conversed with its ship's computer. But HAL (**H**euristically programmed **AL**gorithmic) actually turned against his human crew, to the point of murder.

This was a whole new level of chaos and treachery.

Artificial intelligence, as an academic discipline and scientific reality, began in 1956. In a post-World War II America, the concept of "thinking machines" or an "electronic brain" started to emerge through the work of Norbert Wiener (cybermetrics), Claude Shannon (information theory), and Alan Turing (theory of computation).

Two mathematicians—Walter Pitts and Warren McCulloch—were also highly influential in the development of artificial intelligence. They created a "neural network" to forge a theoretical foundation, but, more importantly, inspired one of their students—Marvin Minsky—to build a "neural net machine" known as SNARC. Consequently, artificial intelligence and Minsky would forever be linked together.[467] Minsky and three other colleagues later organized the 1956 Dartmouth Conference with a simple thesis that "every aspect of learning or any other feature of intelligence can be so precisely described that a machine can be made to simulate it."[468]

It's the day "artificial intelligence" was born and named.

For the next two decades, multiple individuals worked various algorithms in the development of thinking machines. These "computers" and "calculators" were simplistic at first, but as machines learned to communicate in human languages, there was success. Joseph Weizenbaum created a computer program named "ELIZA" that was so human-like it routinely fooled users.[469] In 1972, Waseda University in Tokyo unveiled the first intelligent "humanoid." It could walk, move objects, and measure distances. It was even fluent in Japanese.[470]

In 1984, an artificial intelligence project named "Cyc" was introduced. Its primary goal was to "assemble a comprehensive ontology and knowledge base... about how the world works" in order to enable artificial intelligence devices and applications to perform the difficult cognitive functions of a human.[471] Eventually, computers using AI programs like *Deep Thought* (created by Carnegie Mellon University) and *Deep Blue* (IBM) were winning chess games against the world's finest players.[472]

With the emergence of the Internet in the 1990s, faster processors, and better memory, artificial intelligence grew exponentially in influence. In 2005, a robot vehicle built by Stanford University self-drove for over 130 miles. Six years later, in February 2011, an IBM computer named *Watson* easily defeated the two finest *Jeopardy!* champions in the history of the game.[473] The supercomputer was more than a data bank. It had the ability to learn knowledge and see repetition. After all, *Jeopardy!* is more than a trivia game. It demands intuition and the ability to decipher intelligent puns. Watson "learned" to compete at this high level and beat his competition three times over.[474] In the past decade, artificial intelligence, or AI, has pushed a variety of applications, from weather forecasting to speech recognition to baseball "statcasting." Every Internet search is "smart" and feeds back advertisements that preferentially and personally match your queries.

Yes, it's a bit "creepy."

But for the Robo generation it'll be the norm.

"People are fascinated with robots because
they're machines that can mimic life."
Colin Angle

Since 2010 there has been an explosion of "smart" technologies. Vehicles now employ "lane assist" and navigational systems that automatically brake and accelerate. Vehicles intuitively change mirrors, alter seat positions, pick radio stations, select heating and cooling for specific drivers. Some cars even park themselves.[475] Our homes are loaded with "smart" devices from speakers named *Alexa* to voice recognition searches conducted by *Siri*. We have intelligent doorbells (*Ring*), appliances, heating/cooling, and lighting.[476] We can translate numerous foreign languages through speech recognition. Everything is web-connected and application-driven. The Robo kids will never know a world without watches that didn't monitor health, televisions that didn't connect to the Internet, and devices that didn't answer every question.

But the future of artificial intelligence, particularly in "smart" technologies, is just the beginning. In the near future, everything will be *uber*-intelligent. Clothes will sense hunger, thirst, distress, or tiredness. Vehicles will self-drive, self-navigate, and self-style to every preference. Video screens will interact and share products, destination ideas, and news. Heating and cooling will automatically adjust to personal preference upon entering and leaving a room. Digital assistants will schedule meetings, create agendas, call in orders, book travel, and even start the coffee pot for a morning cup of joe.

One of the more unique AI technologies is personal chatbots like *Replika*. This clever, downloadable application incorporates a neural network that allows a person to create a digital companion that's a perfect replica of themselves. The chatbot can then "hold an ongoing, one-on-one conversation with its user, and over time, learn how to speak like them."[477] Essentially, it's an affectionate, compassionate, thoughtful, digital friend (created in your own image). Its greatest purposes are during seasons of absence, most notably the ultimate departure of death. *Replika* stores memories, ideas, desires, pastimes, preferences, and just about anything else that makes a person unique. Consequently, in times of separation, family and friends can still communicate (via text) with your unique digital self... as if you never left.

If this also sounds slightly creepy, hang on, because the Robo generation might possibly experience the next level of digital memory: humanoid robots that not only look like the deceased person but contain his or her entire brain in a digital format. It's hard to believe that idea, but no one in 1920 could imagine the Internet, touchscreen tablets, video chats, self-driving cars, or smartphones.

A lot can change in a century.

Domo Arigato, Mister Robot

Robots have been around for nearly a century, but only recently have they gotten *smart*. The marriage of AI with robotics has opened an entirely new technological chapter.

"I just want the future to happen faster.
I can't imagine the future without robots."
Nolan Bushnell

The term "robot" was introduced by Karel Capek in his 1921 science fiction play *R.U.R.* (Rossum's Universal Robots).[478] In the Czech language "robot" means "forced labor," and Capek's harsh view of the mechanical beasts created a narrative that persists to this day. In the West, robots tend to be monsters who create mayhem and murder. Movies like *Westworld, I, Robot, Blade Runner, RoboCop,* and *Terminator* promoted this negative stereotype. These killers were sometimes even disguised as beautiful *Stepford Wives* fembots.[479] In 1966, *Star Trek* featured android women in the classic episode titled "What Are Little Girls Made Of?" The creator of a particularly beautiful android extolled her physical features to Captain Kirk:

"Remarkable, isn't she? Notice the life-like pigmentation, the variation in skin tones, the flesh has warmth, there's even a pulse...physical sensation."[480]

Of course, there were softer and kinder portrayals of robots in film and television too. Perhaps the first was Rosie, the dependable robot maid in *The Jetsons*. Or the lovable robo-duo from the *Star Wars* franchise: R2D2 and C3PO. Or Robin William's family-friendly robot in *Bicentennial Man*. *Star Trek: The Next Generation* featured the first fully functional and nearly human-looking android named "Data." Throughout the show, the mechanized Data, incapable of human emotion, struggled to understand his human friends. Even when his creator inserted an "emotion chip" into his computerized brain to improve his relational connections, it still couldn't satisfy Data's longings to be fully human.[481]

This Western "mostly bad, occasionally good" narrative for robots isn't found in the East. To the contrary, in places like Japan, robots are relatively common, embraced, and loved. The Japanese lead the world in designing robots that are more than simply functional. They produce beautiful bots that can perform critical tasks to near perfection. Robots are workers, companions, assistants, and friends.

One of the top robots in Japan is a gorgeous android named Erica. Created by Hiroshi Ishiguro (Director of Intelligence, Robotics Laboratory in Osaka), she is being groomed to replace a human news anchor. Erica looks and feels "human" (even warm to the touch). Her facial recognition technology allows her to focus on faces and track people in motion. She conducts her own interviews and reacts to questions independently. Erica learns from her experiences, stores information, and then operates from that learning. If you think she's "creepy," she'll just reply, "Well, even if I am, get over it."[482] Due to the Japan's failing birth rate, the government is funding research for lifelike android children to comfort childless couples. For example, there's a robo child named CP-2, designed by the University of Osaka, that's remarkably human-like.[483]

It's only a matter of time before Eastern androids catch up to Western utility.

So, how did we get here? The reality is that robots have been working the planet for nearly a century. The first robot was a beastly knight named "Eric," designed by the British in 1928 for an exposition. "Eric" could sit, talk, and generally look fearsome...and eventually he completely disappeared. A decade later, Westinghouse Electric created a robot named "Electro" for the 1939 New York World's Fair.[484] "Electro" stood seven feet tall, weighed 265 pounds, and looked somewhat human for a big, shiny metal object. He could talk, move his head and arms, blow up balloons, and smoke cigarettes. He even had his own robo-dog named "Sparko."[485] In 1950, "Elektro" made a national promotional tour and appeared in a movie.

But at best "Elektro" was a novelty act and a sideshow freak. Nobody took him seriously.

In 1969, thanks to innovations in computer technology and artificial intelligence, creator Charlie Rosen and Stanford Research Institute introduced "Shakey"—the first mobile robot with self-navigation abilities. "Shakey" performed simple tasks like pushing blocks and recognizing when items had been moved. However, "Shakey" might've been better named "Slothy." Every movement required over an hour to complete. It took days for him to walk through a cluttered room.

One of the world's first robotics companies was *Unimation*, founded in 1962 by Joseph F. Engelberger and George Devol. Devol had already patented a robotic arm a decade earlier and introduced the first industrial robot in 1961. This robotic innovation would later be known as PUMA (Programmable Universal Machine for Assembly), and it significantly impacted automation in factories—particularly car factories. The robotic arms could assemble, weld, and paint. Eventually, PUMA technology was attached to robotic vehicles that searched, rescued, carried, and gathered various things. In an Oxford, England factory, 900 robots build a thousand cars every day (with 600 highly-trained humans monitoring production). The advantage to robots building cars is their predictable reliability. Humans make mistakes that machines will not. The payoff? Better quality, faster production, and cheaper cars.

It's no wonder that factories now globally employ millions of robots to do the work.

For most Americans, robotics has historically been non-human machines with wheels, belts, rotors, propellers and tracks. It was "field robot" technology—built by Carnegie Melon University—that helped eliminate dangerous radioactive waste at Three Mile Island, PA in the 1980s. NASA launched a robot called the Pathfinder to explore Mars. And then there was the eight-legged "Dante" robot deployed into an Antarctica volcano in 1992. Dante survived the volcanic inferno but eventually froze in the sub-zero temperatures.[486] In 1988, a company named RedZone produced designer robots for difficult and dangerous jobs related to wastewater management. Their robots inspect tanks for leaks and clean radioactive sludge. Some robots can fold up to enter tight spaces.

Boston (MA) Dynamics has invented the most advanced walking robot. Their robots boldly go where even humans fear to tread, over and under and through any terrain. They can walk up and down stairs, and their use of 3-D printed aluminum means a lighter robot.[487]

Some robots got their start playing keyboards, like the Wabot-2, designed in 1980.[488] The Wabot-2 helped evolve the technology of the mechanical human hand and incorporated micro-computers that modeled the human nervous system. Wabot-2 could hit a key twenty times per second (faster than any human). Robotic appendages have proven helpful for many manual jobs today, but they're also the first step toward a true cyborg culture. In 2018, a Florida man was fitted with the first "mind-controlled robotic arm." Cancer took Johnny Matheny's arm two decades earlier and now science was giving it back.[489] For the emerging Robo generation, no body part (save perhaps the brain) can truly be lost. From arms and legs to eyes and ears, every appendage will eventually be replaceable, either with a robotic or genetically-engineered synthetic parts.

The emergence of recreational drones in the mid-2010s is the "toy robot" for the Robo Generation.[490] These flying pieces of plastic are grooving younger generations towards fresh technological realities and endless possibilities. Drones do more than just supply stunning aerial photographs and backyard entertainment; they're being used to deliver everything from packages to pizzas. Drones have been military tools for decades, serving to gather intelligence and drop supplies. Today, drones film motion pictures, measure crop growth, map wild fires, inspect high-rise buildings, survey land and perform disaster relief. As "smart" drones these flying machines will eventually serve as law enforcement officers, emergency first responders, traffic controllers, home protection monitors and news reporters. Miniature drones will fly into dark, tight and remote spaces (to pollinate plants, search behind walls and make repairs where humans cannot go). Larger drones will serve as taxis, cowboys and lifeguards. They'll even be used for sport-racing.

Drones are now hovering center stage in popular culture.

But it's human like robots that will eventually steal the show.

These humanoids are expected to emerge by 2040 and they will greatly impact both education and entertainment. Robot replicas of famous people for museums and entertainment venues will produce fascinating new attractions. These robots won't use a script that repeats every few minutes and perform clumsy robotic movements. No, these robots will fluidly interact with patrons. They'll discuss concepts, explain history, and inspire decisions. They'll walk, run, shake hands, point fingers, smile and frown. They'll look and behave remarkably "human." This isn't a creepy "RoboChild," but a mechanical humanoid built to impress, persuade and create empathy.

"The danger of the past was that men became slaves.
The danger of the future is that men may become robots."
Erich Fromm

In the coming decade, robots will increasingly become a part of human life, from self-driving vehicles like OTTO to the HelpMate robot that services hospitals. There are now robots that vacuum floors, scrub toilets, wash dishes, and mow lawns. Zume Pizza employs robots to bake their pies.[491] Catalia Health has engineered "Mabu," a friendly robot that monitors home health.[492] "Smart" robots pick fruit, lettuce, and harvest wheat. Starsky Robotics is engineering fully automated tractor trailer trucks.[493] In the future, taxis, trains, buses, and entertainment rides will all be self-driving, automated experiences.

Artificial intelligence and robotics will allow doctors to diagnose disease faster, better...and from a distance. Many futurists believe, as machines learn to think and improve responses, that certain types of jobs will grow obsolete. Machines will do what is simple, repetitive, and programmable. Robots will design and build stuff, police streets, and deliver products. Robots will write and deliver news, perform simple surgery, detect cancers, fight wars, prepare taxes, handle stock exchanges, and pen laws. Columbia University has designed a robot that can uniquely create beautiful art. Eric Horvitz (a technical fellow at Microsoft) employs a digital assistant named "Monica" that controls his schedule. She has even learned which meetings Eric will not attend. Monica knows every personal preference—from food to hobby to travel—for Eric. Again, this might sound "creepy," but for the Robo generation, this type of technology will be as normal as a telephone, photocopier or computer in tomorrow's workplace.

"The job market of the future will consist of those jobs that robots cannot perform. Our blue-collar work is pattern recognition, making sense of what you see. Gardeners will still have jobs because every garden is different. The same goes for construction workers. The losers are white-collar workers, low-level accountants, brokers and agents."
Michio Kaku

Futurist Ray Kurzweil has made a controversial, hotly-contested prediction that nearly half (48 percent) of all U.S. jobs will be lost to artificial intelligence and robotics in the next twenty years.[494] Other experts predict by 2030 that one-third of all current jobs will be robotic. Should that be a concern? Possibly. But we've been here before. Many people were concerned with the Industrial Revolution in the 1800s. They feared that machines and factories would destroy the American way of life. In reality, it just rearranged and enhanced it. The Industrial Revolution is what created a solid working and middle class. It pushed people into the cities and unleashed the greatest human migration in history.

Similarly, the coming robotic transformation will no doubt be disruptive, and it may end many jobs that are taken for granted today. It's clear the Robo generation will face a more highly skilled work environment when they first engage it around 2030. The basic skills that employers will seek include creativity, communication, interpersonal problem-solving, and critical thinking. Education will need to shift from information dispensers to collaborative laboratories that develop soft skills and enhance higher-level thinking.

Similarly, if local churches, community clubs, and other fraternal organizations hope to attract and retain Robo generation members, they'll need to adopt more communal, experiential, and missional models. The Robos will seek sanctuary, embrace community, and pursue service opportunities. They will want to feel "human" and express that humanness through various emotive experiences. After all, it's the capacity for emotion that separates a human from the machine. A robot might think faster and know more, but it will never be emotive. And this is what future generations will crave.

Perhaps the greatest transformation the Robo generation will experience is the augmented self. Bionic technology, as already mentioned, will continue to grow. However, technology that supports—like SuitX's exoskeletal apparatuses—are already helping those with back problems to work longer, harder, and faster.[495] They also give the crippled a new lease on life, permitting paralytics to physically stand and walk. Technically, this cyborg self is nothing new. From prosthetics to artificial organs to fake eyes and wigs, humans have long used artificial means to "augment" their true self. It's just that now we can restore and rebuild. In the 1970s, a popular television show titled *The Six Million Dollar Man* introduced bionics.[496] Today, we're living it.

Naturally, the emergence of intelligent robots has created new philosophical questions. If robots now move like us and look like us, what happens when robots begin to *think* like us? What happens when robots can engineer their own robots? Will they enhance our lives or threaten our existence? Consider a day when robots are so "human" that America will hold a national debate about their "equal rights" under the U.S. Constitution. It sounds preposterous, but some futurists envision this possibility.

If I Only Had A Brain

The Robo generation will also experience advances in genetic engineering that will initiate questions about what it means to be human.

The ability to store human DNA and print 3-D body parts is already possible. In the near future, a lost limb or diseased organ will be easily replaced with another that is 100 percent the person's unique DNA. Consequently, the need for organ and blood donors will disappear. The angst of losing a leg will be gone. The fear of permanent disability due to mutilation will not exist.

Genetic engineering will also allow parents to birth babies without mental retardation, disease, imperfection, and other physical flaws. We'll eventually order our designer offspring like a new blouse from Amazon. Some futurists predict couples will purchase celebrity DNA to seed their progeny. In the future, babies will receive "DNA Report Cards" that'll forecast future lifestyle tastes, addictions, and choices. We'll have the capacity to clone humans just like we clone sheep. In 2018, Chinese scientists performed gene editing on HIV-infected embryos that rendered them immune to the disease.[497] We'll soon possess the ability to heal disease. Just like we cured polio with a vaccination, in the future, every virus, cancer, and illness will be treatable…*before birth*.

In the movie *Jurassic Park*, mathematician Ian Malcom (portrayed by Jeff Goldblum) makes a compelling idea about the genetic engineering which produced the terrifying dinosaurs that roamed the fictional park: "Your scientists were so preoccupied with whether or not they could, they didn't stop to think if they should."

This will likely be the philosophical question that both the iTech and Robo generations will tackle in the coming decades. It's not that we can't do it, but *should* we do it? What will be our limits? At what point are we playing God?

In the future, we might be able to replicate most human parts, including significant organs like the heart, lungs, and liver. But there's one organ that will remain mysteriously and purely human: *our brain*. Machines may be artificially intelligent and physically superior, but it's highly doubtful they'll ever learn the finer nuances of emotional intelligence. Robots might serve sacrificially and work unconditionally, but they can't emote with love, empathy, or grace. They may be smart as a whip, but they will can't possess soulfulness. Consequently, faith and spirituality will never disappear completely. Deep inside our spirits, we have (as Pascal proposed) a God-shaped hole that no machine can replicate or fill.

Its why the Robo generation will need to be a *smarter* generation. To be "educated" will mean the ability to think critically and creatively, and to communicate influentially. In the future, it won't be what you know that matters, but *how* you know *why* it matters…and can you present it clearly and powerfully.

And these Robo kids will have much longer opportunity to do it.

There's a strong likelihood that advances in medicine, environmental sciences, genetics, and living conditions will continue to lengthen the human lifespan. Self-driving vehicles will save tens of thousands of human lives every year as car accidents become increasingly rare. The ability to replicate body parts and organs will significantly slow the aging process. Consequently, the Robo generation should easily live to (and beyond) the century mark, pushing the average lifespan to over eighty years—even ninety years—of age. That means many Robo gen kids will live to see the year 2120.

Tomorrow will be a very "smart" world with very "smart" technology.

The Robo generation will need to be "smarter" as it leads America and the world into the future.

RoboChild was right.

It's time to "wakey wakey."

A TIMELINE OF TECHNOLOGICAL EVENTS (2011–2019):

- 2011: Snapchat debuts. Space Shuttle Discovery docks for last time and is retired. U.S. Defense tests a hypersonic missile able travel five times the speed of sound. The world's first synthetic organ transplant (trachea) in Sweden. Richard Branson opens the first commercial Spaceport in U.S. IBM's "Watson" wins on *Jeopardy!* Microsoft debuts Office 365. FaceTime and Spotify debut. Kindle Fire and Touch announced. Nest Learning Thermostat debuts. "Siri" comes to smartphones.

- 2012: Windows 8 released (designed for tablets and touchscreens). Instagram debuts. Kodak files for bankruptcy. Google Play debuts. Google announces Project Glass. Nook e-reader released. Adobe moves to the cloud. Fitbit Zip debuts. Lyft taxi service starts.

- 2013: Sony releases PlayStation 4 while Microsoft releases Xbox One. Edward Snowden leaks information about NSA's secret Internet and cell phone data gathering program.

- 2014: Google purchases Nest (home automation company). Facebook buys WhatsApp. Amazon releases Fire Phone. Apple Pay debuts. University of Michigan releases M3 (Micro Mote), the world's smallest computer.

- 2015: Apple releases iWatch. Hoverboards and Amazon Echo debut. Sling TV and YouTube Red are launched. HBO and Showtime move to stream. Tesla introduces semi-automatic driverless car. A drone completes first government-approved medical delivery. Radio Shack files for bankruptcy. Google announces powerful TensorFlow open source AI system. Jeff Bezos launches Blue Origin rocket. Mobile livestreaming (Meerkat and Periscope) are popular.

- 2016: Nanotechnologists build miniature machines out of molecules. World's first shipment delivered by self-driving truck. Google's AlphaGo defeats Go champion Lee Se-dol. Bones grown in lab transplanted into humans. Facebook Live and VR headsets debut. Uber announces self-driving cars. UK scientists genetically modify human embryos. Apple factory replaces 60,000 employees with robots. Netflix has more subscribers than any other cable company.

- 2017: Hybrid gaming console released by Nintendo. Echo Dot debuts. Norway is first country to move from FM radio to digital broadcasting technology. Twitter expands from 140- to 280-character limit. Amazon merges with Whole Foods for home grocery delivery. Bitcoin hits the mainstream. High-Dynamic Range televisions debut.
- 2018: Apple introduces Apple HomePod smart speaker. 3-D metal printing debuts. Artificial embryos grown by UK researchers from stem cells. Toronto building world's first "smart neighborhood" called Quayside. Elon Musk sends a Tesla Roadster into space. Fortnite video game a cultural phenomenon.
- 2019: Samsung debuts folding smartphones. Elon Musk launches an unmanned SpaceX. Plant-based meat like "Beyond Beef" and "Impossible Burgers" are sold in stores and restaurants.

INFLUENTIAL BIRTHS IN THE NET GENERATION:

Business, Education, Athletes and Other Leaders:
- Charlotte (2015), princess
- Louis Arthur Charles (2018), prince

Entertainers:
- Fox Messitt (2014), actor
- Meredith Duggar (2015), reality star

Authors/Artists/Social Media Stars:
- Ryan "Toys Review" (2010), YouTube star

A Final Word

Are you still buckled in?

Hopefully so. It's been quite a ride.

The technological turbulence of recent history and its future prospects will no doubt make some of us nauseous. It's hard to imagine a world of holograms, smart appliances, humanoids, and genetically manufactured people. It's hard to believe we even stand on the portal of such a world. It's a thought that cuts against the grain and contradicts our better judgments. For many of us, these technologies could undermine our cherished values, traditional ideas and preferred beliefs. I suspect they might even sound apocalyptic alarms. It's the end of the world as we know it. The whole world is going to hell in a technological handbasket.

And there's a grain of truth to that idea.

But it's also possible that what we fear could be the start of something *new* and *better*.

Every generation faces a technological choice to adopt or abort, to change or conserve. There was a day when automobiles were noisy, slow, and undependable, but we kept improving them. There was a day when television was just three "snowy" channels with nothing worth watching, but we kept transforming the medium. There was a day when computers were the size of a room, but we continued to make them smaller, faster, and more productive.

Today, it's hard to imagine a world without the Internet, smartphones, or high-definition television. We have to admit these technologies have helped us, even if they are riddled with dangerous side effects and consequences. I suspect our great grandchildren will wonder how we ever survived without a personal robot, "smart" clothes, and holographic teleportation.

All I know is every generation has it's "coming of age." We all grow up.

And every generation has its technology that tattoos its personality. We all interact through machines and media that assist, even improve, our lives. It might be automobiles, airplanes, and telephones. It might be motion pictures, radio, and vinyl records. It might be television, satellites, rockets, and gaming. It might be personal computers, cell phones, and the Internet. Or it might be robots.

Whatever our time, and wherever our historical place, technology guided our American story. We are generations of technology.

We are *GenTech*.

"Innovation is what America does best. Whether it is the Apollo Project to the moon, developing the most advanced defense technologies available, the rise of the Internet or the latest advancements in biomedical gene therapies, our nation leads the world in transformative innovations.

Martin Heinrich

Acknowledgements

There are some books that you write, and there are some books that write you. This one is the latter. It's the culmination of years of research, analysis, interviews, and observations. Over the years, I've probably taught this information, in some form or fashion, to tens of thousands of people. It's the product of countless conversations with my students, peers, friends, family, and, occasionally, complete strangers. It's an interesting topic that makes us all think.

Someone once said that writing a book is like giving birth to an elephant. I'm not sure whether that pertains to the two-year gestation (to publish) or the fact that it begins with a conceived idea and births as a huge, glorious work of creation. All I know is it's a painful process that produces a beautiful gift. It's a labor of love and product of discovery. Consequently, I owe the following people some special gratitude.

First, and most important, my wife, Linda. Being a writer's spouse is never easy. There were times when I surely exasperated her as I tried to capture a thought or write a sentence. For several months, other activities were abbreviated, postponed or cancelled. As part of the journey, she listened to me read aloud every finished chapter and yet still graciously cheered me on. I'm thankful for her patience, affirmation, and love. "It is finished!" Let's celebrate. I love you.

I also want to thank my mother-in-law, Karen Swanson. She was one of the first believers in this book. I can't wait for her to read it.

As always, to my children—Becca, Ryan, Kayla and Christopher—thank you for the encouragement, love, and support.

To my publicist Lynette Hoy and her husband Paul, thank you for joining me in this ride. Lynette "gets" me and has proven her worth as we try to take this book to a whole new stratosphere of influence. Everybody needs a "Lynette" in their life to inspire, push, affirm and develop who we really are (and can be).

I must also acknowledge all the churches, organizations, and schools where I taught, spoke and trained. This is where I honed my thinking and found space to present these insights and ideas on generations, cultural change, and technology. This includes Hope International University in Fullerton, CA; the Statehouse Toastmasters Club in Boise, ID; and Star, ID "Life Groups"—my spiritual band of brothers and sisters.

I also want to thank Dr. Leonard Sweet. I spent three years studying under his theological wisdom, cultural insights and revolutionary ideas. He's a historian, futurist, churchman and friend. Thank you for penning the forward to this book.

I'm grateful for Morgan James Publishing's desire to publish this work, particularly **Margo Toulouse** (my author's relation agent) and **Terry Whalin** (who originally saw value in this title). And special thanks to **Aubrey Kincaid** who served as my copy editor. She gave this manuscript a final spit shine to prepare it for print.

I am compelled to mention the help and influence of YouTube, Google, Wikipedia, The History Channel, NBC *Today Show*, and PBS in writing this work. I should also tip my hat to *American Pickers* (**Mike Wolfe** and **Frank Fritz**) and *Pawn Stars* (**Rick Harrison**) for their unique insights and helpful historical understanding of technology. On many occasions something I learned on one of the shows drove me back to the manuscript for rewrite, edit or tweak.

Finally, I want to thank *you* for reading this book. I hope you enjoyed the journey, were challenged in your thinking, and reminisced (as much as I did) about all those fun, cool, and obsolete technologies that we once couldn't live without.

Here's to America's promising future…and to our glorious past.

About the Author

Rick Chromey is a cultural explorer, social historian and generational futurist. He's also served as a pastor, professor, speaker/trainer, and consultant. In 2017, he founded MANNA! Educational Services International to inspire and equip leaders, teachers, pastors, and parents. Rick has a doctorate in leadership and the emerging culture; and travels the U.S. and world to speak on culture, faith, history, education, and leadership topics. He has authored over a dozen books on leadership, natural motivation, creative communication, and classroom management. He lives with his wife, Linda, in Meridian, ID.

Endnotes

Introduction: What in the World Happened?

1   "Digital Photography Timeline Part 2: 1990s": https://practicalphotographytips.com/Photography-Basics/digital-photography-timeline.html

2   Kodak files for bankruptcy: https://www.forbes.com/sites/ericsavitz/2012/01/19/kodak-files-chapter-11/#15c9660c41b2

3   Source: https://www.businessinsider.com/the-us-has-lost-more-than-166-print-newspapers-since-2008-2010-7

4   Source: https://www.crainsdetroit.com/article/20081216/FREE/812169989/detroit-free-press-the-detroit-news-moving-to-3-day-a-week-home

5   Source: http://www.pewresearch.org/fact-tank/2017/06/01/circulation-and-revenue-fall-for-newspaper-industry/

Chapter One: Generations

6   "Baby Buster" was a tag to denote the decline in birth rate in 1965. It was to contrast the previous generation of "Baby Boomers" (traditionally framed from 1946–1964). Douglas Coupland's "Gen X" term, though fictional in context, proved a more accurate and iconic moniker for those born between 1961–1981. In the end, Coupland's tag stuck.

7   Their labels for the generations were noted in others' writings (Missionary, Lost, Gilded, Liberty), but on at least two generations Strauss and Howe have found their tags missing the mark: 13th Generation (instead of Gen X) and Homeland Generation (instead of iTech). Initially they also projected the Millennial Generation to birth until 2003, but this has also proven too lengthy due to the impact and influence of 9-11-01. *Generations: The History of America's Future (1589–2069)* by William Strauss and Neil Howe (New York: Quill Publishers, 1991): 36.

8   In their 1997 follow-up work, Strauss and Howe proposed a "fourth turning" prediction of a "major crisis" in the early 2000s. Their prophetic eye proved correct when the terrorism of September 11, 2001 and the subsequent Great Recession (2007–2009) rearranged America socially, economically, politically and spiritually.

9   In developmental psychology, there are four parts to the human life cycle: youth (ages 0–20), young adulthood (ages 20–40), middle adulthood (ages 40–60) and elderhood (ages 60 and beyond). Similarly, there are four parts to the year that reflect these developmental ages: spring (youth), summer (young adulthood), fall (middle adulthood) and winter (elderhood).

10   Throughout this work I will frame the Millennial generation as 1982–1999 and the iTech Generation as 2000–present. The use of "iTech" is my preferred name for this recent generation, based upon their life with "i" technologies: iPod, iTunes, iPad, iPhone and iWatch.

11   For a visual one-hundred year demographic of birth rates from 1909 to 2009: https://upload.wikimedia.org/wikipedia/commons/6/66/US_Birth_Rates.svg

12   For a general history of oral contraception: https://www.ourbodiesourselves.org/health-info/a-brief-history-of-birth-control/

13   Cognitive sciences have determined we remember very little prior to age six and most of these memories tend to be "passed on" memories by parents and influential adults. https://www.scientificamerican.com/article/when-do-children-start-making-long-term-memories/

14   It's this idea of human memory that has caused me to rethink and readjust time frames for the Millennial (born 1982–1998) and iTech (born since 1999) generations. An iTech obviously cannot recall the terror attacks of September 11, 2001. Even if we liberally allow for three-year-olds to remember that event—which only selected ones can or will—that means the iTechs couldn't have been born any earlier than 1998. Consequently, the Millennial Generation is better framed from 1982–1998 and the iTech Generation from 1999–present.

15   The early phase were tagged as "jaunty optimists" (Walt Disney, John Wayne, Ronald Reagan) while the latter phase were labeled "clean-cut rationalists" (Lee Iacocca, George H.W. Bush, Lloyd Bentson). *Generations* by Strauss and Howe: 261.

16   *Generations* by Strauss and Howe: 74.

17   "iTech" is my unique and preferred label for this post 9-11 generation (born since 2000). Strauss and Howe call them the Homeland Generation and frame their birth years from 1982-2004. http://www.lifecourse.com/about/method/def/homeland-generation.html

18   Wikipedia "Greatest Generation": https://en.wikipedia.org/wiki/The_Greatest_Generation

19   Wikipedia "Silent Generation": https://en.wikipedia.org/wiki/Silent_Generation#Notable_figures

20   "Gen X: Tales for an Accelerated Culture": https://en.wikipedia.org/wiki/Generation_X:_Tales_for_an_Accelerated_Culture

21   "The Blank Generation": http://www.theblankgeneration.com/

22   "35 Pages That Shook The U.S. Education World" by Edward B. Fiske (*New York Times*, April 27, 1988): https://www.nytimes.com/1988/04/27/us/35-pages-that-shook-the-us-education-world.html

23   "Millennials and Gen Xers Outvoted Boomers and Older Generations in 2016 Election" by Richard Fry (Pew Research Center, July 31, 2017): http://www.pewresearch.org/fact-tank/2017/07/31/millennials-and-gen-xers-outvoted-boomers-and-older-generations-in-2016-election/

24   Jean Twenge: http://www.jeantwenge.com/igen-book-by-dr-jean-twenge/

25   "Generation Z": https://en.wikipedia.org/wiki/Generation_Z

26   LifeCourse Associations (Strauss and Howe): http://www.lifecourse.com/about/method/def/homeland-generation.html

Chapter Two: Waves

27   For an atheist's perspective on Friedrich Nietzsche's "God is Dead" quote, visit: https://bigthink.com/scotty-hendricks/what-nietzsche-really-meant-by-god-is-dead

28   LifeCourse Associates (Strauss and Howe): http://www.lifecourse.com/about/method/timelines/generations.html

29   "What's the youngest age a woman can give birth?": https://www.livescience.com/33170-youngest-age-give-birth-pregnancy.html

30   "Abstract Thinking": https://www.goodtherapy.org/blog/psychpedia/abstract-thinking

31   "First Communion": https://en.wikipedia.org/wiki/First_Communion

32   For some orthodox and conservative Jews, a girl will experience her bat mitzvah at twelve years of age, not thirteen: https://en.wikipedia.org/wiki/Bar_and_Bat_Mitzvah\

33   Source: http://amishamerica.com/when-do-amish-get-baptized/

34   "Coming of Age": https://en.wikipedia.org/wiki/Coming_of_age

35   Research reveals the average age for a child receiving his or her first smartphone is 10.3 years. By age 12, half of all American children will have social media accounts. https://www.inc.com/melanie-curtin/bill-gates-says-this-is-the-safest-age-to-give-a-child-a-smartphone.html

36   Strauss and Howe, *Generations*: 72-79.

37   Nine Millennial lawmakers were elected to the U.S. Congress in the 2018 midterm elections, the first time Millennials reached the highest offices in the land. All but one were Democrats. https://www.bustle.com/p/the-millennial-candidates-elected-to-congress-will-bring-so-much-change-to-capitol-hill-13103137

38   Strauss and Howe, *Generations*: 367

Chapter Three: Tipping Points

39   Betamax commercial from 1979: https://www.youtube.com/watch?v=t2v_qEVTh10

40   Betamax: https://en.wikipedia.org/wiki/Betamax

41   93% of all Africans had cell service in 2016 according to a report by *Afrobarometer*. This is both interesting and significant because Africa struggles to be a developed country. "In a lot of communities all over Africa, people can talk on their cell phones, but they can't turn on a light or a water faucet. Never mind flush a toilet. And they may be going hungry," says Winnie Mitullah, director of the Institute for Development Studies at the University of Nairobi. https://www.cnn.com/2016/01/19/africa/africa-afrobarometer-infrastructure-report/index.html

42   The March on Washington drew a quarter of a million people but was "televised live to an audience of millions." https://aaregistry.org/story/martin-luther-king-jr-delivers-his-i-have-a-dream-speech/

43   While the actual assassination of John F. Kennedy wasn't televised, this was the first time that "live" news bulletins were used to communicate the tragedy. The next day, live television captured the murder of Lee Harvey Oswald by Jack Ruby, as well as the subsequent funeral for a slain president on November 25, 1963. https://www.history.com/this-day-in-history/john-f-kennedy-assassinated

44   Around 73 million Americans—two thirds of the whole U.S. population—watched the Beatles perform on the Ed Sullivan Show (February 9, 1964). They gathered around televisions in homes, bars and appliance stores to witness these four lads from Liverpool. The moment not only set off "Beatlemania" in America but shifted popular music altogether. The Beatles changed not just musical tastes but would reimagine the entire industry, format and presentation. https://en.wikipedia.org/wiki/The_Beatles_in_the_United_States

45   Infoplease: "Live Births and Birth Rates, by Year" https://www.infoplease.com/us/births/live-births-and-birth-rates-year

46 Between 1990 and 2000, cell phone subscriptions exploded from 5.3 million to 109 million Americans. Source: https://www.infoplease.com/science-health/cellphone-use/cell-phone-subscribers-us-1985-2010. By 2017, that number was nearly 396 million users. Source: https://www.statista.com/statistics/186122/number-of-mobile-cellular-subscriptions-in-the-united-states-since-2000/

47 "Xennial" is a word that has some cultural traction and has generated some support by those born between 1977 and 1983: https://www.merriam-webster.com/words-at-play/words-were-watching-xennial

48 Xennials: https://mymodernmet.com/are-you-a-xennial/

49 For a history of portable video games: https://en.wikipedia.org/wiki/Handheld_game_console

50 Quote: https://www.brainyquote.com/quotes/frederick_jackson_turner_198281

Chapter Four: Transportation-Telephone

51 Tom Brokaw: https://www.brainyquote.com/quotes/tom_brokaw_372248?src=t_greatest_generation

52 General George Marshall, as quoted in William Strauss and Neil Howe, *Generations*, 1991: 261.

53 "Superman" was created in 1938 by Jerry Siegel and artist Joe Shuster, two members of the "Transportation-Telephone" generation. https://en.wikipedia.org/wiki/Superman

54 The Pure Food Act (1906) inaugurated a number of laws to protect American consumers. Eventually leads to the creation of the Food and Drug Administration. https://en.wikipedia.org/wiki/Pure_Food_and_Drug_Act

55 The "G.I" stood for "general issue" (as in "regular" people) and "government issue" (for their life-time long protection by the U.S. government). They were also "G.I.'s" in two World Wars and then served in leadership over the Korean, Vietnam and Cold War conflicts. Strauss and Howe, *Generations*, 1991: 264-265.

56 Ibid., 261

57 Montana, North Dakota, South Dakota, Washington (1889), Idaho, Wyoming (1890), Utah (1896), Oklahoma (1907), New Mexico and Arizona (1912). Source: http://worldpopulationreview.com/states/states-by-statehood/

58 Luce, H.R.: "The American Century," reprinted in *The Ambiguous Legacy*, M.J. Hogan, ed. (Cambridge: Cambridge University Press, 1999).

59 *The Century* by Peter Jennings and Todd Brewster (New York: Double Day, 1998): 5-6.

60 "The Electric Light System": https://www.nps.gov/edis/learn/kidsyouth/the-electric-light-system-phonograph-motion-pictures.htm

61 In 1900, daily life was brutal and dismal for working-class families—and most American families were working class. In New York City tenements, only half of all households boasted indoor toilets and just 306 of 255,000 residences enjoyed bathtubs. Those who lived in rural America usually had neither. Three-quarters of all industrial laborers worked over sixty hours per week and were routinely laid off (without benefits). Annually, around 25,000 workers were killed and another 700,000 seriously injured in industrial accidents. Poverty and malnutrition were widespread. The average factory job paid $1.50 a day. Thousands of youth under sixteen worked in mines, textile mills or sweatshops. Most children were under-educated because they were forced to work. Half of all kids finished eighth grade and only six percent graduated high school. Many lower income women chose prostitution as their job (more than at any other time in American history) because it would best pay the bills.

62 The skyscraper building was the new "stalk" growing on the city's horizon. It signaled a shift in the new century toward the urban. When Chicago burned to the ground in 1871, from its ashes arose a new modern building composed of steel, concrete and glass. In the coming decades the inner cities of America would be transformed by these giant architectural

wonders. Taller buildings created an unintended consequence: the church steeple was blocked. For centuries the church steeple (and bell) were social signals for where and when to meet. Churches served as schools, assembly halls, voting places and community centers. As taller buildings towered over them, the church and its influence in modern culture was lost in the new urban "trees."

63 Ibid., 12.

64 The Titanic—named after the Greek god "Titan" for its massive size—was considered a marvel of technological wonder. It was an "unsinkable" luxury ship that ferried both rich passengers and poor emigrants to America. Unfortunately, the enormous 78-foot rudder (controlled by its own engine) could not steer out of trouble in the early hours of April 15, 1912. The Titanic struck an iceberg and dented the hull (that buckled its seams allowing water to enter). Eventually the ship sunk and over 1500 people drowned. "RMS Titanic" (Wikipedia: https://en.wikipedia.org/wiki/RMS_Titanic)

65 Ibid., 46.

66 Timeline of Car History: https://www.titlemax.com/articles/a-timeline-of-car-history/

67 In Germany, two different automakers, just sixty miles apart, labored to craft a car: Gottlieb Wilhelm Daimler and Karl Benz. Benz was the first to invent the first real automobile with an internal combustion engine (1885). A year later both Daimler and Henry Ford built their first automobiles, but they were primitive machines at best. Brothers Frank and Charles Edgar Duryea eventually invented the first truly successful gas-powered automobile in the United States (1893).

68 Perhaps that's why, at the turn of the century, a quarter of all automobiles sold used electric engines.

69 In 1909, a 22-year-old Alice Huyler-Ramsey drove her new Maxwell car and three friends from New York City to San Francisco in 59 days. She was the first women to drive coast to coast on her own. At the time, the U.S. had less than 150 miles of paved roads outside of major cities and not one filling station. She bought her gas at general stores. https://en.wikipedia.org/wiki/Alice_Huyler_Ramsey

70 Henry Ford's assembly line not only helped the overall price, it aided greatly in production. Ford Motor Company went from producing 7.5 cars per hour to 146 cars per hour. https://www.titlemax.com/articles/a-timeline-of-car-history/

71 "Car of the Century" (Wikipedia: https://en.wikipedia.org/wiki/Car_of_the_Century)

72 The world's largest automaker General Motors, founded by William Durant (1908), produced the Buick, Oldsmobile, Pontiac and Cadillac. However, Durant financially spread himself too thin and lost control of the company in 1910. He then joined Louis Chevrolet to manufacture "Chevy" cars (1913) but when Chevrolet Motors was acquired four years later by GM, Durant briefly re-assumed control of the whole company (he was fired yet again in 1921). During the 1920s, General Motors surpassed the Ford Motor Company in world-wide sales.

73 For a complete visual history of the automobile: https://www.youtube.com/watch?v=Rb3E8GI0vNM

74 The first vehicle to use a motor was a tricycle, invented by an Englishman named Edward Butler (1884).

75 For half a century, American motorcycles were largely made by either Indian or Harley-Davidson and it created a unique rivalry. In 1953, the Indian motorcycle ceased production of motorcycles for sixty years but never lost favor among motorcycle enthusiasts. Polaris revived and re-marketed the brand in 2013 and it lives on today.

76 Great Britain relied upon its own Triumph model, while the U.S. military commissioned Harley-Davidson to build over 20,000 motorcycles for its purposes. It's one reason why Indian motorcycles eventually failed: the U.S. military used Harleys and they became popular among soldiers when they returned home from war. The police and highway patrols also used Harleys.

77   Sheldon "Red" Chaney created the first drive-through restaurant: Red's Giant Hamburg on
      Route 66 in Springfield, MO. https://en.wikipedia.org/wiki/Red%27s_Giant_Hamburg

78   In 1955, General Motors released the Chevrolet, a fashionable, distinct and highly-coveted car
      to this day. Ford Motors issued the Thunderbird and Jaguar rolled out its first mid-sized sedan.
      Many car collectors consider 1955 the best year ever for car models. https://www.cartalk.com/
      blogs/jim-motavalli/1955-great-year-buy-car-america

79   One of the earliest identifiable biker gangs were the Boozefighters in California. The gang was
      featured in a 1947 *Life* magazine article on the rise of violent biker gangs. Marlon Brando
      would later personify the rebellious attitudes of biker gangs in 1953's "The Wild One." https://
      www.latimes.com/local/lanow/la-me-ln-hollister-marlon-brando-biker-culture-20150519-
      story.html

80   Samuel Pierpoint Langley was the first to build an unpiloted engine-driven model aircraft
      (1896). In 1903, nine days before the Wright brothers flew their plane at Kittyhawk, Langley
      launched a full-size *Aerodrome* piloted plane that failed and crashed due to its fragility. A
      German immigrant name Gustave Whitehead also claimed to be the first to fly a powered
      flight in Fairfield, Connecticut, but this fact remains in dispute.

81   In first two decades of the 1900s, aviators in Europe and America raced to fly faster, farther
      and higher. The early aviation age was pioneered by Europeans named Vuia, Ellehammer,
      Santos-Dumon, Voisin, Farmin, and Bieriot (the first to fly the English Channel). Initially
      planes were used for military purposes and, like motorcycles, World War I proved a watershed
      moment for modern aviation. "History of Aviation" (Wikipedia: https://en.wikipedia.org/wiki/
      History_of_aviation#cite_note-54)

82   "Aviation in World War I" (Wikipedia: https://en.wikipedia.org/wiki/Aviation_in_World_
      War_I)

83   Pilots like Frenchmen Adolphe Pegoud, Rene Paul Fonck and American Eddie Rickenbacker
      became household names during World War I. However, the most notable aviator "ace" was
      a German pilot named Manfred von Richthofen, dubbed more famously as the "Red Baron"
      because of his bright red airplane and superior flight and combat skills (shooting down a
      record 80 planes). "Manfred von Richthofen" (Wikipedia: https://en.wikipedia.org/wiki/
      Manfred_von_Richthofen)

84   The advanced weaponry, particularly of large exploding bombs, created a new debilitating
      psychological condition for World War I soldiers known as "shell shock."

85   For a complete visual history of aviation, particularly its military uses: https://www.youtube.
      com/watch?v=hTwo4vfiK90

86   The Air Commerce Act of 1926 standardized commercial aviation.

87   For an interesting historical perspective on commercial aviation, watch this 1958 Pan Am
      Airlines film on transatlantic flights. Steak dinners. Full size "powder rooms." Smoking
      allowed. https://www.youtube.com/watch?v=QaXZ8Nisyjo

88   In the early 1970s, the lower cost of flights, combined with better jets, created a tipping
      point for air travel. Today, more people fly than ever before in the history of modern aviation.
      In 2017, a record 4.1 billion people flew on airplanes worldwide. https://www.forbes.com/
      sites/ericrosen/2018/09/08/over-4-billion-passengers-flew-in-2017-setting-new-travel-
      record/#64ecd525255b

89   Antonio Meucci invented an early telephone that was not commercially viable in 1854. Six
      years later Johann Philipp Reis constructed a prototype telephone.

90   Another inventor named Elisha Gray may have invented the telephone before Bell. In fact,
      Gray contended that Bell stole his idea. In 1874, Gray produced a "harmonic telegraph device"
      to transmit music (but not a voice). Both inventors submitted telephone patents at the same
      time but, in the long run, only Alexander Graham Bell could prove a working telephone.
      There's also evidence that Gray was aware of Bell's work too. In the end, Bell won both the
      original patent and the praise of his countrymen. "Elisha Gray and Alexander Bell Telephone

Controversy": https://en.wikipedia.org/wiki/Elisha_Gray_and_Alexander_Bell_telephone_controversy

91   "Imagining the Internet: 1870s–1940s Telephone": http://www.elon.edu/e-web/predictions/150/1870.xhtml

Chapter Five: Motion Pictures

92   The earliest cameras required subjects to sit still for up to five minutes for the image to hold. This is why many early photographs often featured blurring.

93   Muybridge invented a lecture aid he called a "zoopraxiscope" to display his running horse animation to audiences. "Zoopraxiscope" (Wikipedia: https://en.wikipedia.org/wiki/Zoopraxiscope)

94   "Art of Ancient Egypt" (Wikipedia: https://en.wikipedia.org/wiki/Art_of_ancient_Egypt)

95   "Roman art" (Wikipedia: https://en.wikipedia.org/wiki/Roman_art)

96   Louis Daguerre's invention of the daguerreotype process created permanent photographs. This was a significant step forward for photography and eventually videography. https://en.wikipedia.org/wiki/Louis_Daguerre

97   The first U.S. President to be photographed was Abraham Lincoln. The use of photography in the Civil War gave people, for the first time, a "real life" look at war. Later, photographs of Indians, pioneers, frontiersmen, outlaws, buffalo hunters and cowboys helped easterners to understand life in the Old West. The photograph was superior to a painting because it was "real" and until the photograph, "real" had never been captured.

98   Inventions like the *phenakistocope* (1833) and *zoetrope* (1834) were popular viewers for early animation. The zoetrope (Greek: for "living things that turn") was invented by William George Horner in 1834). The visual effect of a zoetrope remains common today in the production of animated computer GIFs. https://whatis.techtarget.com/definition/zoetrope

99   Edison's inspiration for his motion picture camera is credited to **Étienne-Jules Marey, a French scientist who invented a photography gun that captured multiple frames per second (1882). Edison met Marey at Paris'** *Exposition Universelle* in 1889. https://en.wikipedia.org/wiki/Kinetoscope

100   Thomas Edison and W.K.L. Dickson soon parted ways, mostly because of Dickson's impatience with Edison to invent a movie projector. Dickson's influence would fade in time, as Edison's star rose. Edison's invention of a movie projector called the Vitascope and early film company that produced movies like "The Great Train Robbery" (1903) helped the inventor stamp his name on early motion pictures. In 1911, Edison still wanted to synchronize sound and picture and invented the kinetophone. A year later he produced a movie that used kinetophone technology to bring sound, including speaking, together into one motion picture experience. He fitted fifty theaters with kinetophones in 1912 and waited for public reaction. The film and sound proved a miserable disaster, often out of synch. Edison eventually left motion pictures, selling off all his equipment and studios, thus ending his dream for synchronized sound in 1918. Nine years later the first "talkie" movie (*The Jazz Singer*) was released.

101   "Auguste and Louis Lumiere" (Wikipedia: https://en.wikipedia.org/wiki/Auguste_and_Louis_Lumi%C3%A8re)

102   The first "Nickelodeon" theater opened June 19, 1905 in Pittsburgh, PA. As the name suggests, the price for admission was one nickel. https://en.wikipedia.org/wiki/Nickelodeon_(movie_theater)

103   *The Great Bank Robbery* was produced by Edison films and was a watershed film for its time. https://en.wikipedia.org/wiki/The_Great_Train_Robbery_(1903_film) Watch the entire film on YouTube: https://www.youtube.com/watch?v=zuto7qWrplc

104 "Classical Hollywood Cinema" (Wikipedia: https://en.wikipedia.org/wiki/Classical_Hollywood_cinema)

105 Marcus Loew's influence was significant upon the young and emerging film industry. Unfortunately, a fatal heart attack cut his life short on September 5, 1927. *Variety* magazine eulogized Loew as "the most beloved man of all show business of all time." *Variety*, September 7, 1927: https://archive.org/stream/variety87-1927-09/Variety87-1927-09#mode/1up

106 Since 1957, MGM Pictures has used "Leo the Lion" to trade mark all its films. However, beginning in 1916, seven different lions were employed to introduce an MGM film and only the last one was actually named "Leo." https://en.wikipedia.org/wiki/Leo_the_Lion_(MGM) For those who sleep through the opening of an MGM movie, here's that famous trademark: https://www.youtube.com/watch?v=OVCxJ1aT24A

107 In the 1920s, the influence of media—particularly motion pictures—encouraged experimentation. From alcohol to premarital sex to cigarettes, America loosened its buttons on a previous Victorian culture. Young women, many of them early "Motion Picture" generation kids pursued illicit activities condemned by parents, priest and preacher. They "cropped [their] hair and flattened [their] breasts" to start a new fashion trend: "flappers." Sexually-suggestive material was found in magazine advertisements, books, plays and films. In fact, the 1920s coined a new term: "sex appeal." *The Century* by Jennings and Brewster, 115.

108 *The Clansman* was originally a book by Thomas Dixon, Jr., a Southern Baptist preacher, penned in an angry response to a stage rendition of the anti-slavery novel *Uncle Tom's Cabin* (1852). Dixon believed *Uncle Tom's Cabin* was pure fiction.

109 Washington Post: https://www.washingtonpost.com/opinions/the-unfortunate-effects-of-the-birth-of-a-nation/2017/07/21/b6fc5920-6c1e-11e7-abbc-a53480672286_story.html?noredirect=on&utm_term=.a50891ff80e9

110 D.W. Griffith's epic three-hour, box office smash could only be unseated by another Civil War era film three and a half decades later: *Gone with the Wind* (1939).

111 The membership of the Ku Klux Klan eroded following the Civil War but found new life in the movie *A Birth of a Nation*. In 1921, the organization had over a million followers and quadrupled that number to four million in 1924. The Ku Klux Klan was a formidable, nearly mainstream, political force in the first half of the century. It didn't just oppose blacks but any race and creed that wasn't white and Protestant. The Klan fought immorality too, from booze to prostitution to gambling, patrolling neighborhoods, back roads and alleys looking for offenders. Membership included prominent businessmen, farmers, policemen and clergy. Future president Harry Truman almost joined the Klan for its political advantages in Missouri but resisted when he learned, if elected, he couldn't hire a Catholic. *The Century* by Jennings and Brewster, 119.

112 On April 26, 1915 over 800 black women gathered a week after *A Birth of a Nation* opened in Boston, MA. The movie had already sparked demonstrations prior to its release in Boston but still drew record white crowds. A speaker at the event the black women attended said, "if there are men here who are afraid to die there are women who are not afraid. This [movie] would not be tolerated if it affected any other race or people." https://www.massmoments.org/moment-details/the-birth-of-a-nation-sparks-protest.html

113 The "new negro" was the title of an influential 1925 anthology of African-American writings edited by Alain Locke. https://en.wikipedia.org/wiki/The_New_Negro:_An_Interpretation

114 "Movie theaters had uniformed ushers and attendants in the rest rooms; pipe organs and orchestras to accompany the film action; and they were sometimes designed so that viewers had to take long, circuitous routes to get to the auditorium itself, giving them a chance to feel that they weren't waiting for a movie at all, but taking a stroll through some raja's palace, admiring the splendor of the rich décor." *The Century*, Jennings and Brewster, 127.

115 News Reel: Stock market crash https://www.youtube.com/watch?v=i2ep3OyX0gM

116 News Reel: Repeal of Prohibition: https://www.youtube.com/watch?v=ZA0AMFyw2ig

117 News Reel: Hindenburg https://www.youtube.com/watch?v=rWeO1q0gHJE

118 News Reel: Pearl Harbor https://www.youtube.com/watch?v=pj_btks99p4

119 News Reel: Death of Franklin D. Roosevelt: https://www.youtube.com/watch?v=xftIpLj4JZ0

120 News Reel: Korean War https://www.youtube.com/watch?v=OF_Ts_6oSi8

121 An artist named Fred Mitzen first painted a Santa Claus enjoying an ice-cold Coke in 1930, but it was Haddon Sundblom's depiction of Santa and Coca-Cola—which appeared in multiple magazines beginning in 1931—that shaped a fresh public image for old Saint Nick. "Five Things You Didn't Know About Saint Nick": https://www.coca-colacompany.com/stories/coke-lore-santa-claus

122 *Baseball: An Illustrated History* by Geoffrey C. Ward and Ken Burns (New York: Afred A. Knopf, 2001): 153.

123 Ibid., 159.

124 The Babe Ruth to New York Yankees deal for $125,000 also included a $300,000 promise by Yankee owner Col. Jacob Ruppert to Red Sox owner H. Harrison Frazee to help him finance his passion for Broadway plays. Frazee went so far to pay for a winning play that he used Fenway Park as collateral for the loan. In the end, the best Frazee got was a hit play (*No, No Nanette*) while the Yankees scored a young slugger who eventually clobbered 714 major league home runs. Some call it the most "short-sighted [deal] in baseball history." Ibid., 155.

125 In 1927, Ruth homered sixty times and finished with 714 lifetime home runs—baseball records that stood for decades. In the 1932 World Series against the Cubs, Ruth allegedly pointed his finger to center field prior to homering in that direction.

126 In 1930 the New York Yankees rewarded their slugger with an $80,000 per year contract, despite the onset of the Great Depression. President Herbert Hoover struggled to lead the nation. In fact, many Americans lived on their last dime in broken-down shanties known as "Hooverville." "President Hoover and Baseball": https://www.whitehousehistory.org/president-herbert-hoover-and-baseball

127 "The Jack Pack": http://www.pophistorydig.com/topics/tag/jfk-and-hollywood/

128 Valentino's death on August 23, 1926 shocked his fans. He was a vibrant, ambitious young man. However, he suffered from appendicitis and gastric ulcers, the reason for his surgery in August of 1926. Valentino had collapsed at a Manhattan hotel and was immediately hospitalized. After surgery he developed peritonitis (swelling of the abdominal walls) and pleuritis (inflammation in the chest cavity) that eventually plunged him into a coma and then death. https://en.wikipedia.org/wiki/Rudolph_Valentino

129 Humphrey Bogart stated "Dean died at just the right time. He left behind a legend. If he had lived, he'd never have been able to live up to his publicity." *Rebel for All Seasons* by Ron Martinetti: http://www.americanlegends.com/bookstore/deanstory/intro.html

130 Concerning James Dean's death: "It's like Valentino," a reporter told Henry Ginsberg, the coproducer of *Giant*, Dean's last movie, referring to the craze that had swept the nation after the Italian actor's death in the 1920s. Ginsberg disagreed, "It's bigger than Valentino." Ibid.

131 In 1928 the first Academy Awards (Oscars) were presented to various films and their stars for excellence in production and acting.

132 Watch *Steamboat Willie* at YouTube: https://www.youtube.com/watch?v=hxf-UHuGobI

133 "Introduction to 1939, Hollywood's Greatest Year" by Roger Fristoe: http://www.tcm.com/this-month/article/238944%7C0/1939-70th-Anniversary-of-Hollywood-s-Greatest-Year.html

134 Additional classic movies from 1939 include: *Stagecoach* (which launched John Wayne's career), *Babes in Arms* (musical), *Goodbye Mr. Chips* (romantic drama), *The Hunchback of Notre Dame* (drama), *Drums Along the Mohawk* (historical drama), *Union Pacific* (western) and *The Little Princess* (Shirley Temple's first Technicolor movie).

135 "Disneyland" (Wikipedia: https://en.wikipedia.org/wiki/Disneyland)

Chapter Six: Radio

136 Paul Harvey carved lanes for later right wing talk radio hosts like Rush Limbaugh, Michael Savage, Mark Levin, Sean Hannity and Laura Ingraham.

137 "Paul Harvey" by Mike Thomas in *Salon*: https://web.archive.org/web/20081201073241/ http://dir.salon.com/story/people/bc/2001/09/25/harvey/print.html

138 The hurricane of 1938 tore a path of destruction throughout New England.

139 Between 1930 and 1933, four million radio sets were sold in America.

140 *Generations* by Strauss and Howe, 279.

141 Strauss and Howe: "The Silent Generation *(Artist, born 1925–1942)* grew up as the suffocated children of war and depression. They came of age just too late to be war heroes and just too early to be youthful free spirits. Instead, this early-marrying Lonely Crowd became the risk-averse technicians and professionals of a post-crisis era in which conformity seemed to be a sure ticket to success. Many found a voice as sensitive rock 'n rollers and civil-rights advocates." https://www.lifecourse.com/ about/method/def/silent-gen.html

142 The senior advisors were Pierre Salinger (Kennedy), Bill Moyers (Johnson), John Ehrlichman (Nixon), Dick Cheney (Ford), Stuart Eizenstat (Carter), James Baker III (Reagan) and John Sununu (HW Bush). Cheney (Vice President) and Baker (Secretary of State, Chief of Staff) would also serve in George W. Bush's administration. Ibid.

143 "Live Births and Birth Rates, By Year": https://www.infoplease.com/us/births/live-births-and-birth-rates-year

144 The radio "unit of frequency" (hertz) is named in honor of Heinrich Hertz.

145 "Wardenclyffe Tower": https://en.wikipedia.org/wiki/Wardenclyffe_Tower

146 The first recorded transmission by Fessenden was weather related: "Hello. One, two, three, four. Is it snowing where you are, Mr. Thiessen?" Source: "Amplitude modulation" (Wikipedia: https://en.wikipedia.org/wiki/Amplitude_modulation).

147 *The Century* by Jennings and Brewster, 110.

148 Listen to Orson Welles "War of the Worlds" radio broadcast: https://www.youtube.com/ watch?v=OzC3Fg_rRJM

149 Listen to Herbert Morrison's dramatic radio report of the Hindenburg disaster: https://www. youtube.com/watch?v=0Ad9tholMEM

150 Watch Orson Welles apology on YouTube: http://www.youtube.com/watch?v=NcRoo0dcxbA

151 Listen to Red Barber and Mel Allen broadcast the 1942 Yankees-Cardinals World Series: https://www.youtube.com/watch?v=p5uP9d40cwo

152 As part of dam construction, a new "model" city was erected next to Vegas to house the workers known as "Boulder City." Nevertheless, Vegas got the most lasting benefit.

153 Mount Rushmore was originally called "The Six Grandfathers" or "Cougar Mountain" by the Lakota Sioux, who believed the Black Hills were sacred lands. Among white settlers it was also known as Sugarloaf Mountain, Slaughter Mountain and Keystone Cliffs. Eventually, it was named Rushmore after Charles Rushmore who prospected the region. https://en.wikipedia. org/wiki/Mount_Rushmore

154 Despite the danger of dynamite and over 400 workers hanging over the cliff's side, not one life was lost.

155 https://en.wikipedia.org/wiki/Mount_Rushmore

156 "During the 20s, there was an average of 70 U.S. banks failing annually. After the crash during the first 10 months of 1930, 744 banks failed – 10 times as many. In all, 9,000 banks failed during the decade of the 30s. It's estimated that 4,000 banks failed during the one year of 1933 alone. By 1933, depositors saw $140 billion disappear through bank failures." https:// livinghistoryfarm.org/farminginthe30s/money_08.html

157 Listen to Franklin D. Roosevelt's first fireside chat at YouTube: https://www.youtube.com/ watch?v=iipnhLTdh-0

158 Listen to Roosevelt's "Fireside Chat #19" on Pearl Harbor, ranked among the five most important speeches of all time: https://www.youtube.com/watch?v=ncXGSV0bLl8

159 "Dust Bowl" (Wikipedia: https://en.wikipedia.org/wiki/Dust_Bowl)

160 "Radio Advertisement" (Wikipedia: https://en.wikipedia.org/wiki/Radio_advertisement#History)

161 National Public Radio (NPR) doesn't rely upon sponsors. It's federally-funded by the U.S. government and established by an act of Congress. National public radio first aired on April 20, 1971 and boasts over a thousand radio stations nationwide. It broadcasts news, public affairs, human interest stories, speeches and music.

162 Alan Freed was a pioneer in rock and roll radio. He played black rhythm and blues on Cleveland's AM WJW. On March 21, 1952, Freed hosted what many consider the first "rock and roll" concert called "The Moondog Coronation Ball" in the Cleveland arena.

163 Tom Miller, *On the Border: Portraits of America's Southwestern Frontier*, 84–85. Source: https://en.wikipedia.org/wiki/Wolfman_Jack#cite_note-5

164 Wolfman Jack encouraged his listeners to "get naked" and to "lay your hands on the radio and squeeze my knobs." Listen to a 1960s era Wolfman Jack Show: https://www.youtube.com/watch?v=4zAagySB7SU

165 Listen to an episode of *American Top 40*: https://www.youtube.com/watch?v=TbMZmPH2iJE

166 "Little Richard" (Wikipedia: https://en.wikipedia.org/wiki/Little_Richard)

167 Elvis Presley served in the U.S. Army from 1958-1960. https://history.army.mil/faq/elvis.htm

168 "Jerry Lee Lewis" (Wikipedia: https://en.wikipedia.org/wiki/Jerry_Lee_Lewis)

169 "The Day The Music Died" (Wikipedia: https://en.wikipedia.org/wiki/The_Day_the_Music_Died)

170 Chuck Berry only served a year and a half in prison (1962-1963). https://en.wikipedia.org/wiki/Chuck_Berry

171 "Payola" (Wikipedia: https://en.wikipedia.org/wiki/Payola)

172 "Alan Freed" (Wikipedia: https://en.wikipedia.org/wiki/Alan_Freed#Legal_trouble,_payola_scandal

173 "Study: 32 Million Listen to Sirius XM Radio Weekly": https://www.adweek.com/tv-video/study-32-million-listen-sirius-xm-radio-weekly-114478/

174 Uses for vinyl records: https://www.pinterest.com/musicstack/interesting-uses-for-vinyl-records/

175 Source: https://web.archive.org/web/19971210103031/http://www.riaa.com/market/releases/statover.htm

176 Watch some 1940s swing: https://www.youtube.com/watch?v=I9zHYkKoL4A

177 "Groovy" originated in jazz and referred to music that's "swinging, tight, funky." http://www.ethanhein.com/wp/2011/how-did-the-word-groovy-come-to-acquire-its-current-meaning/

178 The Civil Rights movement was between 1954 and 1968. https://www.history.com/topics/black-history/civil-rights-movement

179 The Women's Liberation movement emerged in the late 1960s. https://en.wikipedia.org/wiki/Women%27s_liberation_movement

180 The Gay Rights movement started in June 1969: https://en.wikipedia.org/wiki/LGBT_social_movements

181 The Jesus Movement emerged in the late 1960s. https://en.wikipedia.org/wiki/Jesus_movement

182 "Phonograph Record" (Wikipedia: https://en.wikipedia.org/wiki/Phonograph_record)

183 The recording was done by Franco-Swiss pianist Alfred Cortot in 1925. Ibid.

184 Pakenham, Compton (1930), "Recorded Music: A Wide Range". *The New York Times*, February 23, 1930, 118.

185 Sound recordings were initially made of hard rubber, then celluloid and plastic. 78 rpm records continued to have some popularity into the 1950s.

186 "Culture Clubs: A History of U.S. Jazz Clubs": https://www.allaboutjazz.com/culture-clubs-a-history-of-the-us-jazz-clubs-part-i-new-orleans-and-chicago-by-karl-ackermann.php

187 Sinatra's first record was *The Voice of Frank Sinatra* (1946 Columbia Records).

188 The Rat Pack included Dean Martin, Joey Bishop, Sammy Davis, Jr., and Peter Lawford. Marilyn Monroe, Shirley MacLaine and Angie Dickinson were also included as "mascots." https://en.wikipedia.org/wiki/Rat_Pack

189 "Sin-atra City: The Story of Frank Sinatra and Vegas": https://medium.com/@RecordingAcad/sin-atra-city-the-story-of-frank-sinatra-and-las-vegas-5434e557d2f5

190 Tom Santopietro, *Sinatra in Hollywood*, St. Martin's Press (2008), 231. Source: https://en.wikipedia.org/wiki/Frank_Sinatra#CITEREFSantopietro2008

191 "Rocket 88" featured Ike Turner on keyboards. He composed the song.

192 Listen to the "Million Dollar Quartet": https://www.youtube.com/watch?v=vKpg3PkGlZs

193 Hank Williams discography: https://en.wikipedia.org/wiki/Hank_Williams_discography

194 Watch Chuck Berry's "Duck Walk": https://www.youtube.com/watch?v=EqS76TFCCYs

195 "Chuck Berry" (Wikipedia: https://en.wikipedia.org/wiki/Chuck_Berry

196 After Chuck Berry, the Rock Hall of Fame inducted James Brown, Ray Charles, Sam Cooke, Fats Domino, The Everly Brothers, Buddy Holly, Jerry Lee Lewis, Little Richard and Elvis Presley. It would add fifteen more in 1987. Only the Class of 2012 had more than the inaugural (12) and that class included the backing bands for Gene Vincent (The Blue Caps), Bill Haley (The Comets) and Buddy Holly (The Crickets). https://en.wikipedia.org/wiki/List_of_Rock_and_Roll_Hall_of_Fame_inductees

197 Source: https://www.rockhall.com/inductees/chuck-berry

198 The other three albums were Frank Sinatra's *In The Wee Small Hours* (1955), *Songs for Swingin' Lovers* (1956) and Miles Davis' *Kind of Blue* (1959). Rock 'n roll fans argued for then inclusion of *Elvis' Golden Records* album in 1955 that produced four number one songs, including "Heartbreak Hotel" and "Hound Dog."

199 Watch "Ain't That A Shame": https://www.youtube.com/watch?v=Z8dx0oE—VI

200 Watch "Rock Around The Clock": https://www.youtube.com/watch?v=ZgdufzXvjqw

201 Watch Elvis' version of "Hound Dog": https://www.youtube.com/watch?v=MMmljYkdr-w

202 Watch Big Mama Thornton's "Hound Dog": https://www.youtube.com/watch?v=frsBq9MCNVg

203 Watch "Walk the Line": https://www.youtube.com/watch?v=xObSJWIWui0

204 Watch Elvis' third and final "waist up" appearance on the Ed Sullivan show (1957): https://www.youtube.com/watch?v=COFHGFZxtnY

205 *His Hand in Mine* (1960) is considered by many Christian music historians as the first true contemporary Christian record.

206 "Jerry Lee Lewis" (Wikipedia: https://en.wikipedia.org/wiki/Jerry_Lee_Lewis)

Chapter Seven: Vinyl Records

207 "The Scathing Speech That Made Television History" by Lily Rothman (*Time*, May 9, 2016): http://time.com/4315217/newton-minow-vast-wasteland-1961-speech/

208 Source: https://www.youtube.com/watch?v=9dGRgLfaGwo

209 *Generations* by Howe and Strauss, 299.

210 "Generation Jones": https://en.wikipedia.org/wiki/Generation_Jones

211 *Boomer Nation: The Largest and Richest Generation Ever and How It Changed America* by Steve Gillon (New York: Free Press, 2004): 1.

212 Watch a newsreel on Charles Van Doren: https://www.youtube.com/watch?v=oPqryNPuy_o

213 "1960s: First Televised Presidential Debate": https://www.cbsnews.com/news/1960-first-televised-presidential-debate/

214 Walter Cronkite on the impact of television, *Modern Marvels: Television: Window to the World.*

215 John Logie Baird introduced the first working mechanical television on January 26, 1926. https://en.wikipedia.org/wiki/John_Logie_Baird In 1927 Charles Jenkins produces an inter-city transmission of Herbert Hoover using mechanical television. http://history.sandiego.edu/gen/recording/television1.html

216 *Modern Marvels: Television: Window to the World*, The History Channel (1999): https://www.imdb.com/title/tt2164335/

217 Philo T. Farnsworth died March 11, 1971 in Salt Lake City. His wife never stopped championing him as the true inventor of electronic television. In 1999, *Time* magazine named Farnsworth to its list of the "100 Most Important People of the Century." https://en.wikipedia.org/wiki/Philo_Farnsworth

218 The average cost of a television set was $445. Figuring in inflation, the cost today would be over $8000.

219 Earl Muntz also pioneered early television commercials through his use of "unusual costumes, stunts, and outrageous claims." https://en.wikipedia.org/wiki/Madman_Muntz

220 Watch "Milton Berle Show": https://www.youtube.com/watch?v=s09knxgs0mQ

221 Watch "Ed Sullivan Show" (originally titled "Toast of the Town"): https://www.youtube.com/watch?v=k_s7INzHus4&t=35s

222 Watch the 1949 pilot of the "Lone Ranger": https://www.youtube.com/watch?v=YbzSdY2xNf8

223 Watch "Howdy Doody Show": https://www.youtube.com/watch?v=pnUGAe0yqz4

224 Watch snippets of "I Love Lucy" (1951–1957): https://www.youtube.com/watch?v=4t_lFXZKah4

225 Watch Harry Truman's 1952 tour of the White House: https://www.youtube.com/watch?v=GShOK5IZn9g

226 "Number of Televisions in U.S.": https://hypertextbook.com/facts/2007/TamaraTamazashvili.shtml

227 Watch the pilot for "Father Knows Best": https://youtu.be/sXVEWmxkmbQ

228 Watch the pilot for "Lassie": https://www.youtube.com/watch?v=lXquPCNsPzM

229 Watch an episode of "The Donna Reed Show": https://www.youtube.com/watch?v=tYocrksfNEo

230 Watch an episode of "The Andy Griffith Show": https://www.youtube.com/watch?v=zbcHrhzHcEs

231 Watch a 1955 episode of "Gunsmoke": https://www.youtube.com/watch?v=8gFtqE0j9XE

232 Watch an episode of "Have Gun, Will Travel": https://www.youtube.com/watch?v=BNNejXC2hSw

233 Watch the pilot episode of "Bonanza": https://www.youtube.com/watch?v=yJAQ-HdG9K0&t=65s

234 Watch a 1961 episode of "Alfred Hitchcock Presents": https://www.youtube.com/watch?v=mCYM5TMiZ5Q

235 Watch an episode of "The Twilight Zone": https://www.youtube.com/watch?v=NHdJUDBYA0o

236 Watch "The Mickey Mouse Club": https://www.youtube.com/watch?v=nOBlXZyKC6A

237 Watch a classic episode of "The Honeymooners": https://www.youtube.com/watch?v=XUkbd2m0TJg

238 Watch an episode of "The Flintstones": https://www.youtube.com/watch?v=0jjzBs-12tE

239 All five of the original MTV vee jays were born in the Television Generation years: https://abcnews.go.com/Entertainment/mtvs-original-veejays-now/story?id=14204034

240 *Boomer Nation* by Gillon, 5.

241 The McDonald's Big Mac "ingredient" commercials were wildly popular: https://www.youtube.com/watch?v=yEBCV0ic6Tc

242 *Schoolhouse Rock* taught kids through clever cartoons and memorable songs like "Conjunction Junction," "I'm Just a Bill" and "Three is a Magic Number."

243 Other dances included the *Mashed Potato, Watusi, Funky Chicken, Jerk, Swim, Bump, Hustle, Bus Stop, Sprinkler and Lawnmower.*

244 *Boom!* By Tom Brokaw (New York: Random House, 2007): xv.

245 *Generations* by Strauss and Howe, 301.

246 "See It Now" had it most memorable moment on March 9, 1954. In a half-hour special titled "A Report on Senator Joseph McCarthy," Murrow revealed the truth about the controversial senator and his "McCarthyism" anti-communist tactics. The show contributed to the McCarthy's eventual political downfall.

247 Source: https://en.wikipedia.org/wiki/Television_news_in_the_United_States

248 Watch Walter Cronkite's final sign off on March 6, 1981: https://www.youtube.com/watch?v=G5tdqojA26E

249 Watch Walter Cronkite's announcement of JFK's assassination: https://www.youtube.com/watch?v=6PXORQE5-CY

250 Watch Walter Cronkite's commentary on Vietnam: https://www.youtube.com/watch?v=Dn2RjahTi3M

251 Watch the 1952 debut of *The Today Show*: https://www.youtube.com/watch?v=vY4_iv3UbGg&t=58s

252 The longest running television series: *Meet The Press* (November 6, 1947), *CBS Evening News* (May 3, 1948), *Music and the Spoken Word* (October 1949), *Hallmark Hall of Fame* (December 24, 1951) and *The Today Show* (January 14, 1952). https://en.wikipedia.org/wiki/List_of_longest-running_United_States_television_series

253 *Boomer Nation* by Gillon, 8-9.

Chapter Nine: Space

254 Watch Neil Armstrong and Buzz Aldrin's first steps on the moon: https://www.youtube.com/watch?v=HCt1BwWE2gA

255 "The Rockets That Inspired Francis Scott Key": https://www.airspacemag.com/history-of-flight/rockets-inspired-francis-scott-key-180952399/

256 Watch "A Trip to the Moon": https://www.youtube.com/watch?v=xLVChRVfZ74

257 "Konstantin Tsiolkovsky": https://en.wikipedia.org/wiki/Konstantin_Tsiolkovsky

258 Tsiolkovsky built a model space craft in 1903. He called them "sputniks" (the Russian word for "fellow traveler").

259 Quoted from Lehman, Milton (1963). *This High Man: The Life of Robert H. Goddard*. New York: Farrar, Strauss, and Co.: https://en.wikipedia.org/wiki/Robert_H._Goddard#cite_note-Lehman-14

260 The four "founding fathers" of space travel: Hermann Oberth (Germany), Robert Esnault-Pelterie (France), Konstantin Tsiolkovsky (Russia) and Robert Goddard (U.S.A.).

261 Hermann Oberth Raumfahrt Museum: http://www.oberth-museum.org/index_e.html

262 Depending on the source, the number of German physicists and engineers deported in "Operation Paperclip" range from 127 to 1600.

263 While there are many examples of Soviet under-reporting the facts of their space missions, the most famous example would be Voskhod 2 in March 1965 and Alexei Leonov's spacewalk. The Soviet news agency (TASS) happily reported that, "outside the ship and after returning, Leonov feels well." However, this wasn't true. Leonov's spacewalk was nearly deadly. Post-Cold War Soviet documents disclosed that Leonov's space suit inflated to the point he could not bend for re-entry to Voskhod 2. Leonov also violated procedure when he entered the airlock head-first. This caused him to get stuck when he tried to close the hatch. The only way to free himself was to lower his space suit's air pressure (risking decompression sickness and death). He also risked being abandoned altogether by his fellow cosmonaut if he couldn't fully re-enter (thankfully, he did). The Soviet propaganda that Leonov felt "well" and performed the walk

without incident caused Americans to greatly under-estimate the perils of a spacewalk. https://en.wikipedia.org/wiki/Voskhod_2

264 In retrospect, many believed the United States could've beat the Russians (in launching first) but 1950s societal complacency, apathy and contentment held us back. America was living the good life. On July 29, 1957 the Department of Defense formally expressed their unhappiness with space exploration and shelved it. We weren't interested in space. Besides most of our rockets were blowing up on the pads.

265 Watch a "Duck and Cover" civil defense film for 1950s children: https://www.youtube.com/watch?v=l2owGLgCTkg

266 Most of our early rocket work were complete failures. On December 6, 1957, the rocket Vanguard TV-3 exploded violently at lift off. https://www.youtube.com/watch?v=zVeFkakURXM American scientists were demoralized.

267 Alan Shepard flew 116 miles aboard Freedom 7 on May 5, 1961.

268 For the full text of Kennedy's "moon" speech: https://www.space.com/11772-president-kennedy-historic-speech-moon-space.html. To view: https://www.youtube.com/watch?v=TUXuV7XbZvU

269 Other mid-1960s television shows with space or NASA themes, many that equally thrived in syndication for late-birth Space Generation kids, included *The Jetsons, Twilight Zone, I Dream of Jeannie, Lost in Space* and *My Favorite Martian.*

270 Watch Star Trek actors and writers comment on "the kiss": https://www.youtube.com/watch?v=9KGE7HYEie0

271 The NBC decision to end Star Trek in 1969 was later tagged the #4 biggest blunder in television history by *TV Guide*. "25 Biggest TV Blunders 2". *25 Biggest TV Blunders.* July 31, 2011. TV Guide Network. #4 – NBC Cancels 'Star Trek.'

272 "Our World" television show: https://en.wikipedia.org/wiki/Our_World_(1967_TV_program)

273 John F. Kennedy delivered a vision for Americans in space and publicly championed the space program. However, behind closed doors it was a different matter. Space wasn't a high priority for Kennedy, who questioned its extreme cost and importance. https://www.history.com/topics/us-presidents/kennedy-has-doubts-about-space-race-video

274 Watch the astronauts read Genesis 1 on December 24, 1968: http://www.youtube.com/watch?v=njpWalYduU4

275 For a full review of 1968: https://en.wikipedia.org/wiki/1968_in_the_United_States

276 Watch Neil Armstrong's first steps on the moon and CBS News commentary: https://www.youtube.com/watch?v=5F6B1U77dgs

277 Watch Alan Sheppard play golf on the moon: https://www.youtube.com/watch?v=f-FxhCZold0

278 Apollo 13—piloted by Jim Lovell—was scheduled to be the third moon landing, but an oxygen tank exploded and severely crippled the craft (also manned by astronauts Fred Haise and Jack Swigert) on April 13, 1970. The mission got off on a bad foot when Ken Mattingly (exposed to measles) was replaced by Swigert three days prior to launch. Apollo 13 was over 205,000 miles from earth when the accident happened. Lovell, famously radioed Mission Control in Texas with the infamous phrase, "Houston, we have a problem." Given the severity of the situation (less than 10% chance of success), only pure American ingenuity, toughness and perseverance—by both astronauts and Mission Control—saved their lives. Even though Apollo 13 never officially landed on the moon, only circled it, their mission has been called a "successful failure." https://en.wikipedia.org/wiki/Apollo_13

279 Watch an NBC report on the Challenger explosion: https://www.youtube.com/watch?v=yibNEcn-4yQ

280 Christa McAuliffe was born two years shy of the Space Generation's initial birth year (b. 1948) but she could certainly still be included. She had dreamed of space since her youth. In fact, she wrote on her NASA application: "I watched the Space Age being born, and I would like

to participate." https://en.wikipedia.org/wiki/Christa_McAuliffe McAuliffe's backup was an elementary school teacher and Space Generation member (b. 1951) from McCall, ID named Barbara Morgan. https://en.wikipedia.org/wiki/Barbara_Morgan

281 "Space Challenger Shuttle Disaster": https://en.wikipedia.org/wiki/Space_Shuttle_Challenger_disaster

282 "Richard Branson": https://en.wikipedia.org/wiki/Richard_Branson

283 Watch the launch and entire first hour of MTV (without videos): https://www.youtube.com/watch?v=i1QDSmflFtM

284 Members of the Space Generation born after 1960 have saved between $35-70K for retirement and will be all be 65 and older in the year 2035 (15 years from now). As a rule, this generation carries more debt, has less financial stability and endures more economic downturns (layoffs, unemployment, inflation) than other generations. https://www.marketwatch.com/story/all-the-ways-gen-x-is-financially-wrecked-2018-09-12

Chapter Ten: Gamer

285 Strauss and Howe argued that "13" was a great name for this generation. It was a "non-label label" that was "a little Halloweenish, a little raffish, a little heavy." They pointed out that high-rises don't have thirteenth floors and a "baker's dozen" meant thirteen doughnuts. This generation was also the thirteenth removed from the American revolution. Fortunately, these two boomers relented on reducing an entire generation of kids to a cursed number. Eventually they would join everyone else and employ "Gen X" to describe those born between 1961 and 1981. Neil Howe and William Strauss, *13th Gen: Abort, Retry, Ignore, Fail?* (New York: Vintage books, 1993): 16-17.

286 The origin of the "Generation X" name begins in London, England and a book titled *Generation X* by Jane Deverson and Charles Hamblett. The book was later purchased at a garage sale by Billy Idol's mother, who gave it to her son. Idol loved the title so much he named his late 70s' punk band "Generation X." In America, the moniker wouldn't find traction until it was used as a title for Douglas Coupland's 1991 book: *"Gen X: Tales for an Accelerated Culture."* http://mentalfloss.com/article/542159/how-generations-named-baby-boomers-generation-x-millennials

287 "Generation X": https://en.wikipedia.org/wiki/Generation_X

288 Between 1973 (when abortion was legalized) and 1980 (the last birth year for the Gamer Generation), abortions doubled from 19.6 per 100 live births to 35.9 per 100 live births. Essentially one in three pregnancies were aborted by the end of the 1970s. https://www.statista.com/statistics/185286/legal-abortions-per-100-live-births-in-the-us-since-2000/

289 "Marriage and Divorce Rates": https://www.washingtonpost.com/news/wonk/wp/2015/06/23/144-years-of-marriage-and-divorce-in-the-united-states-in-one-chart/?noredirect=on&utm_term=.606b4d03b6ca

290 The title of the 1983 report was *A Nation at Risk*. It was a landmark study of American schools that revealed the nation's children were receiving an inadequate education in comparison to other countries around the globe. The commission proposed 38 recommendations to correct the problem. https://en.wikipedia.org/wiki/A_Nation_at_Risk

291 As quoted in *13th Gen* by Howe and Strauss, 16.

292 As quoted in *13th Gen* by Howe and Strauss, 25.

293 Ibid.

294 Ibid., 27.

295 "Decades of Drug Use: the 80s and 90s": https://news.gallup.com/poll/6352/decades-drug-use-80s-90s.aspx

296 AIDS emerged in the 1980s. In 1981 there were 270 reported cases and 121 deaths. By 1983 there were 3,993 deaths. In 1989, there were 66,493 deaths. AIDS was fatal to those who

contracted it, and it forever ended the "free love" sexual attitudes and behaviors of the 1970s. http://www.factlv.org/timeline.htm

297 Since the early 1980s, church attendance has been in decline despite a Boomer-led evangelical megachurch revival at the same time. Gen X was the first generation to not return to church attendance once kids arrived. https://religionnews.com/2014/01/27/great-decline-religion-united-states-one-graph/

298 "The Jail Generation" by Dan Hoyle: https://www.alternet.org/2004/04/the_jail_generation/

299 *13th Gen* by Strauss and Howe, 85.

300 "Young Voted Clinton, Old Voted Trump": https://www.forbes.com/sites/niallmccarthy/2016/11/09/the-2016-elections-generation-gap-infographic/#32a4cd08497b

301 Alex P. Keaton was a character in the 1980s sitcom *Family Ties*. Keaton (played by Michael J. Fox) was an ultra-conservative Reagan-loving Republican born to ultra-left wing, liberal hippie parents.

302 The checkers program was designed on the Ferranti Mark 1 computer by Christopher Strachey in 1952 as part of a research project. Source: https://en.wikipedia.org/wiki/History_of_video_games

303 Alexander Douglas invented "OXO"—a tic-tac-toe video game—on the EDSAC computer in 1952. Source: https://en.wikipedia.org/wiki/History_of_video_games

304 "Space War!" (1961) is considered one of "the ten most important video games of all time" by the Library of Congress. Source: https://en.wikipedia.org/wiki/Spacewar!

305 Released in 1979 by Atari, Inc., the goal of the game is to shoot down invading "flying saucers" while avoiding getting tagged by asteroid rocks. The player can also shoot the rocks, but beware, the smaller the rock fragment the faster it travels. Consequently, failure to completely explode a lumbering giant asteroid can come back to bite you. Source: https://en.wikipedia.org/wiki/Asteroids_(video_game)

306 Released in 1979 by Namco. Source: https://en.wikipedia.org/wiki/Galaxian

307 Released in 1980 by Atari, Inc. Source: https://en.wikipedia.org/wiki/Missile_Command

308 Released in 1981 by Williams Electronics. Source: https://en.wikipedia.org/wiki/Defender_(1981_video_game)

309 Released in 1981 by Midway Manufacturing. Source: https://en.wikipedia.org/wiki/Galaga

310 The point of Pac-Man was to eat up the dots of a giant maze while avoiding capture from four ghosts named Blinky, Pinky, Inky and Clyde. In each corner of the maze was a special dot that when consumed allowed Pac-Man to turn on the ghosts and eat them for bigger points. Unfortunately, that special power was limited and eventually Pac-Man was back to running. Pac-Man was designed by Namco and released in 1980. Source: https://en.wikipedia.org/wiki/Pac-Man

311 "Pac-Man Fever" by Buckner and Garcia peaked at #9 on the Billboard charts and has over 2.5 million sales. VH-1 ranked the song #98 in its "100 Greatest One Hit Wonders of the 1980s." Hoping for lightning to strike twice, Buckner and Garcia also released "Do the Donkey Kong" but it flopped. Listen to "Pac-Man Fever" at YouTube: https://www.youtube.com/watch?v=0-MONIvP6kI

312 Released in 1982 by Midway Manufacturing without permission by Namco. Source: https://en.wikipedia.org/wiki/Ms._Pac-Man

313 For most of its history Nintendo dealt in playing cards, but in the early 1960s ventured into other businesses including taxis, noodles, hotels and even vacuum cleaners. Nothing worked, except their toys and games. In 1971, Nintendo and Odyssey partnered to create a "shooting gallery" game. And while Odyssey eventually failed, Nintendo kept that shooting concept alive in Japan and even sold Odyssey game consoles in Japan. Source: https://en.wikipedia.org/wiki/History_of_Nintendo

314 Source: "The History of Video Games": https://www.youtube.com/watch?v=z7-BN0qdZDk&t=50s (26:18 mark).

315 Also known as the "video game crash of 1983–1985," this gaming recession was costly to Atari, Mattel and other gaming publishers. Revenues dropped from $3.2 billion in 1983 to a paltry $100 million in 1985 (-97%!). Source: https://en.wikipedia.org/wiki/Video_game_crash_of_1983

316 Twenty-two million Commodore 64s were sold in 1983 for $600 each. It was the first affordable home computer.

317 Apple Computers used the Super Bowl on January 24, 1984 to spread its message of the MacIntosh. The famous Super Bowl ad features an Orwellian universe, mindlessly operating in lock-step to a giant talking head, when a young woman runs into the room and hurtles a sledgehammer at the screen and blows it up. The tagline: "On January 24th, Apple Computer will introduce MacIntosh. And you'll see why 1984 won't be like '1984.'" Watch the commercial: https://www.youtube.com/watch?v=axSnW-ygU5g

318 Trip Hawkins desired to create video games that were art forms. His company Electronic Arts developed games that only could be played on computers (using floppy disks). Packaged like a record album, his sports games used real athletes and coded the games to behave like real sports stars. Football legendary coach John Madden was recruited for the football game but when he saw the early version (which featured only seven players), he resisted. Electronic Arts eventually coded the football game for eleven players per side and *Madden Football* was released (1988). Every version of *Madden* got more "real" and the video game became the crown jewel of the company. Hawkins is now the most successful video game creator in history.

319 Roberta Williams is considered one of the most important game designers. She single-handedly created the graphic adventure video game genre. Other games she created include *Wizard and the Princess* (1980), *The Dark Crystal* (1983), *Mickey's Space Adventure* (1984), *Mixed Up Mother Goose* (1987) and *Phantasmagoria* (1995). Source: https://en.wikipedia.org/wiki/Roberta_Williams

320 Nintendo Entertainment System: https://en.wikipedia.org/wiki/Nintendo_Entertainment_System

321 Sega SG-1000: https://en.wikipedia.org/wiki/SG-1000

322 Tetris: https://en.wikipedia.org/wiki/Tetris

323 *Myst* was a 1993 game designed for the Mac by two brothers named Robyn and Rand Miller. The game sold 250,000 copies in one year and remains a perennial best-seller. https://en.wikipedia.org/wiki/Myst

324 Will Wright was fascinated by how cities worked. In 1989 he released a computer program called *Sim City*. It initially struggled for sales but after a positive review in *Newsweek* everything changed. A variety of spin off games followed, including *The Sims,* which allows players to build actual people and then control their lives.

325 Eric Harris and Dylan Klebold—the two teenaged gunmen in the April 20, 1999 school shooting at Columbine High School in Littleton, CO—played violent video games. Harris once confided he wanted to shoot his school up like *Doom.*

326 Joseph Lieberman advocated to ban violent video games. He took special interest in *Mortal Kombat*: "I was startled. It was very violent, and as you know, rewarded violence. And at the end, if you did really well, you'd get to decide whether to decapitate… how to kill the other guy, how to pull his head off. And there was all sorts of blood flying around." https://gamicus.gamepedia.com/Joe_Lieberman

327 In 1983 a program named *Battle Zone* was developed for use in military maneuvers. Gamers actually helped the military to create interfaces. When the military wanted to recruit young people for war, they created a video games called *America's Army*. https://www.military.com/daily-news/2018/11/09/uncle-sam-wants-you-play-video-games-us-army.html

328 These teams of players are called "clans." Some of these clans have an annual gathering called "Quakecon." Today it's become a yearly vacation for gamers to meet and play, including

children and seniors. In 2016 over 8,600 people convened. https://en.wikipedia.org/wiki/QuakeCon#2017

329 "EverQuest": https://en.wikipedia.org/wiki/EverQuest
330 "Guitar Hero": https://en.wikipedia.org/wiki/Guitar_Hero
331 Nintendo Wii: https://en.wikipedia.org/wiki/Wii

Chapter Eleven: Cable Television

332 "The Heidi Game" is one of the most famous NFL games of all time. https://en.wikipedia.org/wiki/Heidi_Game. Watch it on YouTube: https://www.youtube.com/watch?v=zJAn3cTMXW8

333 *Sports Illustrated* writer Paul Zimmerman later wrote about the 1967 Jets-Raiders game: "The 1967 game was one of the most vicious in Jet history. [Joe] Namath was slugged to the turf; he was hit late, punched in the groin. They aimed for his knees, tried to step on his hands…And [Ben] Davidson got Namath. He got him on a rollout, with a right that started somewhere between Hayward and Alameda. It knocked Namath's helmet flying, and broke his jaw, but Namath didn't miss a play, and he threw for 370 yards and three TD's in that 38-27 loss." "Heidi, Ben, Warren and Memories" by Paul Zimmerman, *Pro!* (Oakland edition). August 13, 1976. NFL Properties.

334 "That Clutch Raiders Win" by Bob Valli, *The Oakland Tribune* (November 18, 1968): 33,39.
335 Television was never more popular than in 1968. The U.S. had over 25 million television sets.
336 The home video tape recorder was introduced into American homes in the mid-1970s. Initially there were two competing formats: BetaMax (Sony) and VHS (JVC). Eventually, the VHS format won the format war. In 1980, there were around two million video cassette recorders in America. It was mostly a luxury for the rich. As prices for the machines dropped and legal battles over video-taping copyrighted shows were resolved, the VCR experienced rapid sales in a 1980s materialistic culture. By the end of the decade over 63 million units were wired to American televisions. https://en.wikipedia.org/wiki/Video_tape_recorder

337 "Cutting The Cable Cord: 2015": http://mediashift.org/2015/04/cutting-the-cord-2015-a-special-series-on-streaming-tv/ See also *PC Magazine*: https://www.pcmag.com/news/322824/experian-cord-cutting-on-the-rise-especially-among-netflix

338 "Sorry, But Cable TV Won't Exist in 2030" by Chris Mills: https://bgr.com/2017/12/04/cable-tv-cord-cutting-streaming-services-omg-what/

339 Ronald Reagan used the phrase "Make America Great Again" in various political speeches throughout the 1980s but he first used it to kick off his 1980 presidential campaign at New York's Statue of Liberty. Watch on YouTube: https://www.youtube.com/watch?v=5N9c6DbRvAo

340 "Morning in America" was the theme for Ronald Reagan's 1984 presidential re-election campaign. It must have worked. Reagan was elected in a landslide. Watch the commercial: https://www.youtube.com/watch?v=Vx2Ik1Rckss

341 Unemployment fell from 10.8% in 1982 to 3.9% in 2000. https://www.thebalance.com/unemployment-rate-by-year-3305506

342 U.S. home prices more than doubled between 1980 and 2000. https://fred.stlouisfed.org/graph/?g=1jZT

343 The U.S. government estimated between 200,000 and 500,000 Americans were homeless in the 1980s and 1990s. A concerted effort to feed and house the homeless was initiated in the 1990s. https://en.wikipedia.org/wiki/Homelessness_in_the_United_States

344 In 1980, a year of instruction at a public university (tuition, room and board) cost $2400. By 2000 it was $7600. When adjusted for inflation, a $2400 bill in 1980 would be $5,300 in 2000, producing a true increase of $2300/year between 1980 and 2000. Private colleges and universities are considerably higher. In 1980, a year of instruction at a private school (tuition, room and board) cost $5500. By 2000 it was $21,400. When adjusted for inflation, a $5500

bill in 1980 would be roughly $12,000 in the year 2000, producing a true increase of $9,400/year. Source: National Center for Education Statistics https://nces.ed.gov/programs/digest/d07/tables/dt07_320.asp

345 From 1981 to 1989, among Americans age 25 to 29, the number of homeowners declined by 11 percent—while the number of renters rose by 16 percent ("Housing in America" report by the U.S. Department of Commerce, 1992). Source: *13th Gen: Abort, Retry, Ignore, Fail?* by Neil Howe and William Strauss (New York: Vintage Books, 1993): 100. Home ownership, a sign of a healthy middle class, has risen since 2015 (64.4% of Americans owned a home in 2018 as compared to the 63.4% in 2015, which at the time was a 48-year low according to the Census Bureau). https://www.chicagotribune.com/business/ct-older-first-home-buyers-20150817-story.html

346 Cable Center (2014): "Cable History Timeline": 1. https://www.cablecenter.org/images/files/pdf/CableHistory/CableTimelineFall2015.pdf

347 Ibid., 2.

348 Ibid., 7.

349 Ibid., 10.

350 Another "superstation" was Chicago's WGN (taken from the Chicago's Tribune slogan "world's greatest newspaper"). Like Turner's TBS, this Chicago station carried movies, classic television shows and their hometown Chicago Cubs, White Sox, Black Hawks and Bulls. Eventually TBS dropped the Braves games but WGN to this day still offers Cubs fans over forty games a year. WGN, Harry Carey and Cubs baseball still says it's "summer" in Chicago. https://wgntv.com/station-history/

351 Watch the first hour of CNN (June 1, 1980): https://www.youtube.com/watch?v=rWhgKuKvvPE

352 O.J. Simpson's defense counsel included a "who's who" of lawyers, including Robert Shapiro, Johnnie Cochran, F. Lee Bailey, Alan Dershowitz and Robert Kardashian. https://en.wikipedia.org/wiki/O._J._Simpson_murder_case

353 *Crossfire's* political pundits included (from the left) Tom Braden, Michael Kinsley, Bob Beckel, Geraldine Ferraro, James Carville and Van Jones. From the right there were conservatives like Pat Buchanan, Robert Novak, John Sununu, Tony Snow, Lynne Cheney, Mary Matalyn, Tucker Carlson and Newt Gingrich. The show aired from 1982-2005, took a hiatus and returned for a final run in 2013-2014. https://en.wikipedia.org/wiki/Crossfire_(U.S._TV_program)

354 Bill O'Reilly's *Factor* spawned a Comedy Central parody known as *The Colbert Report* (Stephen Colbert). Colbert and Jon Stewart's political "comedy" shows were popular among younger "Millennial" viewers.

355 The top ten cable news shows in 2018: *Hannity* (Fox), *The Rachel Maddow Show* (MSNBC), *Tucker Carlson Tonight* (Fox), *The (Laura) Ingraham Angle* (Fox), *The Five* (Fox), *Special Report with Bret Baier* (Fox), *Last Word with Lawrence O'Donnell* (MSNBC), *The Story* with Martha MacCallum (Fox), *All In* with Chris Hayes (MSNBC) and *America's Newsroom* (Fox). Source: https://www.adweek.com/tvnewser/the-top-cable-news-programs-of-2018-are/388730

356 "History of Cable": https://www.calcable.org/learn/history-of-cable/

357 For more information on ESPN: https://en.wikipedia.org/wiki/ESPN

358 Watch "Video Killed The Radio Star" by The Buggles: https://www.youtube.com/watch?v=Iwuy4hHO3YQ

359 Watch Michael Jackson's "moon walk": https://www.youtube.com/watch?v=7lvsBBNV-U4

360 "Live Aid": https://en.wikipedia.org/wiki/Live_Aid

Chapter Twelve: Personal Computer-Cell Phone

361 *Millennials Rising: The Next Great Generation* by Neil Howe and William Strauss (New York: Vintage Books, 2000): 3.

362 Ibid., 4.

363 The use of cell phones in-flight was strictly forbidden in 2001. In fact, most larger aircraft featured phones in the headrests for passenger use (but they were expensive calls and few used them, especially in coach). When United 93 passengers experienced the hijacking about forty minutes into the flight, the cell phone was used exclusively for information. Flight 93 was the last flight to be hijacked (to be crashed into a significant American location) and passengers soon realized they were destined for a similar fate. Consequently, they forcibly re-took control of the cabin. The hijackers flying the plane realized they probably wouldn't reach their intended destination (which many believe was either the U.S. Capitol or White House) and crashed the plane into the ground near Shanksville, PA. https://www.history.com/topics/21st-century/flight-93

364 As quoted in episode twelve ("Millennium"): *America: The Story of Us* television series, broadcasted on the History Channel in April and May of 2010.

365 Intel: https://en.wikipedia.org/wiki/Intel

366 "Moore's Law": https://en.wikipedia.org/wiki/Moore%27s_law

367 The Altair 8800 was an affordable computer. So much so that even the average college student could buy in. The machine created various computing communities who gathered to create various uses for the Altair 8800.

368 The California counter culture of the early 1970s greatly helped the personal computer to develop. The counter culture believed in sharing everything, including information. The Homebrew Computer Club was cut from this cloth. It was a place where ideas were cooked and improved within a programming community. It was out of this creative stew that Apple Computers was born.

369 The Apple I was their first computer. It was a primitive machine, but Steve Jobs and Steve Wozniak still sold around 200 of these computers for $500 each.

370 To advertise their IBM computers, Big Blue used the iconic Charlie Chaplin as a promotional mascot. Watch early 1980s IBM computer advertisements: https://www.youtube.com/watch?v=kQT_YCBb9ao

371 The Palo Alto Research Center was started in 1971 by Xerox. The paper company saw the writing on the wall. The future was actually a "paperless" office and Xerox needed to rethink their business strategy. Bob Taylor ran the PARC computer science lab—which boasted 58 of the top one hundred computer researchers in the world. There was total intellectual freedom to explore every idea. PARC researchers envisioned a future office with WYSIWYG ("what you see is what you get") computer technology using graphic user interface programs. Unfortunately, these researchers couldn't persuade their Xerox executives to pursue that future.

372 As quoted in the Mark Stephens/Robert X. Cringely PBS documentary (1996) *Triumph of the Nerds: The Rise of Accidental Empires*. Cringely was an insider and tech columnist for InfoWorld magazine. https://www.pbs.org/nerds/part3.html Watch the documentary on YouTube: https://www.youtube.com/watch?v=AIBr-kPgYuU&t=93s

373 The "macintosh" apple is one of America's favorite apples particularly popular to cook and eat raw. Apple picked the "macintosh" to further brand its personal computers. https://en.wikipedia.org/wiki/McIntosh_(apple)

374 The Super Bowl ad featured an Orwellian universe with cloned participants living in lock-step to a "big blue" screen (a pointed jab at IBM computers). It was played during the third quarter to an estimated 77.5 million viewers on January 22, 1984—two days prior to the official launch. Watch the ad on YouTube: https://www.youtube.com/watch?v=2zfqw8nhUwA

375 Pepsi CEO John Sculley was persuaded to move cross country to assume the leadership of Apple Computers thanks to a famous query by Jobs: "Do you want to sell sugared for the rest of your life? Or do you want to come with me and change the world?" The line worked. Sculley led Apple as it's CEO from 1983-1993. https://www.pbs.org/nerds/part3.html

376 Watch Steve Jobs announce his "iCEO" status at a company meeting: https://www.youtube.com/watch?v=bSWzWV4nvOs

377 Source: https://hypertextbook.com/facts/2004/DianeEnnefils.shtml

378 By 1989, more Americans had credit cards than voted. The number of shopping malls surpassed high schools.

379 In 1983, there's a ten-year waiting list to buy a mobile phone in New York, one of the few places in the U.S where there is cell service.

380 Watch the epic "brick phone" scene at YouTube: https://www.youtube.com/watch?v=UDCmNFD18nQ

381 In 1987 seven out of ten mobile phone users earned over $50,000 annually (adjusted for inflation that's nearly $111,000 today).

382 Between 2001 and 2007 an estimated 16,000 people were killed in traffic accidents related to texting while driving, and most of these deaths were drivers under thirty. In 2008, nearly six thousand "texting" deaths occurred. "Talking to Death" by Maggie Fox: https://www.reuters.com/article/us-cellphones-driving/talking-to-death-texts-phones-kill-16000-study-idUSTRE68M53K20100923

383 "Triumph of the Nerds," part three: https://www.pbs.org/nerds/part3.html

384 The only feature Larry Ellison missed was the camera. The smartphone has replaced the digital camera and video camera. It's essentially a photography and videography device.

385 A 2018 Pew study of American phone habits revealed that 99.5% of the PC Generation (ages 18-38) had a cellphone and 92% owned a smartphone. Pew Research Center Study: http://www.pewInternet.org/fact-sheet/mobile/

Chapter Thirteen: Internet

386 Watch "Revolution" by The Beatles on YouTube: https://www.youtube.com/watch?v=BGLGzRXY5Bw

387 "Christchurch" shooting: https://www.cnn.com/asia/live-news/new-zealand-christchurch-shooting-intl/index.html

388 "Selfie Deaths Are Epidemic" by Kathryn Miles; Outside magazine (April 16, 2019): https://www.outsideonline.com/2393419/selfie-deaths

389 "Rise in Teen Suicide Rate Connected to Social Media Popularity: Study" by the Associated Press (November 14, 2017): https://nypost.com/2017/11/14/rise-in-teen-suicide-connected-to-social-media-popularity-study/

390 J.C.R. Licklider was posthumously inducted into the Internet Hall of Fame in 2013: https://Internethalloffame.org/inductees/jcr-licklider

391 Robert Taylor was inducted into the Internet Hall of Fame in 2013. https://Internethalloffame.org/inductees/robert-taylor

392 Lawrence Roberts was inducted into the Internet Hall of Fame in 2012. https://Internethalloffame.org/inductees/lawrence-roberts

393 Roberts placed his "interface message processors" (IMPs) initially at four universities: UCLA (Sigma 7), Stanford Research Institute (SDS 940), Un. Of California at Santa Barbara (IBM 360/75) and Un. Of Utah (PDP-10).

394 Leonard Kleinrock was a 2012 inductee into the Internet Hall of Fame. https://Internethalloffame.org/inductees/leonard-kleinrock

395 "Roads and Crossroads of the Internet History" by Gregory Gromov: http://www.netvalley.com/cgi-bin/intval/net_history.pl?chapter=1

396 Lawrence Roberts asked over a hundred companies, including IBM and AT&T, to bid on ARPANET "packet switching" work but they all refused. They saw no revenue in the technology. Consequently, Roberts and his team created "packet switching" on their own.

397 Robert Kahn and Vint Cerf were both inducted into the Internet Hall of Fame in 2012. https://Internethalloffame.org/inductees/robert-kahn https://Internethalloffame.org/inductees/vint-cerf

398 Raymond Tomlinson was inducted into the Internet Hall of Fame in 2012. https://Internethalloffame.org/inductees/raymond-tomlinson

399 "The Number of Emails Sent in 2019": https://www.lifewire.com/how-many-emails-are-sent-every-day-1171210

400 Al Gore is the only politician inducted into the Internet Hall of Fame. His contributions weren't so much engineering the science as promoting its uses. He authored several academic papers on the value of the Internet, initiated legislation to open it to the masses and personally committed to connecting every classroom to the Internet by the year 2000. https://Internethalloffame.org/inductees/al-gore

401 Tim Berners-Lee was inducted into the Internet Hall of Fame in 2012. https://Internethalloffame.org/inductees/tim-berners-lee

402 Mark Andreesson was inducted into the Internet Hall of Fame in 2013. https://Internethalloffame.org/inductees/marc-andreessen

403 Netscape and Navigator soon found itself battling Bill Gates and Microsoft in an epic battle over who would control how people went online. Microsoft developed their own web browser called Explorer and bundled it with every Windows-driven computer. Consequently, Netscape got squeezed out of the market. It eventually re-emerged with America Online in the mid-2000s but by then Windows Explorer owned the browser market. https://en.wikipedia.org/wiki/Netscape_Navigator

404 Watch the *Today Show* hosts inquire about the Internet in 1994: https://www.youtube.com/watch?v=UlJku_CSyNg

405 "11% of Americans Don't Use the Internet: Who Are They?": Pew Research https://www.pewresearch.org/fact-tank/2018/03/05/some-americans-dont-use-the-Internet-who-are-they/

406 Amazon website visits: https://www.statista.com/statistics/623566/web-visits-to-amazoncom/

407 "Big Internet Brands of the 1990s": https://www.npr.org/sections/alltechconsidered/2016/07/25/487097344/the-big-Internet-brands-of-the-90s-where-are-they-now

408 Google Library Project: https://www.google.com/googlebooks/library/

409 Wikipedia is number five among Americans (as of September 2018). Ironically, if you google "history of Wikipedia," the top entry is from Wikipedia and that page carries a modest request to "update the information to reflect recent events." Wikipedia is always evolving with new information. https://en.wikipedia.org/wiki/History_of_Wikipedia

410 The first chat room was created by Dave Woolley and Douglas Brown at the University of Illinois. It was known as "Talkomatic." https://en.wikipedia.org/wiki/Talkomatic

411 Message or bulletin boards emerged in the early 1980s. https://en.wikipedia.org/wiki/Bulletin_board_system

412 America Online released the first instant messaging communication in 1997.

413 "Open Diary" is considered the first social networking "blogging" site. https://en.wikipedia.org/wiki/Open_Diary

414 At its zenith, Friendster enjoyed over 115 million users. https://en.wikipedia.org/wiki/Friendster

415 LinkedIn: https://en.wikipedia.org/wiki/LinkedIn

416 MySpace: https://en.wikipedia.org/wiki/Myspace

417 Facebook: https://en.wikipedia.org/wiki/Facebook

418 On March 12, 2019, federal prosecutors revealed how Net Gen parents paid more than $25 million to Rick Singer—a college admissions consultant—to bribe administrators, testing officials and coaches at nine of America's finest universities (including Stanford, Georgetown, UCLA, USC, Yale and Wake Forest). Several notable celebrities like Lori Loughlin and Felicity Huffman were caught in the scandal. https://www.nytimes.com/news-event/college-admissions-scandal

419 The term "snowflake" originated from the 1996 *Fight Club* novel, by Chuck Palahniuk, where a character states: "You are not special. You are not a beautiful and unique snowflake." In 2017, Palahniuk took credit for coining the term and felt it represented the current younger generation. Claire Fox wrote a book titled *I Find That Offensive!* and outlined various cases where the younger generation has been particularly insensitive and intolerant to any view that contradicts his or her own worldview. In 2016, Collin's Dictionary recognized "snowflake" as one of its words of the year. https://en.wikipedia.org/wiki/Generation_Snowflake

420 YouTube has over 5 billion uploaded videos and 50 million unique users posting content. Every minute 300 hours of video is uploaded. Demographically, 62% of users are male. The 35+ and 55+ age groups are the fastest growing demographic (many of them watching YouTube for nostalgia). https://www.minimatters.com/youtube-best-video-length/

421 Ibid.

422 "Nomophobia" is a shortened use of "no mobile" phone. https://mashable.com/2014/08/02/tech-phobias/#7BXGjNpWqsq7

Chapter Fourteen: iTech

423 Beloit College: 2018 Mindset List http://themindsetlist.com/2018/08/beloit-college-mindset-list-class-2022/

424 Generational expert Meagan Johnson prefers the tag "Linksters": "We chose the term Linkster Generation because it is the first generation to be linked into technology from day one…[they] may never hold a textbook, read everything from a tablet and never learn cursive writing. The Linkster Generation may never write a check or walk into a traditional bank" https://www.independent.co.uk/life-style/millennials-generation-z-linksters-what-next-generation-x-baby-boomers-Internet-social-media-a7677001.html

425 Neil Howe and William Strauss prefer "Homeland Generation" because this cohort was born in the shadow of September 11, 2001 world. https://www.lifecourse.com/about/method/def/homeland-generation.html

426 Jean Twenge has used the term "iGen" since 2006 to describe those born between 1995–2012: "Why the Label iGen?": http://www.jeantwenge.com/faq-items/why-the-label-igen/

427 *Millennials Rising: The Next Great Generation* by Neil Howe and William Strauss (New York: Vintage): 6.

428 "Move Over Gen Z, Generation Alpha is the One to Watch": https://adage.com/article/cmo-strategy/move-gen-z-generation-alpha-watch/316314

429 Jean Twenge prefers a more traditional route with other generations: Baby Boomers (1946–1964), Gen X (1965–1979), Millennials (1980–1994) and iGen (1995–2012. http://www.jeantwenge.com/faqs/

430 Source: https://www.lifecourse.com/about/method/def/homeland-generation.html

431 Pew Research Center: "Defining Generations: Where Millennials End and Generation Z Begins" https://www.pewresearch.org/fact-tank/2019/01/17/where-millennials-end-and-generation-z-begins/

432 The Center for Generational Kinetics takes a traditional path for the Baby Boom generation (1946–1964) but shortens the Gen X frame to 1965–1977 and expands Millennial birth years to 1977–1995. Gen Z, iGen or Centennials are born after 1996. https://genhq.com/FAQ-info-about-generations/

433 *iGen: Why Today's Super-Connected Kids Are Growing Up Less Rebellious, More Tolerant, Less Happy—And Completely Unprepared for Adulthood—and What That Means for the Rest of Us* by Jean Twenge (Atria Books, digital e-book, 2018): loc. 75.

434 Source: https://www.metro.us/news/map-timeline-of-mass-shootings-in-the-us-since-2000/ tmWmll-14WH11UWCww

435 "2001–2011: The Decade of Great Change & Tragedy" by Scott Stenholm: https://www. huffpost.com/entry/20012011-the-decade-of-gr_b_1131422?ref=tw

436 Mainline U.S. denominations saw a 23% decline or a loss of 5 million members between 2007 and 2014, according to a Pew Research Study: https://www.pewresearch.org/fact-tank/2015/05/18/mainline-protestants-make-up-shrinking-number-of-u-s-adults/

437 Network news has been in decline since 1980 but continues to slide further as news shifted first to cable and then to the Internet and social media. https://www.journalism.org/numbers/ network-evening-news-ratings/

438 Most of the CD's decline in sales happened after 2007 with the introduction of the smartphone. https://www.statista.com/chart/12950/cd-sales-in-the-us/

439 In 2017 alone, DVD sales declined 14% to $4.7 billion while DVD rentals fell 17% to around $2 billion. "Disc Sales Declines": https://variety.com/2018/digital/news/home-entertainment-spending-2017-1202658638/

440 "Cable and Satellite TV Are Dying: AT&T Suffers Largest Pay TV Subscriber Drop in History" by Mike Brown (May 17, 2016): https://www.inverse.com/article/15741-cable-and-satellite-tv-are-dying-at-t-suffers-largest-pay-tv-subscriber-drop-in-history

441 Source: https://fr.slideshare.net/sparksandhoney/generation-z-final-june-17/39-They_are_ hyperaware_and_concernedabout

442 "PC Sales Keep Falling": https://www.pcmag.com/news/361916/pc-sales-keep-falling-but-big-manufacturers-are-doing-just

443 "Teens, Social Media and Technology 2018": https://www.pewInternet.org/2018/05/31/teens-social-media-technology-2018/

444 As reported by the Center for Generational Kinetics in the *State of Gen Z: 2018* report: 7-8.

445 Ibid.

446 "Should the Parkland Shooting Change How We Think About Phones, Schools and Safety?" February 17, 2018: https://www.npr.org/sections/ed/2018/02/17/586534079/should-the-parkland-shooting-change-how-we-think-about-phones-schools-and-safety

447 "Mark Zuckerberg is Trying to Transform Education. This Town Fought Back." By Nick Tabor (October 11, 2018): http://nymag.com/intelligencer/2018/10/the-connecticut-resistance-to-zucks-summit-learning-program.html

448 Digital Learning Collaborative. (2019). Snapshot 2019: A review of K-12 online, blended, and digital learning. Retrieved from https://www.digitallearningcollab.com.

449 Pew Research Study (November 13, 2018): https://www.pewsocialtrends.org/2018/11/15/ early-benchmarks-show-post-millennials-on-track-to-be-most-diverse-best-educated-generation-yet/psdt-11-15-18_postmillennials-00-00/

450 "US White Population Declines" by the Brookings Institution: https://www.brookings.edu/ blog/the-avenue/2018/06/21/us-white-population-declines-and-generation-z-plus-is-minority-white-census-shows/

451 Ibid.

452 "Atheism Doubles Among Gen Z" (Barna Group): https://www.barna.com/research/atheism-doubles-among-generation-z/

453 "Red and Blue States": https://en.wikipedia.org/wiki/Red_states_and_blue_states

454 "Why Democrats Should Be Losing Sleep Over Gen Z": https://www.forbes.com/ sites/ashleystahl/2017/08/11/why-democrats-should-be-losing-sleep-over-generation-z/#c50770c7878c

455 "New Survey Shows Gen Z More Conservative, Favors National Focus over Globalism": https://marketresearchfoundation.org/2018/10/22/new-survey-shows-generation-z-more-conservative/

456 Source: http://java.candidjava.com/tutorial/Java-program-to-delete-vowels-in-a-given-string.htm

457 "50 Popular Internet Acronyms": https://www.smart-words.org/abbreviations/text.html

458 "12 Meanings of LOL": https://www.buzzfeednews.com/article/katieheaney/the-12-meanings-of-lol

Chapter Fifteen: Robotics

459 Watch the Turbo Tax RoboChild commercial on YouTube: https://www.youtube.com/watch?v=JIRX3yWhgZI

460 "Number of Smartphones sold, 2007–2018": https://www.statista.com/statistics/263437/global-smartphone-sales-to-end-users-since-2007/

461 Australian Mark McCrindle projects the generation born between 2010 and 2025 will surpass 2 billion births. That's 200 million more than those born between 1995 and 2009. "Move Over Gen Z, Generation Alpha is the One to Watch" by Ardrianne Pasquarelli and E.J. Schultz (January 22, 2019): https://adage.com/article/cmo-strategy/move-gen-z-generation-alpha-watch/316314

462 Ibid.

463 Visit Ryan's Toy Review at YouTube: https://www.youtube.com/channel/UChGJGhZ9SOOHvBB0Y4DOO_w

464 Wikipedia: "Dennis Gabor" https://en.wikipedia.org/wiki/Dennis_Gabor

465 Wikipedia: "Holography" https://en.wikipedia.org/wiki/Holography

466 "The Dawn of the Age of Holograms" by Alex Kipman (April 18, 2016): https://www.youtube.com/watch?v=1cQbMP3I5Sk

467 Wikipedia: "Artificial Intelligence" https://en.wikipedia.org/wiki/History_of_artificial_intelligence

468 The Dartmouth Conference originates in "A Proposal for the Dartmouth Summer Research Project on Artificial Intelligence" (August 31, 1955) by J. McCarthy (Dartmouth College), M.L. Minsky (Harvard University), N. Rochester, I.B.M. Corporation and C.E. Shannon, Bell Telephone Laboratories. http://www.formal.stanford.edu/jmc/history/dartmouth/dartmouth.html

469 Wikipedia: "ELIZA" https://en.wikipedia.org/wiki/ELIZA

470 Wikipedia: "Humanoid Robot" https://en.wikipedia.org/wiki/Humanoid_robot

471 Wikipedia: "Cyc" https://en.wikipedia.org/wiki/Cyc

472 On May 11, 1997, the *Deep Blue* computer played Gary Kasparov, the world champion in chess and beat him. *Deep Blue* processed an astounding 200,000,000 moves per second. https://en.wikipedia.org/wiki/Deep_Blue_(chess_computer)

473 Wikipedia: "Watson" https://en.wikipedia.org/wiki/Watson_(computer)

474 Watch the "Watson" computer compete *on Jeopardy!* https://www.youtube.com/watch?v=P18EdAKuC1U

475 Watch a Mercedes commercial featuring their self-parking car: https://www.youtube.com/watch?v=7-BjYp_JNoA

476 Watch a commercial by Beko on tomorrow's smart home: https://youtu.be/d36M4CCCXRw

477 "The Emotional Chatbots are Here to Probe our Feelings" by Arielle Pardes (January 31, 2018): https://www.wired.com/story/replika-open-source/?fbclid=IwAR1ALHSb-otH3ciD-I4PjaFaq3tPqRISUTg9-YdhlRZiEGGlzogNrWdm4Rk

478 "The Wired Guide to Robots" by Matt Simon (May 17, 2018): https://www.wired.com/story/wired-guide-to-robots/

479 "Killer Robots in Film-In Pictures" by Greg Whitmore (February 22, 2014): https://www. theguardian.com/film/gallery/2014/feb/22/killer-robots-in-film-in-pictures-alien-blade-runner-terminator

480 Watch the android scene from Star Trek: https://www.youtube.com/watch?v=YbeyivYA7sI

481 Wikipedia: "Data" https://en.wikipedia.org/wiki/Data_(Star_Trek)

482 "Meet Erica, Japan's Next Robot News Anchor" by Brandon Specktor (January 30, 2018): https://www.livescience.com/61575-erica-robot-replace-japanese-news-anchor.html

483 CP-2 features two cameras in the eyes and two microphones in the ears so the android can fully see and hear. The Japanese have a special talent for engineering lifelike robots.

484 Watch a 1939 demonstration of "Elektro": https://www.youtube.com/watch?v=AuyTRbj8QSA

485 Wikipedia: "Elektro" https://en.wikipedia.org/wiki/Elektro

486 "Robot Named Dante to Explore Inferno of Antarctic Volcano" by Warren E. Leary (New York Times, December 8, 1992): https://www.nytimes.com/1992/12/08/science/robot-named-dante-to-explore-inferno-of-antarctic-volcano.html

487 Boston Dynamics: https://www.bostondynamics.com/

488 Wabot-2 humanoid robot: https://www.youtube.com/watch?v=ZHMQuo_DsNU

489 "Florida Man Becomes First Person to Live with Advanced Mind-Controlled Robotic Arm" by Chelsea Gohd (February 2, 2018): https://futurism.com/mind-controlled-robotic-arm-johnny-matheny

490 "A Short History of Drones and their Rise in Popularity": https://didyouknowscience.com/a-short-history-of-drones-and-their-rise-to-popularity/

491 Zume Pizza: https://zumepizza.com/about

492 "Mabu" (Catalia Health): http://www.cataliahealth.com/introducing-the-mabu-personal-healthcare-companion/

493 Starsky Robotics: https://www.starsky.io/

494 "Will AI and Robots Force You Into Retirement?": https://www.forbes.com/sites/stephenchen/2019/04/04/will-ai-and-robots-force-you-into-retirement/#2ce48044133d

495 SuitX Industrial Exoskeletons: https://www.suitx.com/

496 Watch the introduction to "The Six Million Dollar Man": https://www.youtube.com/watch?v=0CPJ-AbCsT8

497 CRISPR Babies: Stumbling Over Mankind's Next Giant Leap by Tiffany Vora (December 4, 2018): https://singularityhub.com/2018/12/04/crispr-babies-stumbling-over-mankinds-next-giant-leap/#sm.00008gue5y4n1fjhtay24d24vvmn0

CPSIA information can be obtained
at www.ICGtesting.com
Printed in the USA
BVHW031627060520
579293BV00002B/75